Schools and Schooling Practices in Pakistan

Lessons for Policy and Practice

Schools and Schooling Practices in Pakistan

Lessons for Policy and Practice

Edited by

Rashida Qureshi

and

Fauzia Shamim

OXFORD
UNIVERSITY PRESS

Great Clarendon Street, Oxford ox2 6DP

Oxford University Press is a department of the University of Oxford.
It furthers the University's objective of excellence in research, scholarship,
and education by publishing worldwide in

Oxford New York

Auckland Cape Town Dar es Salaam Hong Kong Karachi
Kuala Lumpur Madrid Melbourne Mexico City Nairobi
New Delhi Shanghai Taipei Toronto

with offices in

Argentina Austria Brazil Chile Czech Republic France Greece
Guatemala Hungary Italy Japan Poland Portugal Singapore
South Korea Switzerland Turkey Ukraine Vietnam

Oxford is a registered trade mark of Oxford University Press
in the UK and in certain other countries

ISBN 978-0-19-547629-3

Typeset in Adobe Caslon Pro
Printed in Pakistan by
Kagzi Printers, Karachi.
Published by
Ameena Saiyid, Oxford University Press
No. 38, Sector 15, Korangi Industrial Area, PO Box 8214
Karachi-74900, Pakistan.

Contents

Part II: Leadership and School Improvement Practices

Foreword

While the research presented in this book is geographically situated in Pakistan, it is intellectually situated in contemporary theories, practices, and research on teacher development and school improvement—action research, reflective practice, teacher mentoring, cooperative group learning, active learning, school-based instructional leadership by teachers, effective schools, and comprehensive school reform (or whole school improvement). Thus, the research findings and implications presented here should be of relevance to teacher educators, school developers, education researchers, and other education stakeholders worldwide, not simply in South Asia and in developing countries. The authors explore and critique the implementation, adaptation, and consequences of those ideas and practices for teachers and their students within the challenging socio-cultural and organizational contexts of public and private schools in Pakistan. They offer new, empirically grounded insights into the teacher development practices, instructional methods, school effectiveness and school improvement strategies studied, and present a more optimistic view of the potential for improvement in education quality in Pakistan (and similarly challenging contexts) than reported in Warwick and Reimers' mid-1990s investigation and critique of public school education in Pakistan (entitled *Hope or Despair?*). This book contains no panacea for education improvement on a large scale. What it offers is a variety of up close accounts and analyses of school-based teacher learning and school development efforts associated for the most part with participation in teacher development and school improvement programmes sponsored by the Aga Khan University Institute for Educational Development (AKU-IED) in Karachi, Pakistan. The researcher-authors are all AKU-IED faculty or former participants in the IED Master's in Education programme for teacher leaders in schools cooperating in IED's whole school development strategies. Their accounts do not hide or minimize the challenges of changing the thinking and practices of teachers and school administrators in ways that will contribute to improvements in the quality of teaching and learning. If anything, they provide a pragmatic and deep understanding of how this can actually happen, albeit accompanied by the daunting realization that to do so will depend on the sustained presence and professional knowledge and skills of committed local teacher and school development agents such as those being prepared and supported by AKU-IED. The chapters in this book provide research-based accounts of good people doing good things in challenging circumstances to improve the quality of education in this corner of the world. From my perspective as a researcher, teacher, and consultant working in the field of educational change for the past twenty-five years in Canada, the US, Pakistan, and East Africa, much can be learned from the experiences, findings, and insights contained in this book that has theoretical and practical significance for school improvement worldwide.

Stephen E. Anderson
International Centre for Educational Change
Department of Theory and Policy Studies in Education
Ontario Institute for Studies in Education of the University of Toronto, Canada

Introduction

The state of education in Pakistan has been described by authors and researchers writing on this issue as being far from satisfactory (see for example, Hoodbhoy, 1998; Warwick and Reimers, 1995). More specifically, there is a general sense of dissatisfaction with the low quality of teachers and teaching and learning in Pakistani schools. The government of Pakistan, which still remains the largest education provider particularly in the rural areas despite the proliferation of private schools in the last two decades or so (Harlech-Jones, 2005), has undertaken a number of initiatives during the last few years, particularly in the wake of the Jomtien and Dakar meetings. The objective is to achieve EFA goals in terms of improvement in the enrollment of girls in particular, and increase in the retention of students at least during their early years to complete primary schooling and attain basic literacy skills (Education Sector Reforms, 2001). However, both, the standard of teachers and quality of teaching and learning processes leave much to be desired. The teachers in public sector schools generally have gaps in their content and pedagogical knowledge due to the low quality of their learning experiences in their education and professional training (Warwick and Reimers, 1995). They are low paid with low social status and morale. Similarly, the quality of teaching and learning is characterized by passive learners, outdated or irrelevant curricula and textbooks, and a system of assessment that focuses on rote learning (Bergman and Mohammad, 1998; Greaney and Hasan, 1998). Therefore, there is a need to improve teaching and learning in different ways such as more active engagement of learners in the teaching-learning process, provision of a variety of learning experiences based on inquiry methods, and development of critical thinking to improve the life chances of learners in terms of widening their participation in both the local and global contexts.

In the wake of this scenario, a few successful attempts have been made to improve the quality of teachers and teaching in Pakistani schools. One such attempt is the establishment of the Institute for Educational Development of the Aga Khan University in 1993 with a specific aim to improve the quality of education in Pakistan through teacher education. The vision and mission of the Institute is illustrated in the following speech of the Chancellor of the Aga Khan University as quoted by Pardhan and Theissen (2006):

> The Institute for Educational Development targets a very important, low status profession: teaching. The very creation of IED highlights the importance of teaching, and the programmes of IED are crafted to amplify that message. The technical work of the Institute is designed to raise the competence of teachers, both in their substantive areas of specialty and in their teaching skills, with the expectation that a truly excellent teacher will inspire others by example. Greater competence may not ensure higher status, but it will make it easier to achieve. Neither publicity nor good training is likely to make much difference, however, unless an environment is created in which good teachers can be more effective. IED is planning to devote much of its work to creating such an environment (p. 11).

The IED model of school improvement is characterized by building partnerships for developing a 'critical mass' in schools (cf. Farah and Jaworski, 2006). The assumption is that an ongoing engagement of this critical mass in 'critical reflection' will lead to collaborative learning and continuous improvement that would be responsive to the needs and realities of varied teaching-learning contexts. Hence the various programmes of AKU-IED focus not only on the professional development of individual teachers but also on developing leadership and management skills of head teachers and other educational managers in its cooperating schools.[1] (For a detailed description and critical analysis of AKU-IED's programmes and other initiatives for school improvement in Pakistan and other developing countries in eastern Africa, and south and central Asia, served by the Aga Khan University, see Farah and Jaworski, 2006).

The programmes of AKU-IED are both school-focused and school-based. Critical reflection is a key concept underpinning the design of all its programmes. Farah and Jaworski (2006) argue that reflection in practice is difficult not only for the inexperienced but also for experienced practitioners, 'In this respect IED programmes have drawn on action research models as a basis for encouraging critical engagement with issues' (p. 257). Action research is taught formally in IED's programmes. At the same time course participants are supported to conduct inquiry on their own and their colleagues' practice in schools and classrooms. Unsurprisingly, many graduate students and researchers from AKU-IED work with teachers in the school to study their practice and/or to study their own innovations in methodology, as well as their strategies for school-based teacher education. Thus, over the last few years of IED's operations a great deal of indigenous knowledge has been accumulated about the implementation of innovative strategies in teaching, teacher education, as well as the whole school improvement initiated by AKU-IED's satellite Professional Development Center in Gilgit. Most of this research work has been undertaken by students for their M.Ed dissertations at AKU-IED or faculty pursuing their Ph.D. studies at universities abroad (e.g. Khamis, 2000, Mohammad 2002, Halai, 2001).

Research on the impact of the AKU-IED model and schools and schooling practices promoted by AKU-IED is part of faculty's ongoing inquiry and critical reflection (e.g. Retallick and Mithani, 2003, Shamim, 2005, Halai and Anderson, 2005). Thus, while some published work is now available about the 'experiment' in school improvement undertaken by AKU-IED (e.g. Farah and Jaworski, 2006), there is still a need to bring together in a coherent form, the wealth of research knowledge available in unpublished student dissertations and research reports. The description and critical analysis of using innovative strategies for improving schools and schooling practices in Pakistan presented in different chapters of the book aim to bring in a breath of fresh air or hope in a scenario of either skepticism or extreme despair (cf. Warwick and Reimers, 1995). The major objective of this book is therefore to share a set of experiences of implementing innovations with other educationists, practitioners, and policy makers in Pakistan and similar contexts elsewhere. All the contributors have taken a critical stance on the innovations introduced by them. Thus, the authors share both their achievements and challenges. We hope that the book will help in starting a dialogue on issues in schools and schooling practices for improving students' learning experiences and achievement levels in schools in Pakistan.

One limitation of the research work reported in the book is that all the reported innovations are located within one or a few schools in Pakistan. Also, the studies are mainly qualitative in nature. In addition, many of these research studies have been done in the context of private or community-based schools. While we accept that the scope of the research work presented in this book may seem narrow to some readers, we would like to point out that small-scale qualitative studies help us immensely in gaining an in-depth understanding of issues in implementing innovations in classroom methodology, teachers' professional development, leadership styles and strategies, and whole school improvement. This understanding is necessary for scaling up these innovative practices and/or starting a large-scale school reform programme.

In addition to this, based on our rich experience of conducting programmes for and in different developing countries served by AKU-IED, we contend that while the empirical investigations reported in this book are grounded in the contextual reality of schools and schooling practices in Pakistan, the lessons learnt in the process of implementing innovative techniques and strategies at the level of the classroom and/or school, may be generally applicable to other developing countries as well. Hence, the book would be able to inform the practitioners and policy makers in similar contexts elsewhere.

Fauzia Shamim
Rashida Qureshi

NOTE

1. AKU-IED's cooperating schools are those schools with which the Institute has a partnership arrangement. AKU-IED invites their teachers and mangers to participate in its various programmes. In return, the schools open up their classrooms for IED's course participants for applying innovative practices and understanding their feasibility and impact through inquiry and research.

Part I
Teaching and Teacher Development Practices

Introduction to Part I

The first two articles outline and discuss the process and outcomes of using innovative teaching strategies in primary classrooms in Pakistan in public and private schools respectively. While both Mehrun-Nisa and Anjum Halai focus on learner participation, they do so from different perspectives. Mehrun-Nisa as a teacher is rightly interested in enhancing learner participation in the face of all odds in a government science primary classroom through using questioning as a teaching strategy. Her findings indicate that if the teachers have the required content knowledge and the will to implement innovative teaching strategies, the dynamics of a classroom can change from passive to active learners who are curious and inquisitive to find out things instead of asking procedural questions only. Halai goes a step further in her quest to see how teachers who are already using innovative strategies for teaching mathematics 'succeed' in their efforts in creating new social norms (and socio-mathematical norms) in the classroom. More importantly, she wants to find out to what extent engaging students in small cooperative learning groups in solving problems related to students' everyday lives facilitates their understanding of mathematics. Her findings and following discussion give an important message. We generally think of innovations from the perspective of the teachers only. Currently, very few studies are available (e.g. Shamim, 1996) that include students in their discussion of initiating and managing change in Pakistani classrooms and similar contexts elsewhere. The tension between the varied agendas of the participants in the teaching-learning process highlighted by Halai brings the students centre-stage in the process of change and innovation. She states, rightly in our view, that all innovations in the classroom need to take account of the students' understanding of the change effort. Lack of congruence between the understandings of the focus of change amongst the two major participants, i.e. teacher and learner can lead to tensions which unless identified and resolved may 'sabotage' the change effort.

The next five chapters are on practices of teacher development: mentoring, reflective dialogues, and action research. While mentoring and reflective dialogue in some sense can be subsumed under action research, they have been included as two major strategies currently being used in several schools for school-based professional development of teachers, particularly in the private sector schools in Pakistan. There are three chapters on action research—each focusing on a different aspect of this very practical but complex strategy for teacher development currently being 'promoted' in teacher education programmes in Pakistan and internationally (e.g. see Dean et al., 2005). Jane Rarieya shares with us her experience of using reflective dialogue, both process and outcomes, for helping teachers reflect on their lessons to improve their practice. She identifies the role of the reflective coach as integral to the process of helping teachers become reflective practitioners. According to Rarieya, the reflective coach needs to be very active, asking questions, challenging teachers' current beliefs and strategies, while at the same time supporting them in their efforts, even modelling teaching strategies, if required. This role of the reflective coach, as defined by Rarieya, is very different from that mentioned in the literature where the reflective coach is mainly seen as a catalyst for teachers' professional development. Here, the reflective coach needs subject knowledge in addition to facilitative skills mainly due to gaps in teachers' content or subject knowledge. Karim and Halai, in their study of the process and outcomes of 'mentoring' in a similar kind of school context in Pakistan arrive at the same conclusion. Both schools are eager to promote teachers' school-based professional development. This is evident in the fact that these schools provide time and space for engaging teachers in reflective dialogue or developing mentor-mentee relationship for their ongoing professional development. However, we learn that teachers' personal and professional lives such as their prior background and experiences require both the reflective coach and mentor to be a subject specialist in addition to facilitating the development of teachers' content pedagogical knowledge and skills.

Action research was used successfully by Rahat Joldoshalieva as a tool for developing her skills as a teacher educator, as part of her master's programme at AKU-IED. Bernadette Dean, a university-based researcher, also reports the potential of action research as a tool for teachers' professional development. Dean helped some teachers use action research in varied school settings, as a way of continuing their professional development. She found that engaging in action research improved the teachers' capacity and confidence, which in turn was empowering both for the teachers and their learners. Similarly, Razia Fakir Mohammad and Roshni Kumari's work with teachers from the rural context who had recently graduated from a teacher education programme at the Aga Khan University's Institute for Educational Development, Karachi, revealed that action research has a lot of potential as a strategy for teachers' continuing professional development. However, they have identified some contextual constraints which, in their view, would deter teachers from continuing with action research as a means of their personal and professional development in rural public sector schools. These include both personal and organizational factors such as teachers' limited understanding of the new pedagogical approaches, gaps in their subject knowledge and lack of incentives and rewards for continuing professional development in the government sector in Pakistan.

Thus, on the one hand the above accounts of 'good practice' in teaching and teacher education challenge the state of despair, based probably on the experience of many unsuccessful school reforms in the past; these accounts, we hope, would serve as a ray of hope in this era of extreme pessimism about improving the quality of school education in Pakistan. On the other hand, these critical accounts of innovative practices, grounded in the reality of schools and classrooms in varied contexts, invite the readers to think about contexts and conditions that may need to be established for scaling up these and similar kind of reform efforts for improving teaching and teacher education practices for school improvement in Pakistan and similar settings elsewhere.

Fauzia Shamim

1

Using Questioning as a Teaching-Learning Strategy: Opportunities and Challenges

Mehrun-Nisa

INTRODUCTION

Asking questions in the classroom is one of the regular activities in the teaching-learning process. This study explored the role of teacher's questioning as a teaching-learning strategy for enhancing students' participation in a primary science classroom in Pakistan. The main research question was: How can teacher's questioning as a teaching strategy enhance student's participation in the primary classroom? And the following subsidiary questions helped in answering the main research question:

1. What are the existing questioning practices and how effective are these in enhancing students' participation in a primary science classroom?
2. In what ways, and to what extent, can an intervention enhance students' active participation in a primary science classroom?
3. What factors facilitate teachers in using questioning techniques?
4. What challenges do teachers face in implementing questioning techniques?

THEORETICAL FRAMEWORK

What is a Question and Questioning?

Brown and Edmondson (1996), define a question as, 'any statement intended to evoke a verbal response' (p. 99). Cotton (1999) elaborates that in the classroom setting the 'teacher's questions are defined as instructional cues or stimuli that convey to students the content elements to be learned and directions for what they are to do and how they are to do it' (p. 1). By examining the above definitions it appears that questioning strategy is used to evoke responses from individuals or groups to enhance their learning.

The general purposes of teachers' questioning stated in the literature are to elicit information, probe prior learning before introducing new material, revise and consolidate learning, and stimulate students to ask questions (Cohen and Manion, 1989; Dillon, 1988). Brown and Wragg (1993), cited the work of Pate and Bremer (1967), who in a study of 190 teachers in the United States elementary schools asked teachers to provide reasons for asking questions:

> 69 percent of the statements emphasized questions to check knowledge and understanding, 54 percent were concerned with diagnosing pupils' difficulties, 47 percent stressed recall of facts and only 10 percent stressed the use of questions to encourage pupils to think. (p. 4)

Looking at the summary of the reasons discussed above, the conclusion can be drawn that teachers have varied intentions in asking questions. Moreover, research shows that compared to other kinds of questions, teachers' questions which stimulate children's thinking are in a low proportion. For example, Galton, Simon and Croll, (1980) found that time spent in questioning by teachers in junior classrooms amounted to 12 per cent of teacher activity. However, the types of questions most closely related to promoting thought and imagination represented only 5 per cent of the total questioning.

Questioning Skills and its Effect on Students' Participation

Although the context of questioning varies from subject to subject, many basic skills are the same (Kerry 1982). Firstly, identifying key questions during lesson planning is essential. Secondly, distribution of questions around the class is important because it not only provides opportunities to students to participate in teaching and learning but it also reduces the risk of losing attention.

Kerry (1982) has identified some factors which affect students' participation. This includes 'zone of maximum interaction' in the class. Some teachers have a left hand or right hand bias, i.e. they are more conscious of what is happening on one side of the room rather than the other. Others may suffer from tunnel-vision. Adams and Biddle (1970) analysed several hours of videotaped lessons, and found that most of the questions were directed at children sitting in a V-shaped ledge in front of the class. Children sitting outside that V-shaped wedge appeared out of the action zone (questions). Teachers need to be aware of these factors which affect students' participation. Several other factors have been identified which facilitate or hinder students' participation in the teaching and learning process (Sotto, 1994). The major constraint on students' participation is when the teacher acts as knowledge imposer and the students are supposed to listen to the teacher. In contrast, factors which facilitate students' participation include, firstly, the willingness of teachers to listen to students' ideas. This caring attitude of the teacher encourages students to participate. Second, learners feel encouraged to participate when they know that their teachers will not evaluate them each time they speak. Third, students feel encouraged to participate when they feel that the teacher values their ideas.

According to Cobb (1986), 'children's learning takes place through interaction and participation within the social environment', (p. 21). This only happens in those classrooms where the teacher listens to children and facilitates them in learning from one another. In questioning practice the teacher should have the role of a supporter and facilitator, to help learners to build on what they already know (Sotto, 1994). In addition, teachers should encourage children to participate in class not only by responding to teachers' questions but also by asking questions (Dillon, 1988). A class where the teacher wants to implement questioning as a teaching strategy to make the class more interactive demands a lot of skill and effort on the part of the teacher. I agree with Goodwin, Sharp, Cloutier and Diamond (1999) that 'effective questioning sessions in classroom require advance preparation' (p. 8). To summarize, it seems that questioning could be used to encourage learner participation in teaching-learning and is, therefore, an integral part of effective teaching. However, lesson planning plays a key role in using questioning effectively.

Factors to be Considered in using Questioning as a Teaching-Learning Strategy

Kinds of Questions

There are various ways of classifying questions. Many of these systems are based on the seven levels, as listed in Bloom's Taxonomy of Educational Objectives (Cotton, 1999). Researchers have also identified more simple comparisons, that is, high and low order cognitive questions (Cotton, 1999). Lower cognitive level questions are also referred to as factual and closed questions. Higher cognitive questions are also called open-ended, interpretive, evaluative, inquiry and synthesis questions. Closed questions are those for which there are a limited number of acceptable answers or 'right answers'. On the other hand open questions anticipate a wide range of acceptable responses rather than one or two 'right answers' (Kerry, 1982). Both levels of questions are important for students according to their age level, cognitive abilities, and teachers' purpose of questioning.

Wait Time

Literature shows that one of the factors which can have an effect on students' outcomes is the amount of wait time. Rowe (1969) has defined two types of wait time: Wait time I, as the duration of the pause after a teacher utterance, and wait time II, as the duration of the pause after a student utterance. Rowe (1969) further discussed the significance of wait time I and II. Wait time I, i.e., pausing after asking a question provides opportunities to students to think about the teacher's question and formulate a response. While wait time II or pausing after a student's response provides the student with the opportunity to add, modify or elaborate the response.

Rowe's (1969) research on classroom questioning indicated that students need at least 3 seconds to comprehend a question, formulate an answer and begin to respond, whereas, on the average, classroom teachers allow less than 1 second of wait time. Rowe found that when teachers increased wait time I and II, there were certain positive outcomes as follows:

- The length of student's response increased (p. 11)
- The number of questions asked by students increased
- There was greater participation by slow learners

Moreover, research has indicated a relationship between wait time and students' variety of outcomes. For example, Samirondon (1983) cited in Tobin, Trippins and Gallard, (1994) investigated the relationship between higher cognitive level questions, wait time, and students' achievement. Teachers in two experimental groups were trained to use wait time of 1 to 4 seconds or 4 to 7 seconds, respectively. Seventeen teachers each taught 60-minute lessons to two 11 grade biology classes. Only eight teachers achieved the desired wait time lengths. Results indicated that classes receiving the extended wait time treatment achieved at a significantly higher level than those receiving the short wait time treatment.

Similarly, Tobin's (1983) review of wait time shows that pausing can elicit longer answers, encourage more pupils to take part in answering questions and produce more questions from pupils. Much of this work goes back to the seminal studies of Rowe (Rowe, 1969, 1974). Looking at the research evidence we can conclude that there is a positive relationship between length of wait time and students' response.

Most studies on teachers' questioning have been done in Western countries. This study applied some of the strategies suggested in the literature on teachers' questioning and wait time in a primary science classroom in Karachi, Pakistan, to explore its effectiveness as a teaching strategy, particularly in enhancing students' participation level in the classroom. In this study students' active participation means not only responding to teacher's questions but also posing questions to the teacher during the teaching and learning process.

METHODOLOGY

Research Design

Action research method, within the qualitative paradigm, was used in the study. Cohen and Manion (1994), cited in Cohen, Manion and Morrison, (2000), define action research as 'a small- scale intervention in the functioning of the real world and a close examination of the effects of such an intervention.' (pp. 276-7) McNiff (1988), defines action research as 'an instrument used willfully by teachers to improve their practice' (p. 5). Action research has been defined by many researchers in different ways, but almost all of them agree that this method helps the teacher-researcher understand classroom problems and improve the teaching-learning process. Kemmis and McTaggart (1982), describe the process of action research as a four-step process, 'plan, act, observe and reflect more carefully, more systematically, and more rigorously than one usually does in everyday life.' (p. 10)

I began the research by identifying an area for inquiry, i.e. using questioning as a teaching-learning strategy to enhance students' participation in the class. I planned some strategies, took action in the class, observed, reflected on the process, and planned for improved action in the next lessons. Thus an attempt was made to understand the use of questions as a teaching strategy to improve the teaching-learning process in a primary science classroom in Pakistan.

Sample and Sampling Procedure

The criteria for selection of sample, school, teacher, and level of class, were based on different factors. I selected a primary science classroom in a government school where teacher questioning is the only mode of teacher and student interaction in the teacher-centred classrooms. I worked with a volunteer teacher to gain in-depth understanding of the opportunities and challenges in using questioning as a strategy in a primary science classroom.

On the very first day of my fieldwork, I had an informal meeting with the head teacher in order to select my sample teacher and class and share the purpose of the study as integral part of the M.Ed course. He mentioned that one teacher is responsible for teaching science to both sections of class 5. With the permission of the head teacher, I had an informal meeting with her to share the purpose and other details of the study. After her agreement, we discussed the data collection schedule; I tried to carry out the study within the teacher's timetable and syllabus.

Context of the Study

The research study was conducted in a co-educational government school located in the central part of Karachi and run by the Directorate of Primary Education. The school operates in two shifts: morning and afternoon. The first shift is for primary classes, both boys and girls, and the afternoon shift is for girls' secondary classes only. The research study was conducted in the morning shift of the school.

It was a small school with six classrooms and one office. The rooms were dark and small. The school building was hardly sufficient to accommodate the 300 students in the school. Each class had two sections and the number of students in each section ranged from twenty to twenty-five students. The staff included a head teacher, twenty-one teachers and support staff. These included two male and nineteen female teachers. The education level of these teachers ranged from matriculation (grade 10) to Bachelors degree. Some of them had professional qualifications such as Primary Teaching Certificate (PTC), or Certificate in Teaching (CT). One of the male teachers had a B.Sc degree but he taught mathematics only while other general classroom teachers taught science.

Like other government schools in Pakistan, the school had classes 6 days a week. The duration of each period was 30 minutes. The course of studies used in the school was prescribed by the Sindh Government.

Data Collection Procedure

First of all I observed the participant teacher's class, which provided the baseline information about the existing questioning practices and students' level of participation in the class. Then during the intervention I planned and delivered lessons based on the textbook but keeping in mind the focus of inquiry. The lessons were recorded and transcribed for analysis. The participant teacher observed my class in the intervention stage, whenever available. During the intervention stage, I had the dual role of researcher and teacher. I maintained my reflective journal to record my thoughts and questions about the process of using questioning as a teaching-learning strategy to enhance students' participation. The reflective journal also assisted me in my ongoing data analysis and enabled me to arrive at some tentative conclusions.

Data Analysis Procedure

First of all I constructed a grid, in which I organized the information from each lesson's transcripts such as questions asked, students' responses, and kinds of questions (closed, open), wait time, origins of questions and answers. From these grids, descriptions of lessons were written. Then I selected three lessons of the teacher observed during the pre-intervention stage and four lessons of my own conducted during the intervention stage for further analysis and discussions.

Figure 1: Framework for Data Analysis

Questions asked	Pupil responses	Types of questions	Wait time	Origin of questions	Origin of responses
		open closed procedural		Teacher Student	Teacher Student

Limitations of the Study

As I worked with one teacher and one class at the primary level in a particular school, the findings of the study may not be generalized to other kind of settings or situations. However, descriptive information about the researcher's role, sampling procedures and the data collection and analysis methods can be replicated in another setting.

FINDINGS: ANALYSIS AND DISCUSSION

This section presents the findings of the study with the focus on teachers' questioning as a strategy for enhancing students' participation in a primary science classroom in a government school in Pakistan. Data and evidence for answering the research questions come from various sources such as classroom observation of the teacher, observation and reflection on my own teaching and interviews with the teacher and students at the post-intervention stage.

Existing Questioning Practices and their Effect on Students' Participation

Following is a summary of questions observed at the pre-intervention stage.

Table 1: Categories of questions asked by teachers and students and wait time

Questions asked by	Types of questions asked			Wait time I
	Open-ended	Close-ended	Procedural	
Teacher	2	6	6	Less than one second
Student	None	None	5	

The analysis of three lessons shows that the teacher asked six close and two open-ended questions and the questions were taken from the textbook. For instance, which animals give birth to their babies? Which animals feed and protect their babies? Why do animals lay eggs? How do plants reproduce themselves? Usually students answered in chorus, for example: (teacher) Does mother take care of the babies? (students) Yes, miss. Few questions were answered by individual students e.g (teacher) Which animals lay eggs? Hanif: Hen and sparrow.

It was interesting to note that the two open-ended questions that demanded thinking and divergent answers from students were answered by the teacher herself immediately after posing these questions. In all cases wait time was less than one second. It was also observed that sometimes students asked questions to clarify the task when the teacher assigned written work, e.g 'How to write the answers and date'?

From classroom observation it was evident that the general pattern of science teaching in the classroom started with the teacher's reading of the text and students following the text in their textbooks. While reading, the teacher had little eye contact with the students. The teacher asked questions from the textbook. Mostly these were close-ended questions. Students' responses were from the text and consisted of one or more than one word answers. The type of questions asked and the responses given did not promote discussion and foster thinking. There were no probing questions or questions to generate a discussion in the class.

Another problem with the teacher's questioning techniques was that sometimes the teacher first selected a student and then asked a question. This situation might have decreased the interest of the rest of the students. Cotton (1999) confirms that 'if you call the student's name first, the rest of the class may not listen to the question' (p. 13). More important, the teacher's wait time was less than 1 second. Research (Rowe 1969) shows that when wait time is very short, students tend to give very short answers. It was also evident from observation that students asked only procedural questions. Leverhulume's study of questioning in twenty lessons, cited in Brown and Wragg (1993), also found that students asked twenty questions and most of these questions were procedural, such as 'Should we put the date?'

There were other factors which might help to explain the teacher's practice in the classroom. Firstly, the teacher had very low expectations from the students. From the interview it appeared that she believed that since most of the children came from lower class backgrounds they had less interest in learning. It seems that her belief hindered her from encouraging students' active participation in the class.

Secondly, teacher's reluctance to ask open-ended questions could be attributed to a lack of confidence in her own understanding of the subject area; the teacher shared her difficulties regarding the textbook content and questions: 'There are some questions in different chapters for which I cannot find answers in the textbook. How can I write the answers of these questions?' Analysing the teacher's statement it seems that content knowledge is very important for teachers to help students in understanding abstract concepts and allowing children to ask questions in order to enhance their level of participation and learning. We need to remember that the participant teacher had been assigned by the head-teacher to teach science to class 5. The situation of this teacher reflects a very well-known scenario of primary science teaching in Pakistan:

> In the primary schools science is taught by the general classroom teachers and there are more than hundred thousand such teachers. Most of these teachers have done 10 years of schooling with one year professional training. At school they have done either a two years course in 'general science' or two years of physics, chemistry, and biology. At the one year of professional course these teachers are prepared for the teaching of all the primary school subjects, thus they have little time for good grounding in subject matter and teaching methodology of science (Sheikh, 1977, p. 8).

Based on this evidence, I concluded that the teacher's questioning practices were characterized by several factors such as dependence on the textbook and less wait time. Similarly, my observations suggested that lack of background knowledge may restrict teachers in asking higher level or open-ended questions, which in turn, hinders students' active participation in the teaching-learning process. Hence, I agree with Wragg (1993) that teachers' lack of confidence in key subjects such as science suggests the need for keeping a balance in content and pedagogical knowledge in teacher training programmes.

Ways of Enhancing Students' Participation through Questioning

This section reports the findings based on the analysis of four lessons taught by the researcher during the intervention stage of the study. For my study I decided to continue with the lesson which the teacher was teaching from the textbook. As the focus of the study was to enhance students' participation through teacher's questioning, I included in my lessons a combination of closed, open-ended, and probing questions. I also maintained closely the wait time for my questions. Following is a summary of questions asked during the intervention stage

Table 2: Categories of Teacher's Questions and Wait Time during the Intervention Stage

Lesson # Topic	Closed questions	Open questions	Teacher's wait time I
Lesson # 1 Needs of plants	16	12	3-5 seconds
Lesson # 2 Health and hygiene	7	15	3-5 seconds
Lesson # 3 Sound	4	8	3-4 seconds
Lesson # 4 Air occupies space	4	6	3-5 seconds
Total	31	41	

Classroom Vignette

One episode is shared to give an idea of the questioning and classroom interaction pattern. A combination of closed and open questions were asked during the demonstration of a lesson. A glass, a tub of water, and a piece of paper were used for demonstration purpose.

> Researcher: [before putting the paper in the glass] What is in the glass?
> Students: Glass is empty.
> R: [after putting the paper in the glass] What else is in the glass apart from paper?
> S: Nothing.

After getting children's ideas the researcher invited the children to predict what would happen to the paper when the glass is put upside down in water. Most of the children responded that it would get wet but two of them said it would not get wet. In this situation there were two groups with different views and this certainly encouraged discussion. The teacher-researcher invited children to explain and give reasons for their opinions by asking questions.

> T: Imran, would you like to share with us why you think the paper will not get wet?
> S: Miss, last year I did this activity so, it will not get wet.
> S: It's interesting.
> T: Yes, Rana, in your opinion why will it not get wet?
> S: Miss, I am not sure. I am thinking.
> The other thirteen children said it would get wet.

The researcher demonstrated the activity (put the piece of paper into the bottom of the glass and put the glass upside down in the tub of water) and invited the children to observe the result. When the children observed that the paper did not get wet they were curious to know the reason. The researcher encouraged the children to solve the problem themselves, and then the students started asking questions. For example:

> S: Miss did you add something to the water?
> T: (smiling) What do you mean by something?
> S: Miss…(pause) any chemical?
> T: No.
> S: Miss, did you apply anything to the paper?
> T: Could you please explain what you mean?
> S: Miss, like gum.
> T: No.

The students started discussion amongst themselves. Here is a section of the students' discussion.

> S1: There is something in the glass.
> S2 (interrupting): If there is something in the glass we should be able to see it.
> S1: Is there anything between the water and paper?
> T: Yes.

Subsequently, one of the students asked if he could do the activity. The researcher agreed. The following dialogue took place.

> S: Miss, water will not go inside because it is filled with air.
> T: Are you sure?
> S: Yes miss, air is inside.
> S: Miss, see now it will get wet. When I do like this (holding the glass slightly tilted).
> S: Miss, we discussed that we cannot see the air but air is in the room.
> S: Miss, we also classified air as a gas.

At this stage the researcher decided to explain the discrepancy for the children that air occupies space.

This episode shows the student–student and student-teacher interaction during the demonstration of an experiment. The episode reflects students' active participation as they were responding to the teacher-researcher's questions, justifying their answers, asking questions for clarification, and beginning to relate their previous learning to the new concept (air occupies space). It seems that generating curiosity amongst the children was very important for developing their participation. Curiosity motivated them to ask questions. It appears that demonstration with questioning helped children understand an abstract science concept.

One of the issues that emerges from the above episode is whether the level of participation was due to the demonstration or the use of questioning by the teacher, or both. The possible explanation could be that it has more to do with questioning as the activity could have been done simply by doing it with an explanation of the concept. The alternative way is asking questions to engage students in discussion in order to enhance their participation and understanding of an abstract concept. It was found that children ask questions when they are encouraged to do so by the teacher. It was also observed that in the beginning students were only responding to the questions asked by the teacher. However, with the passage of time and increased familiarity with the teaching style and encouragement from the teacher-researcher, the students developed confidence and started asking questions. Thus, the class became more interactive with enhanced student participation.

The findings of the study suggest teachers' questioning as a strategy for encouraging students' active participation in a primary science classroom. In addition to key questions during teaching, probing for further clarification appeared important. For example, 'Can you give me an example?' 'Is there any other view?' These questions also helped me in assessing the children's understanding of the concept. Open-ended questions also provided opportunities to students to respond from their daily life experiences, prior knowledge, and from the textbook. The students' answers to these questions were longer; there were also different individual responses for each question.

Giving clear instructions at the beginning of the lesson about the activity and how to respond to questions appeared important to keep the students on task. I used to remind the children to think before sharing their ideas and to put their hands up and take turns while responding to questions. This helped me in maintaining a longer wait time, which in turn provided opportunities to students to comprehend the question and respond accordingly. This also helped me in maintaining discipline in the class and changed the pattern of students' answering from responding in chorus to more individual responses. It was recognized that classroom management skill is vital in implementing questioning as an effective teaching strategy.

Using different strategies for student selection and nomination to respond to teacher's questions, such as addressing questions to the whole class, inviting volunteers and non-volunteers, and calling students by name after posing questions, also helped in enhancing students' participation in the class. For example, sometimes, when one student responded immediately after the question was posed, I encouraged others by asking, 'Do you agree'? This strategy also encouraged other students to get involved in the discussion. In addition, teacher's verbal responses like 'that is a good answer', 'that is interesting', 'thank you for asking questions', and non-verbal responses like eye contact with the student who was responding, nodding and appropriate facial expressions played an important role in encouraging students' active participation in the lessons.

Similarly, different strategies were used as a vehicle to ask questions in the class. Sometimes I used supplements such as pictures, concrete materials (rubber band and ruler), and demonstration as means to provoke students' curiosity and spur them to ask questions. Questioning was found to be more effective when coupled with activities in a science classroom. It was found that interactive demonstration helped to create more student-student interaction in the lessons. Since textbooks are generally used as the only resource in the primary science classrooms in Pakistan, the activities were taken from the textbook and questions were formulated around them.

The research indicates that teachers questioning can play a significant role in making the classroom more interactive and enhance students' active participation in the teaching-learning process.

TEACHER'S QUESTIONING TECHNIQUES: OPPORTUNITIES AND CHALLENGES

There were some facilitating factors in implementing questioning as a teaching strategy. Firstly, maintaining a reflective journal helped me in writing detailed reflections on my questioning strategies and students' responses. Reflections on the teaching-learning process facilitated me in improving my questioning skills, and exploring ways to enhance students' participation in the class. For example, by listening to the recorded lessons, I realized that sometimes I had talked more than the students. The reflection helped me reduce my talking time, and encouraged children to participate more in the lessons. The reflective journal also helped me in ongoing data analysis. Secondly, using a shared language was found a facilitating factor in implementing questioning as a teaching strategy. As the students were well-conversant in the Urdu language, the use of Urdu in the classroom allowed them to express their thoughts and feelings well. Thirdly, teacher's positive attitude and the overall friendly classroom climate played a significant role in increasing students' involvement in the teaching-learning process. The importance of creating a classroom climate where students feel comfortable and confident is cited by several writers as an important factor in enhancing students' participation (Sotto 1994; Harlen and Holroyd 1997). Biddulph, Symington and Osborne (1986) also found in their study that '...the number of questions asked by children may have been influenced by the attitude of the teacher and the general atmosphere of the classroom' (p. 81). And lastly teacher's content knowledge appeared important in using questioning as a teaching strategy effectively to enhance students' participation in the class.

Some issues also emerged while using questioning as a teaching strategy for enhancing students' participation in the teaching-learning process. For example, if the teachers encourage students' participation in the lesson by allowing them to ask questions, the students might ask some 'difficult' questions. This could be very threatening or frustrating for teachers with weak subject or content knowledge. For example, in one of the lessons a student asked, 'Miss, how is energy stored in the food?' At that moment it was difficult for me to answer the question in a simple manner. However, the question was later addressed in a lesson entitled 'Where does the food energy come from?'

Completing the syllabus, doing the given exercises in the textbook and assigning homework appeared to be the major concerns of my teacher participant, 'Parents check children's homework. If we do not complete exercises of the chapter, parents will complain about it' (Teacher interview). Moreover, it was also realized that use of probing questions, extending wait time, and engaging students in critical thinking and discussion made the lessons much longer. This situation could be perceived as an issue by teachers following a tight time schedule and who are under pressure to complete the syllabus and prepare the students for examinations.

Another issue identified during the study was the difficulty in equal distribution of questions in the class. Some of the talkative students tried to dominate the quieter ones. It was challenging to encourage the quiet students to participate without discouraging other children. To cope with this situation, often the quieter students were encouraged to respond by calling their names and observing a longer wait time for their response. It was observed that gradually the quiet students also started responding to the teacher's questions. However, sometimes, this irritated the bright children in the class.

One of the significant issues was measuring the wait time. As mentioned earlier, I recorded all the lessons and transcribed them using a stop watch. I focused on wait time I or teacher's wait time after asking the question only because handling another variable might not have been possible within the limited time frame of the study. I agree with Sotto (1994) who indicates the importance of content knowledge, desire for encouraging participation and 'the presence of someone who is supportive and knowledgeable' (p. 183) in the class to overcome the problems of introducing new ideas or interventions. I had reasonably good content knowledge with my background of being a science student and teacher; additionally, I had the desire to encourage students' participation. However, I discovered that the process of implementing an innovative instructional strategy can be very challenging if it is not supported by a mentor or other colleagues in the school context.

SUMMARY OF FINDINGS

To summarize, the study findings indicate that teacher's questioning does play a significant role in making the classroom more interactive. Thus the study supports earlier findings about wait time being an important variable in using questioning for enhancing students' participation in teaching-learning in the class. In particular, it was found that a longer wait time encouraged the quieter students to participate more actively in the class. A number of factors were also identified in encouraging students to respond to teacher's questions. These are: advance preparation or lesson planning focusing on identifying key questions, giving clear instructions at the beginning of the lessons, teacher's positive attitude, a conducive classroom environment, and teachers' ongoing reflection on the process and consequences of using different kinds of questions in the teaching of science and other subjects. However, issues such as the possibility of students asking 'difficult' questions (questions to which the teacher does not know the answer), pressure of syllabus completion, skills required for equal distribution of questions in the class, maintaining wait time, and teachers' content knowledge and support available to her at the initial stages of introducing questioning as a teaching strategy can also affect the effectiveness of this strategy for enhancing students' participation in teaching-learning process.

The study indicates that the process of action research facilitates the use of innovative instructional strategies through planning, acting, reflecting, collecting, and interpreting the data in a real classroom situation. However, it was realized that teachers need support from a 'mentor' while introducing an innovative teaching strategy. Otherwise, it is possible that they might not be able to recognize and/or face the issues faced during data collection and analysis (see also Chapter 3 in this book).

IMPLICATIONS FOR SCHOOLS AND SCHOOLING PRACTICES

Contemporary classroom practices in primary science classrooms in Pakistan do not provide opportunities for using questioning as a strategy to increase students' participation and learning.

Therefore, teachers of primary science need substantial guidance in developing their questioning skills.

Moreover, teachers who are unsure of their own knowledge base or teachers who interpret science teaching as transmission of facts may feel uncomfortable in enhancing students' active participation in the teaching-learning process. It is therefore, recommended that teacher training institutions and school-based teacher development programmes should have a balance between content and pedagogical knowledge, and incorporate 'teachers' questioning as a teaching strategy' as an important skill for all teachers, who can thereby develop the use of questioning effectively in their classrooms.

Textbook developers also need to incorporate various kinds of questions such as closed and open-ended in textbooks as generally most teachers use only textbook questions to assess students' learning and for assigning homework.

2

Initiating Change in Mathematics Classrooms

Anjum Halai

INTRODUCTION

This chapter reports on a study of students' learning in the context of mathematics classrooms where the teacher had initiated change in classroom practices. The changed practices included use of cooperative learning strategies and introduction of mathematics tasks that were richer, open-ended, and related to everyday experiences of students. Researching students' learning in the classroom context necessitates taking account of those shared understandings and invisible meanings that establish classroom culture and that provide meaning to the interpretations being made by the participants of the classroom, i.e. the students and the teacher.

Classroom culture is governed by invisible yet shared ground rules and patterns of interaction. The teacher necessarily represents the culture of the mathematics classroom, and of the discipline of mathematics, therefore, the teacher is a significant force in initiating and stabilizing ground rules that implicitly govern classroom interactions (Edwards and Mercer, 1987; Yackel and Cobb, 1996). If these invisible yet shared ground rules govern the discourse in the classroom, the question is how do these rules come to be established in the first place, so that interpretations made by various participants in the classroom are compatible? And, how does one describe or recognize these implicit rules?

Patterns of interaction do not stabilize through teacher's initiation alone. For this to happen, teachers and students need to negotiate mutual expectations and obligations that are constituted in the classroom. The collaboration among the various participants would then take place as a consequence of fulfilling these expectations and obligations.

A sociological construct used to describe the shared understandings of a culture is 'norm', which refers to understandings or interpretations that become normative or taken-as-shared by the group (Yackel, 2001). Yackel goes on to elaborate that these norms are inferred by identifying regularities in patterns of social interaction in the classroom. Those classroom participation structures that are stable facilitate in inferring the social norms prevalent, while the notion of taken-as-shared implies that individual interpretations fit with the purpose at hand.

The understanding that students have about socially interacting with other students and with the teacher is regarded as a manifestation of social norms. However, it is important to recognize that within social norms there are socio-mathematical norms, and it is these socio-mathematical norms that make a mathematics classroom different from other classrooms.

Yackel (2001) holds that,

> The distinction between social norms and socio-mathematical norms is subtle. For example, the understanding that students are expected to explain their solutions is a social norm, whereas the understanding of *what counts* (emphasis in original) as an acceptable mathematical explanation is a socio-mathematical norm. (pp. 13-14)

Hence, a socio-mathematical norm would be a shared criterion of what is valuable, or what matters in a mathematical explanation or solution. As with social norms, socio-mathematical norms could be inferred by identifying regularities in patterns of social interactions. The idea of socio-mathematical norms is significant in order to distinguish the differences in the ways students learn mathematics in different classes.

THE STUDY

This study examined the role of social interactions in students' learning of mathematics and was located in two secondary schools in Karachi, Pakistan. Over a period of one academic year two small groups of students (11–13 yrs.) were observed, each engaged in working at mathematics tasks set for them by their respective teachers. The research question was:

What is the role of social interactions in students' learning of mathematics as they work in small groups (in the context of classrooms in Pakistan)?

The subsidiary questions were:

1. What is the nature of social interactions in the classrooms?
2. What is the nature of students' learning of mathematics in the classrooms?
3. What conclusions can be drawn about the processes of students' learning of mathematics in small group settings?

Methodology was qualitative in nature. Participant observation was the primary mode of conducting the research. Questions emerging from ongoing observations were followed up in stimulated recall interviews with students. Meetings were scheduled with the teachers who were seen as a significant part of the socio-cultural context. Classroom observations were recorded on videotapes and interviews were audiotaped. While the audio tapes were transcribed, the video tapes were logged using the techniques suggested by Graue and Walsh (1998, p. 139).

I used grounded theory procedures and techniques for analysis (Strauss and Corbin, 1998). This meant that I read and re-read the video logs and coded them line by line. The codes emerged from the ongoing analysis, and were clustered together in broad categories. Moreover, my emphasis on meanings emerging from my interaction with data meant that in coding and naming categories, I tried to capture the experience or the issue being represented by the category. For example, categories like 'students' beliefs about mathematics' or 'students' interpretation of the purpose of task' kept the issue being described by the category in the foreground.

The Setting

This study draws on one of the two schools, the Karachi Boys' School (pseudonym). The school is part of a larger system which regularly sponsors teachers to the Aga Khan University, Institute for Educational Development (AKU-IED), which provides in-service teacher education. It offers Mathematics education programmes at certificate and advanced diploma level. Working collaboratively with others and introducing cooperative learning in the classroom is an important part of the curriculum at AKU-IED (Halai, 2006; Halai, 2001; Jaworski, 1996). Based on my previous experience of working with teachers in this school, I had reasonable expectations of seeing group work and other collaborative forms of learning in the classrooms.

Amina Karim (pseudonym) was a mathematics teacher in the Karachi Boys' School. I first got to know Amina when she came to attend some courses in mathematics education that were being offered at AKU-IED and which I was teaching. When I approached Amina Karim to work with me in my research project it was almost a year since she had graduated from the mathematics education programme at AKU-IED.

She informed me that since her graduation, she had been working at improving her own teaching practices. Hence, for the academic year in which I approached her for the research, she had already asked the principal to assign her all classes of year seven to teach. Previously, she had taught some classes in year seven and others in year six. She said that she was implementing her learning from AKU-IED which required, among other things, planning the provided mathematics syllabus in ways that were appropriate for group tasks. Being the sole teacher responsible for all year seven classes, she would cover the curriculum for year seven, but be free of potential constraints of keeping up with other teachers.

The small group of students, from class 7, whom I observed were three boys named (pseudonyms) Faizullah, Mansoor, and Saleem (age range 11-12 yrs.). They came to be part of the research as a result of a process of selection I undertook in consultation with the teacher.

CHANGING THE CLASSROOM PRACTICES

Amina told me that she had introduced in her class co-operative learning strategies (Johnson, Johnson and Houlbec, 1993) to which she had been introduced in the course at AKU-IED. According to Johnson et al. (ibid., pp. 6-12), there are five basic elements that should be incorporated in small group work to make it co-operative learning. These include, a) individual accountability, i.e. when performance of each individual is evaluated, feedback is given both to the individual and the group, and the student is held responsible by the group if not working responsibly, b) face-to-face interactions, i.e. when individuals encourage and facilitate each group member's effort to achieve group goals, c) positive interdependence, i.e. all group members believe that they, and all other members of the team are essential for the success of the team, d) group processing, e.g. reflection on group sessions to describe what actions of the members were effective and which were ineffective and deciding which actions to continue with, to modify or discard, and e) social skills, i.e. to use appropriately interpersonal skills in small group work.

Hence, to ensure students' individual accountability as they worked in groups, she usually invited the group members to label themselves a, b, c or d and at the time of whole class presentation, she invited students by their labels. For example, she would say, 'Person 'b' from group one please come forward'. This strategy was to ensure that all members of the group would be ready to share the group's work with the whole class. Periodically, she invited students to assess how they were working in groups and to monitor how far the responsibilities of working in groups were being met by each of the students within the group and the various groups within the class. For example, she encouraged them to take on the responsibility of monitoring each other in the group, and the groups to monitor other groups to ensure that each one participated in the group task. However, the assessment and monitoring of work in groups was mostly about organizational aspects of group work such as sharing resources or taking turns when speaking or using soft voices and so on.

The result of introducing co-operative learning strategies in the classroom was that the classroom organization of working at mathematics tasks in small groups preceeded by some introductory work by the teacher, and followed by the whole class presentation and discussion, was very consistent across the lessons observed. In a typical 40 minute lesson there would be whole class work for about 5 to 10 minutes. Here the teacher would introduce the group task. This was followed by work in small groups for about 20 to 25 minutes. The whole class sharing session would be for the remaining 10 to 15 minutes. In this session, different groups of students shared their work by going to the front of the class and explaining their work, often by writing on the blackboard.

Throughout the course of my research, the students and the teacher spoke about their responsibilities regarding work in groups and towards one another when working together in the classroom. There was no explicit conversation among them about the nature and process of mathematical thinking and developing understanding of mathematics being learnt. I inferred that the change in socio-mathematical practices was being introduced through problem tasks which were designed or selected by Amina and were in the form of worksheets. The context of the problem was familiar and within the realm of real world experience of the students. Students were not required to follow fixed procedures for solving the problems. Instead they were free to use the solution strategies they found suitable and were expected to explain them to others in the group and in the classroom. Moreover, the directions in the problem tasks required students to explain their solutions to others in the group or the teacher. In addition to the problem tasks, resources like teacher-made worksheets, cardboard cut-outs of geometric shapes, and the real-world experiences of the students were used to enable students to learn mathematics.

In the course of the study, several classroom examples were generated which illustrated the process of students' learning in the context of classroom change. For instance, these included students' learning proportional reasoning through comparing strong and weak drink prepared with water and Rooh Afza; learning mode in the context of 'favourite drinks'; and exploring relationships of quadilaterals by looking for 'other names'. These examples have been documented in some detail in Halai (2001). However, for depth of discussion one illustrative example is drawn upon to provide a context for discussion of findings.

Vignette: *Chand Raat*

At the time of teaching it was the month of Ramadan. In the task below, the teacher provided a real life situation of setting up a small business on *Chand Raat*. The night the new moon is sighted is called *Chand Raat*. The new moon after the end of Ramadan heralds Eid celebrated by setting up stalls to sell bangles.

Chand Raat Task:

Suppose two of your friends had decided to set up for *Chand Raat* a bangles stall on Tariq Road. One friend contributed Rs 500 and the other contributed Rs 1000. They made a profit of Rs 1000.

- What would be a fair way of sharing the profit?
- What would be each friend's share in the profit?
- Can you explain the method you used to share the profit?

MATHEMATICS BEING LEARNT AND BELIEFS ABOUT MATHEMATICS

Faizullah and Mansoor worked at the *Chand Raat* task while Saleem was absent. The mathematical topic of ratios and proportional division was being considered in this lesson. The setting and the amount of money involved in the task was such that the students could be expected to have had experience of it. When they began the work, Faizullah suggested that in sharing the profit the friend who had put in 1000 rupees would get double the share in profit. He thus informed Mansoor that they should divide the profit into three shares because one person had put in double the amount of the other. Mansoor did not agree and suggested dividing the profit equally among the two friends, which meant each friend would get Rs 500.

The following extract from the video transcript illustrates how the students approached the mathematical idea of proportional division. In the conversation below, both, Faizullah and Mansoor are referring to the problem statement, *Chand Raat*.

1. Faizullah: (he) has put in 1,000 rupees, (he should) get more on it.

2. Mansoor: (reads from the worksheet) 'What would be each…'. The profit is the same. You know, if he gets twenty rupees the other will also get twenty rupees. He should not get twenty-one. He should get twenty. (reads again) 'What would be each friend's share in the profit?' See, it is saying the same thing. Both friends should get the same (amount of) money. If this one gets a thousand, that one will also get a thousand.

(Data item: 5, Video Transcript)

In line 1 above, Faizullah gives evidence that according to his understanding, the profit would be divided in proportion to the investment. Hence, he suggests that the friend who had put in a 1000 rupees should get more (as compared to the one who put in 500 rupees). Mansoor, however, thinks differently. In line 2, he suggests that an equal share of the profit should go to both friends in the business. He names different amounts of money to make his point that irrespective of whatever sum one friend invests, the other would get the same. Both of them repeated their proposed solutions. Faizullah then wrote that he proposed dividing the profit in a ratio of 1:2, and showed his solution to Mansoor. Mansoor reiterated his point of equal share in the profit and suggested that the profit be divided by two. Faizullah also wrote out the solution proposed by Mansoor.

Mansoor looked at what Faizullah had written and declared that their work was wrong. He suggested that they should consult the teacher and beckoned the teacher.

1. Mansoor: We were doing wrong, brother. Teacher! (Beckons the teacher).

(Pause, the two wait for the teacher)

2. Mansoor: You are doing it wrong, call the teacher.

(Data item: 6, Video Transcript)

Faizullah and Mansoor waited for the teacher. In the transcript below Faizullah held out their work for the teacher to see. The work showed both the solution procedures, that of dividing the profit in two shares (1:1) and of dividing it in three shares (1:2). The teacher in line 2, looked briefly at the work, pointed to the solution in the ratio 1:2 and asked one of them to come up and explain.

1. Faizullah: (showing their written work to the teacher) Teacher we have done. Teacher, I...is this right?
2. Teacher: Can you come and explain?
(looks at what Faizullah is showing and points to the solution in the ratio 1:2).
3. Mansoor: Ooooh!
4. Teacher: (to the whole class). Okay, discussion is over.
5. Mansoor: (refers to going to the blackboard) Go, you go. You go, I will not go.
6. Teacher: (to the class) All eyes here. All eyes here.
7. Mansoor: (to Faizullah) How is this right? How is this right?
8. Faizullah: Teacher....
9. Mansoor: (to Faizullah) How is this right?

10. Faizullah: Teacher.
11. Mansoor: (To Faizullah) How is this right?
Faizullah is seen getting up to go towards the blackboard.

(Data item: 7, Video Transcript)

Evidence shared so far shows students' overriding concern to find out, whether or not their answer was right. The sample of work shows Faizullah had thought through the problem and had a rationale for sharing the profit in the ratio 1:2. However, he is also not sure whether his answer is 'right'. He therefore asked me first and then showed his work to the teacher. The teacher (line 2) invited the students to come and explain their work at the blackboard. Mansoor's questions in lines 7, 9 and 11 indicate that he interpreted the teacher's invitation as a declaration on the teacher's part that the 'answer is right'.

It appears that each boy believed he was right, and each had his rationale but could not convince the other. Also significant is the students' referral to the teacher to confirm which answer is right. It seems from their need to use an outside source to decide the veracity of their work that the nature of argument being used to convince themselves and others was not based on their own reasoning, rather the acceptance or otherwise was based on the authority of the teacher. There were tensions in the students' implicit belief in the value of the right answer even at the expense of one's own reasoning and the socio-mathematical practices being initiated that solutions should be meaningful, which implied a focus on reasons along with conclusions. Further, the focus on right answers implies that students viewed mathematics as a fixed body of knowledge leading to certain truths in the form of right or wrong answers.

NATURE OF THE PROBLEM TASK

A pattern emerging in my analysis showed that there were certain assumptions implicit in the task, which led to issues for students' learning. The problem task *Chand Raat* drew upon the specific socio-cultural experiences from the real world that the students might be expected to be familiar with. Assumption implicit in the task was that the real world context familiar to the students would facilitate their learning. The mathematics involved was relatively simple. The three questions in the task were aimed at enabling the students to rationalize the procedure they might come up with in the course of proportional division of the profit. While the problem aimed to draw on the real world context, implicit in the intention of the teacher were the limits to the extent that the real world context would be evoked. For example, in a real world context, two friends setting up a small business on *Chand Raat* may not necessarily be doing it for financial gains. The motive may be to have fun and participate in the festivities. The issue of sharing profit might not be the primary consideration in such a business. Moreover, in the real world situation, variables such as time and effort put in by each partner in the business could also be a consideration. However, set within the context of the mathematics lessons on ratios and proportions, the teacher's purpose is implicit that the task should enable students to learn the formal mathematical interpretation of fair share, i.e. proportional share. Mansoor's case showed that he had difficulty in being able to abstract the required mathematics from the real world context.

Discussion on Findings

In the following section, I synthesize my discussion on findings and identify the outcomes and implications for students' learning.

Students' Beliefs about the Nature of Mathematics

Observations revealed that students appeared to view mathematics as a fixed body of knowledge leading to certain truths in the form of right or wrong answers. This view was in conflict with the view implicit in the teacher's change initiatives: that of mathematics knowledge as discursive and socially constructed.

For example, during the work on mathematics' tasks a strong emphasis in the classroom was laid on finding the 'right answer'. From the student's side this emphasis was evident in the uncertainty they had in the validity of their own argument because belief in the right answer meant that two different answers could not both be right. Hence, they needed someone to say which answer was right. Their reasons for accepting an answer as being right or wrong were not based on a rational argument. Instead, it was the teacher's authority that was used as a criterion to decide right or wrong. A recurring question was, 'Teacher, is this right?' This focus on right answer suggests that students believed that mathematics was a body of fixed knowledge leading to right or wrong answers. It was an implicit criterion against which mathematical activity was being judged by the students and the teacher.

These beliefs about the nature of mathematics being prevalent among the students raised the issue of a possible conflict with the new socio-mathematical practices that the teacher was trying to establish. For example, the socio-mathematical practice of 'meaningful solutions' required that the nature of arguments put forward for accepting or rejecting an answer or a solution would be based on students' own reasons. I sensed a tension here in students' learning. On the one hand, classroom practices were initiated by the teacher to enable students to rationalize their solutions. On the other hand, they had to ensure that their answer was right from the perspective of the teacher. An implication of the implicit classroom practice of focus on the right answers seemed to be that the students could not explore their own thinking to make sense of the solution.

Ernest (1994) extends these ideas about the nature of mathematics to contend these (fallibilist) views to assert that the status of mathematical truth is determined to some extent, relative to its context and is dependent, at least in part, on historical contingency. A consequence of adhering to fallibilist philosophy could be that the arguments that students in the classroom put forward would be social in nature and would not use authority (teachers/textbooks) to rationalize their answers. An implication of the above discussion on the nature of mathematics is that if students' and teachers' views about mathematics are absolutist rather than fallibilist they can impede learning. This is because the absolutist views could lead to teaching in ways that might encourage students to believe that mathematics is a fixed body of knowledge with right or wrong answers.

However, there are issues involved in extending these conceptions of the nature of mathematics into the classroom to ensure that students recognize the fallibilist nature of mathematics. In the classroom, the young learners are expected to learn the 'body of knowledge' that has been acknowledged by the community of mathematicians as acceptable mathematically. By the time this body of knowledge reaches the classroom all the detours, different lines of thought, and messiness that might have been involved in the process of this body of knowledge coming to be accepted are ironed out. Hence, for the student this body of knowledge has an 'objective status' outside of him or her (Lakatos, 1976). This state of affairs creates a tension when the teacher tries to set up learning situations that have an implicit constructivist philosophy but the student adheres to the philosophy of naïve realism leading to epistemological beliefs about an objective body of knowledge outside the knower.

Communicating the Purpose of Changed Practices

The teacher's communication of her changed expectations from the students was explicit where the forms of social behaviour were concerned. However, her communication was largely implicit regarding how the change in social practices would lead to mathematics knowledge development. Evidence showed that students appeared to have oriented their activities to suit the change in the social practices. However, there appeared to be some confusion regarding what the students saw as the purpose of these changes with regard to mathematics learning. The suggestion is that there was a need for more explicit communication between students and the teacher with regard to socio-mathematical norms being initiated. For example, classroom interaction patterns showed that a social norm that was stable in classroom was that group representatives share their solutions with the rest of the class. The new social norm of sharing group work with the whole class had raised the issue that students became too preoccupied with preparing for what to say when called to the blackboard to engage seriously with the mathematical thinking of the task. An implication was that students were participating in small group work but their purpose for doing so was different from the teacher's purpose of planning the group work. The students' purpose in group work appeared to be to use group work as an opportunity to get ready for the ultimate task of presenting their work to the whole class. According to my inference, the teacher's purpose in setting up group work was to enable students to learn mathematics meaningfully. The students' motivation for participation in small group activities was different.

My analysis suggests that a reason could be the manner in which the teacher had communicated the change in classroom practices to the students. She had overtly and explicitly emphasized her focus on co-operative learning, including her expectation from students to share their work in groups with the whole class. However, she had left implicit the purpose of group work to exchange ideas and engage in the process of meaning-making that could be inferred from her various change initiatives in the classroom. Hence, students attributed significance to what they interpreted as the teachers' real purpose of the classroom change, i.e. students' presentation at the blackboard. An implication is that for teachers to initiate a change in the classroom practices would require that they communicate their changed expectations through explicit and implicit means.

Contradictory Messages in the Teacher's Practice

The teacher's role was an important element in the socio-cultural setting of the classroom. She was instrumental in initiating the changes in the social setting of the classroom, including initiating the new social practices and the socio-mathematical practices. Certain issues and tensions arose as a result of the teacher's mode of work in the classroom. For example, implicit in the context of the problem-solving tasks was the teacher's purpose of mathematising (Bauersfeld, 1992) everyday phrases like 'other names', 'strongest drink' and 'fair share'. Implications of mathematising everyday terms and words are that these words are used by the teacher to carry specific meaning and usage that the teacher has in mind. However, these words carry with them social and cultural meanings not always compatible with mathematical meanings. The result is a narrowing of meanings and interpretations that would be acceptable in the classroom. In the research classroom the teacher's funnelling (Bauersfeld, 1992) of meaning became apparent in the students' presentation of their work in the whole class. The teacher responded differently to the various groups' presentation in the whole class presentation session. She remained non-committal towards answers that were apparently unacceptable to her and accepted the right answers.

The practice of mathematising raised the issue of students' ritualized participation in the classroom activities. Edwards and Mercer (1987) remark on the teacher's dilemma.

> ...to have to inculcate knowledge while apparently eliciting it. This gives rise to a general ground rule of classroom discourse, in which the pupil's task is to come up with the correct solutions to problems seemingly spontaneously, while all the time trying to discern in teacher's clues, cues, questions and presuppositions of what that required solution actually is (p. 126).

The suggestion is that the teacher's selective acceptance of student response suppresses, however unintendedly, alternative interpretations. An implication of the teacher's selective acceptance of solutions was that the focus on learning appeared to be narrow, ruling out alternative interpretations and meanings. To an observer it appeared that students were getting contradictory messages from the teachers' practice. On the one hand, they were encouraged to explore alternative interpretations of problem tasks through strategies such as using their own solution methods and explaining solutions in their own words. On the other hand, their alternative interpretations were dismissed without the students being provided an opportunity to explain their interpretations.

The Classroom and the Broader Context

The focus of the study was students' learning in the classroom. However, there were certain issues and questions that emerged because of the factors outside the classroom. I used the diagram adapted from Price (2000) to represent pictorially how the classroom mathematics learning of the child was being influenced by forces outside the mathematics classroom.

The shaded box in Figure 1 shows that mathematics learning is not limited to the mathematics lesson only. Rather, it crosses over to the classroom, school, and the society. Factors such as students' experiences of cultural activities like business, pressures such as examination or the teaching that was drawing from the teachers' experience of AKU-IED, influenced the teaching-learning process. The classroom appeared in a relationship of being nested in the school and in the larger box titled 'the society'.

This perspective of classroom being nested enabled me to make sense of some issues and raised new questions for the study. For example, the people in the society in which the school is located do not usually speak English as their first language. The medium of instruction was English in the school. A question arose for me: To what extent were students' difficulties in learning exacerbated by the fact that the teaching was in English? Could language issues be contributing to the difficulty that the students appeared to face in making meaning in the classroom? This question gained further pertinence, given that the students in my research reverted to the Urdu language when speaking amongst themselves. This observation of students reverting to Urdu suggests that they were more comfortable sharing their

**Figure 1: Factors influencing a Child's Learning of
Mathematics in a Pakistani Classroom**

	Family		The Society		Friends
Shops			The School		
		Peers	Other teachers		
		Social Studies	The Classroom		Syllabus
			Discipline,		
	Costs	English	Languages	Mathematics	Learning
		Religious Education	Science	Problem tasks	Exams,
				Group work	Textbooks
Other Language	Sports	Individual Work			
				Discipline	Shopping
				Bilingual	Business
				AKU-IED	Cricket
				Chand Raat	
	Religion				

thinking in Urdu. Hence, the use of the English language might be problematic for them. However, an alternative interpretation could be that the group interactions being in Urdu were aiding students in their effort to learn mathematics meaningfully. As the diagram illustrates, a mathematics lesson is but a part of the students' classroom experiences. The students' classroom experiences in lessons other than mathematics were not based on group work. What were the implications of different practices in the other lessons for the teacher's efforts at changing the social and socio-mathematical practices in their lessons?

Finally, as shown in the diagram, learning experiences in the classroom and the school are nested in the largest square, i.e.

society. While I do not have direct evidence, I know from my experience and research in Pakistani schools that the role of a teacher is understood as that of a knowledgeable adult who is responsible to transmit this knowledge to students, whose role is to receive this knowledge. What are the implications of these understandings of teacher's and student's role for classroom change where learning is seen in the process of active participation and in cooperative interactions with others, not necessarily in teacher transmission?

CONCLUDING REFLECTIONS

In this study, it was established that a change has been initiated in the social and socio-mathematical practices in the classroom. The students worked at mathematics tasks which were different in nature; and the ways of working were more socially interactive, i.e. students were expected to work in small groups and rationalize their thinking. The focus on the process of developing mathematical thinking through rationalization was a significant step forward because research has shown that Pakistani mathematics classrooms are mainly characterized by an emphasis on only the product of mathematics tasks obtained through application of rote memorized rules (Halai, 2004, Warick and Reimers, 1995).

However, students appeared to work in groups through interpretations made from the perspective of old norms prevalent in the classroom. Hence, while ways of working in groups came to be taken as shared to some extent, mathematics rationalization in the group did not. For example, working at specially designed problem tasks in groups and later presenting this work to the whole class appeared to be an accepted part of the classroom practice. Besides these new practices in the classroom that were regarded as normative, there were certain old understandings that also appeared to be taken as normative by the students. For example, a norm prevalent in the classroom was that the purpose of the mathematics problem task was to find the right answer.

Hence, there appeared to be agreement among the students regarding this purpose when they engaged in mathematics tasks in the classroom. A wide experience of prevailing norms in Pakistani classrooms supports this interpretation.

Two main factors led to students working through old ways in new settings. First, the teachers' communication of the purpose of change was largely implicit in her practice so that the students were expected to infer the purpose implicit in the change. Second, students' perceptions of mathematics and the purpose of classroom tasks did not support critical reasoning of mathematical ideas. Hence, classroom evidence led me to conclude that students and teacher are both participants in the classroom culture, so that meanings do not come to be taken as shared as a consequence of teacher initiation alone.

These findings and conclusions lead to several recommendations for teachers and teacher educators. First, teachers need to consider students as participants in the change process in the classroom and not simply as receivers of change. This difference in stance towards students would have implications for the teacher's own role, which would be that of a participant in classroom processes and not the manager of classroom culture. Second, introducing new teaching strategies in teacher education courses should be seen as a complex process requiring a critical consideration of assumptions underpinning the new teaching strategies and their implications for the individual teacher's beliefs and practices. Third, beliefs about the nature of knowledge and about the discipline, in this case mathematics, have a strong influence on how classroom interaction patterns change. Hence, teacher education in mathematics courses needs to challenge teachers' conceptions of mathematics and how it is learnt.

3

Exploring Reflective Dialogue as a Strategy for Teacher Development

Jane F. A. Rarieya

INTRODUCTION

Despite the tacit acknowledgement that reflective practice is important in the field of education and that teachers need to be reflective practitioners, this development has largely been in the West. Teachers in Pakistan are generally unaware of what reflective practice means; and those who do know about it, do not know how they can effectively engage in it. In most classrooms in Pakistan, the classroom is often a teacher's private world and many teachers view it as a weakness to step outside their classroom and ask for assistance. As a result, they face a host of perplexing issues in the classroom, alone. Exchanges about teaching and learning are either done during staff meetings or during the occasional moments when teachers get to chat, maybe over a cup of tea during recess. Most of the dialogue at this time is often perfunctory and hardly reveals much.

My observations and experiences of working with teachers have made me appreciate the importance of reflective dialogue in trying to help teachers improve themselves. I have noted on numerous occasions that teachers are unable to look at their classrooms with critical eyes, and hence find it difficult to try and change their practice in any way. I have often had to probe the teachers through conversations to get them to reflect on their lessons, and consequently try to improve their practice.

This chapter, therefore, presents findings of a study that sought to explore the possibilities, challenges, and effects of engaging in reflective dialogue; it aimed at finding out what effect reflective dialogue has on teachers using it in the context of Pakistani schools and indicate the way forward for teacher educators in Pakistan in their attempts to bring about change and improvement in schools.

The chapter begins with a review of literature on reflective dialogue. It then presents the methodology of the study and provides a background of the research questions, the participants, and the setting. Findings of the study and the implications of these findings for schooling and teacher education practices are also discussed. The chapter also briefly looks at the role of those who help teachers to become reflective (the reflective coach) as the reflective coach is an integral part of the process of engaging in reflective dialogue. The role of the reflective coach in this study was also significant because the teacher participants had never encountered the notion of reflective dialogue and therefore had to be assisted in understanding and engaging in it.

What is Reflective Dialogue?

Reflective dialogue as a concept means different things to different people. A number of researchers and writers do not use the term 'reflective dialogue' to describe their own activities or understanding. Instead, they use terms like, 'reflection,' 'reflective practice,' 'teacher talk,' or teacher conversations' interchangeably. In this chapter, I too use them interchangeably for I feel that they encompass what reflective dialogue is.

A review of literature and research (e.g. Stephens and Reimer, 1993; Thomas and Montemery, 1997; Risko, Vukelich and Rosicos, 2002; Serafini, 2002; Fendler, 2003) reveals that reflective dialogue is viewed either as the maintenance of a dialogue journal or participation in reflective conversations in groups or pairs. In this study, I used the term to include both the notions of dialogue journals and reflective conversations.

Certain features are peculiar to reflective dialogue and distinguish it from other forms of reflection. The first of this is that reflection is done through talk. This talk can be verbal or written as in the form of dialogue journals, which Holly (1994) describes as talk with oneself. However, if this talk is to be termed reflective dialogue, then it is talk shared with others by giving them access to one's thoughts in the journal to read and respond accordingly. So, reflective dialogue is not an individual activity. It is reflection with others who ask questions of one another, thereby helping each other gain new insights about situations, beliefs, and values. Moreover, the perspectives are usually shared in an atmosphere of mutual support. Hence, collaboration is also a significant aspect of reflective dialogue.

Reflective dialogue necessitates the presence of the other person who responds to the teacher's reflections, thereby facilitating the process of reflection. Thomas and Montemery (1997) talk of 'reflective coaching' (p. 380), which they describe as the role one plays in posing thought-provoking questions to help the process along. They point out that all teachers need these kinds of reflective coaches. The role of the reflective coach is one that has been labelled differently by different people. For example, Dobbins (1996) refers to it as 'facilitators of reflection' and 'mentors' and Day (1993) as 'skilled helpers.' Dobbins (ibid.) points out that the role played by the reflective coach is important because, 'one cannot assume that teachers will explore issues or challenge their thinking on their own' (p. 276).

Certain qualities seem to be required of those who play the role of the reflective coach. Day (op. cit.) claims that reflective coaches should be '…critical friends, trusted colleagues who have not only technical abilities but also human relating/inter-personal qualities and skills as well as time, energy and the practice of reflecting on their own practice' (p. 88). Elliot (1991) adds that those who support teachers must relinquish their expert status and adopt partnership roles as facilitators and collaborative teachers.

Ashcroft (1992) advocates the recognition of the role of peers in promoting teacher learning. She points out that 'peers can act as non-threatening observers, they can challenge interpretations, they can help each other gain insights by being an audience for each other's explanations and evaluations' (p. 41). Pugach and Johnson's study (1990) of collaboration between novice and experienced teachers revealed that reflection with peers raised teacher tolerance at two levels: the teacher's ability to listen to others' views and the teacher's ability to tolerate what was going on in their classrooms by looking at what was happening without getting angry.

Studies on reflective dialogue (Thomas and Montemery, 1997; Reinhold, 1999; Risko et al., 2002, Reed, Davis and Nyabanyaba, 2002,) reveal that as a result of engaging in reflective dialogue, participants in the study (a) spent more time thinking about the affective aspects of teaching instead of the cognitive, (b) found reflective dialogue a valuable planning and teaching tool, (c) adopted a different stance to understand their experiences from a different perspective, and (d) thought reflective dialogue was useful for helping them understand and learn about their role as teachers.

Reflective dialogue provides 'windows' into teachers' thinking (Thomas and Montemery, 1997) as it enables the teacher to open up her/his teaching to the public through writing or talk. Its value in teaching and learning is that it encourages one to view problems from different perspectives (Rarieya, 2005).

Russell (1993) suggests that a reflective teacher is not necessarily a good teacher and I am inclined to agree with him. We are predisposed to assume that being reflective and being successful go hand in hand. Nonetheless, it is best when a strong teacher is reflective and when reflective practice is used to make a weak teacher stronger. This is because teaching, as Wesley (1998) points out, is largely a thinking life, a constant reflection; forward to a plan, backward to an evaluation.

Research Setting

I think it is important to describe the context of the school where the study was conducted because the school's aim of trying to develop it into a good institution, as well as the prevailing culture in the school was significant for the study.[1]

The school in which the study was conducted is situated in central Karachi. It is a private, co-educational, well-equipped community school run by a board of trustees. At the time of the study, the school was only ten years old and comprised kindergarten, primary, secondary and higher secondary sections, all situated within one campus.

There is a general policy in the school to make it one of the good schools in Karachi. The school's management feels that the best way to achieve this is through its teachers. There is also a great emphasis on non-traditional ways of teaching. Both the vice-principal and the primary section-head, who are responsible for helping teachers improve their classroom practice, carry out classroom observations to ensure that teachers do away with the traditional ways of teaching. Teachers are encouraged to pursue professional development courses, which are often paid for by the school. So, any activity that helps the teachers to develop professionally is welcomed by the school's management.

The school's endeavours to improve teaching have been mixed. Some teachers have been able to meet the challenges posed by this kind of expectation from the administration and are relatively 'good' teachers. On the other hand, there are some who feel pressured and uncomfortable in meeting these demands. The feelings of anxiety are heightened by the fact that the administration does not hesitate to drop any teacher from its staff who is not willing to improve his or her teaching to conform to the administration's expectations.

Research Question

The study sought to know whether, and in what ways, engaging in reflective dialogue affects teachers in the context of a private school in Pakistan. It was informed by several questions, four of which are pertinent to this chapter:

- What are the challenges faced by the teacher in integrating the concept of reflective dialogue in his or her practice?
- How are teachers affected by reflective dialogue?

- Do teachers attribute any benefits to reflective dialogue? If so, what are they?
- What is the role of the reflective coach in reflective dialogue?

METHODOLOGY

The study employed a qualitative case study approach and involved four teachers in the same school. I wanted to examine the process and outcomes of engaging in reflective dialogue and in doing so, seek a deeper understanding of this experience from the participants' perspectives because as Silverman (1993) points out 'meaning is of essential concern to the qualitative approach' (p. 32). The qualitative paradigm also allows one a certain degree of flexibility as one goes about his/her research. This flexibility was appropriate for my school-based research for it accommodated the possibility of changes in my study should teachers drop out of the study or should they not be available for any of the research activities that I may have planned. Finally, as I was also studying my own actions and consequences as a reflective coach, using the qualitative approach enabled me to do so comfortably.

Data sources included interviews, personal conversations, observations, and teachers' as well as the researcher's reflective journals.

Reflective dialogue took place at three levels:

- Each teacher maintained a dialogue journal, which she shared with me as the reflective coach throughout the study.
- Each teacher had a chance to engage in individual reflective dialogue with me after a classroom observation (one-to-one reflective sessions).
- All the teachers took part in a group reflective dialogue session once a week for one hour (group reflective sessions).

These opportunities to engage in reflective dialogue served as data sources too. Reflective dialogue focused on issues related to teaching, either with regard to the teachers' practice or thoughts about teaching, school-related issues, personal issues, as well as the process of reflection that the teachers were undergoing.

Participants' Profiles

Below are brief profiles of the research participants which I believe partly account for the individual teacher's responses to reflective dialogue:

Shafia is a science graduate and at the time of the study had five years of teaching experience. In addition to teaching English, Mathematics and Science to class three, she was a class teacher and a housemistress. At the time of the study, she was a single woman who lived with her parents and had no family responsibilities. She had a good reputation as a teacher both at the school and the institute where she taught English after school hours and had won the best teacher award in the school the previous year. She had also been to a number of in-service courses/workshops and had learnt various teaching strategies, which she used in her classroom and which she felt had made her a better teacher.

Aliya, a political science graduate, had six years of teaching experience. At the time of the study, she had only been in the school for five months. In addition to being a class teacher, she taught social studies to classes 4 and 5. At the time of the study, Aliya was engaged to be married and expected to give up teaching once married.

Maryam, who at the start of the study had only four months teaching experience, taught English to class 7. She was single, lived with her parents and had no family responsibilities.

Razia is a political science graduate and had five years of teaching experience. At the start of the study, she had only been in the school for five months. Razia taught social studies to classes 6, 7 and 8. She was divorced and lived with her parents and daughter. Being a single parent, she was solely responsible for bringing up her daughter.

REFLECTIVE DIALOGUE IN ACTION

I will now look at what happened in each form of reflective dialogue so as to illustrate why the teachers responded the way they did. In addition, I briefly analyse my role as a reflective coach during each of these forms of reflective dialogue and explain why my role took the various dimensions that it did.

Group Reflective Sessions

These sessions took place weekly after school for one hour. During these sessions, the teachers would review their week. They would talk about things that went well or did not go well in their classrooms and the lessons they learnt from them. The group members would comment or ask questions about some of the things that they had heard. It was also during these sessions that the teachers sought advice on how to handle certain events in their classrooms. The teachers also often reflected on the impact certain existing school structures had on them or their teaching. These sessions also served as extensions to the one-to-one reflective sessions that I had with individual teachers. The teachers would talk about the difficulties they experienced, especially if they felt dissatisfied with what had gone on during our one-to-one reflective sessions.

The dialogue during this time was frank and open and this, I think, is what helped the teachers to talk to each other freely as well as not mind any of the criticism or questioning they were subjected to. In addition, a feeling of trust developed among the group members. As one of the participants remarked at the end of the study, 'at first, I felt frightened that what we discussed would leak out but I learnt to trust everybody in the group. You see, you allowed us to speak freely.'

The multiplicity of perspectives was what the teachers considered to be of utmost benefit about this form of reflective dialogue as the following statement by Maryam illustrates, 'It [group reflective sessions] gave one an opportunity to get ideas from others. You see, when I was reflecting with you only, what I'd give to the students would only be your ideas and mine. But with the group sessions, I'd take away with me other people's suggestions, and maybe many suggestions.'

One-to-One Reflective Sessions

These sessions would last from 35 minutes to one hour. The main focus of these sessions was the lesson that I had observed. They often took place immediately after the classroom observation. During these sessions, I often played a very active role because the teachers were unable to reflect on their own, especially at the start of the study.

These sessions were often held after a lesson and the teachers found these sessions an 'eye-opener' to what was going on in their classrooms as well as what their teaching was all about. They liked this form of reflective dialogue because of the individual attention they got from me as well as the time I actually gave to them. They all felt that this type of reflective sessions had the most impact on their classroom practice. For example in the case of Shafia, she felt that this type of reflective dialogue contributed greatly to her growth as a reflective teacher because it was based on actual teaching events that we had both witnessed and it was done within the school hours so that it seemed very much a part of her teaching. Aliya, too, expressed a similar view.

Reflective Journals

All the teachers had to maintain a reflective journal. There was neither a fixed number of entries one had to make nor a specific format to follow when making those entries. Furthermore what they wanted to write about was left to their discretion. It was, however, expected that they would write on issues that were related to their teaching. The teachers were required to share their journals with me once a week.

Initially, the teachers did not find journal writing easy. In fact, I had to address this issue at a group reflective session to find out what the problem was. They claimed that they did not know how and what to write in their journals. Shafia in fact told me:

> Basically, we're not used to this [journal writing]. Over here in Pakistan, hardly any teacher keeps a journal. I don't remember ever being told to write freely as you are asking me to. I was always told to write in a particular way, especially during exam time. You know three of my close friends and my cousin who are all teachers, when I tell them that I'm writing a journal, they ask me, 'What's this stupid thing of keeping a journal?' I tell them that it is a good thing and they ask me if I am sure.

The paradox of keeping a journal for the teachers was expressed by Maryam, when she said, 'You see, on one side, I see that I will improve a lot by keeping a journal, but on the other hand, what a headache!'

However, once the teachers began to write in their journal, they began to enjoy the process of writing and reflection. Aliya, who had actually had the most difficulty writing her journal and had seemed quite reluctant to do so, said, 'It was difficult for me to express my feelings but funnily enough, now that I have started, I'm enjoying it.'

The journal served different purposes for the teachers. Some viewed it as a way of getting some control of their life. For example, Maryam said:

> I have not written much but whatever I have written these three weeks has helped. Frankly, whatever I would teach would just disappear from my mind. There are so many things that are happening. I'm studying for examinations, there are weddings in the family, our house is being painted and so many things. I find I'm beginning to forget so many things but when I write down things about my teaching, everything comes back and it's there; what I did. This makes me feel much better.

The reflective journal also enhanced the teachers' reflection. Shafia said:

> When you asked us to keep a journal, I thought it was a horrible idea and that I could not keep it. But when I started to keep it, I realized that it was one way of really looking at my teaching. Sometimes, when I observed that my lesson was not going well, I would just keep at it. But when I go home and start writing in my journal, then I begin to realize where exactly I may have gone wrong and it is also then that alternatives come to mind....

The teachers found it the most time-consuming form of reflective dialogue. One of them pointed out, 'I need time. I need to sit quietly in a separate room and reflect on the things that happened. It takes me about an hour to reflect on one lesson.'

Razia, who later dropped out of the study, claimed that she was not comfortable with the process of reflective dialogue, especially journal writing. 'I don't know why it is so, but I'm not feeling comfortable,' she said at a group reflective session. In addition, she felt that her demanding workload and family obligations made it impossible for her to engage in any form of reflective dialogue. She said:

> You are telling me to try this and try that in my class and that means that I have to carry home my work. That is extra work for me. I am not used to this. I just can't. I don't have the time. I am divorced. I have a baby daughter and when I go home, she is my responsibility. I also have to help with the work at home. So, how can I write my journal?

Nonetheless, the other teachers' commitment to journal writing was enhanced by the fact that I would respond to their entries. Maryam, in fact, said, 'Keeping a journal is good in so far as you know somebody is going to read it.'

The Reflective Coach

My role as a reflective coach took on different dimensions depending on which form of reflective dialogue I was involved in. In order to have a reflective dialogue session with an individual teacher, I would observe the teacher's lessons and then we would critique the lessons together. In this type of reflective dialogue, I found myself playing a very active role, in fact, almost dominant, especially at the beginning of the study because of the teachers' lack of readiness to reflect on their teaching. I asked most of the questions, suggested alternatives, provided teachers with reading material and sometimes modelled some teaching technique. I had to be careful of how I did this because I did not want to alienate the teachers. How I did this was viewed differently by individual teachers. One said, 'I like the way you tell me my weaknesses....You never give me an impression that things that have gone wrong are really bad....The manner in which you tell me my weaknesses is good; I never feel threatened.' Yet another said, 'How can you feel there are mistakes in my lesson? I have been teaching for five years and nobody has ever made me feel that my teaching was not up to standard.'

During the group reflective dialogue sessions, I did not really come to the foreground as in the one-to-one sessions. Maryam said of my role during group reflections, 'You were there as an observer....You sort of had a backseat over there and we were the main people discussing things there.' During these sessions, I facilitated the meetings and took care of the logistics of the meetings regarding time, venue and so forth. In addition, I initiated the reflective sessions, co-ordinated the tempo of the dialogue, as well as ensured that all the members participated in the session. I had to constantly ask questions of the participants to raise the level of the dialogue to a reflective one and not just mere descriptions and complaints about whatever had happened to be the issue.

As for the journal writing, my role was that of responding to the teachers' entries. My responses would range from asking questions to raising the teachers' thinking about some of the issues they had written about, to commiserating with them about something, to praising them and even sharing my experiences as learning points or just showing plain appreciation for some of the things they had done or were doing in their classrooms.

Responding to the teachers' entries seemed to enhance the depth of their reflectivity as well as their commitment to maintaining the journals. As Shafia said:

> When I first wrote in my journal, I had thought that you'd only take it and just read it. But when you wrote some remarks and it struck me that somebody has responded to what I had written, at that time I started to write more seriously. It was not that I wanted to please you but I felt that there was someone who was taking note of my problems, someone who could help me when she read my journal.

DISCUSSION

It is evident that the teachers did see some benefit in engaging in reflective dialogue. However, they were unanimous in their preference for the one-to-one and group reflective dialogue sessions. This was because issues were discussed in the light of what actually went on in their classrooms. In addition, during the one-to-one reflective sessions, they received individual attention from me. Furthermore, this particular session did not go on after school hours. The teachers felt that they would have liked the group reflective sessions more were it not for the fact that they were held after school hours. With the exception of Aliya, the others were not in favour of journal writing because they found it too time-consuming, a view that was shared by Aliya, despite the fact that she enjoyed reflecting through her journal.

It appears that there was a clear demarcation on the contents of each form of reflective dialogue. In the one-to-one reflective sessions, the content of reflections was based on the teachers' classroom concerns. In the group reflective sessions, the content of reflections was extensive. The teachers reflected on their classroom practice, events in the school and the larger society and their effects on their classrooms. Whereas in the dialogue journal, the teachers reflected on their classroom concerns as well as themselves as individuals; that is, what was happening to them and why and how they felt about the happening.

All the three forms of reflective dialogue required the teachers to take risks of a different nature in order to be reflective about their teaching. In their attempts to be reflective through their dialogue journals, the teachers found themselves having to take risks with their own selves. They had to allow themselves to look inwardly towards themselves and question themselves about their thoughts, actions, and motives. In the group reflective sessions, the teachers had to take a risk with their peers. They had to allow their peers to question them as well as let them gain access to their teaching thereby letting them see how fallible they were. As for the one-to-one reflective sessions, the teachers took a risk with an 'expert.' They had to open their classroom to someone they hardly knew and allow her to question their teaching beliefs and actions in ways they had never been questioned before. The teachers were able to take all these risks because of their desire to improve their teaching, as well as the support they received from the school's administration and the reflective coach. Support from the school's administration was evident in the interest they displayed in the teachers' activities as well as their provision of time for the teachers to engage in reflective dialogue.

The role that was played by the reflective coach was quite a multifaceted one and this is perhaps an indication of the nature of support teachers in this context need from a reflective coach. In order to help the teachers become reflective, I needed to do much more than just raise questions for the teachers. I had to give a lot of time and energy to the teachers. In addition, I had to be quite knowledgeable as far as pedagogy is concerned because teachers like Aliya and Razia, who are not trained, definitely needed more help with pedagogical skills. I also took on the role of resource person and this included the provision of reading materials for teachers, as well as modelling some teaching. It was also necessary that I possess some interpersonal skills, because as the teachers began to question their teaching and try out new alternatives, they needed some scaffolding. The teachers in this study gained from having opportunities to reflect upon their teaching with the reflective coach and their peers and they saw these as collaborative-learning situations. As shared earlier, they viewed the responses to their reflections by the reflective coach and their peers as immensely valuable in helping them become more reflective. Though Elliot (1991) suggests that those who support teachers must relinquish their 'expert role,' I found that this was not possible. The teachers were willing to listen because of my 'expertness'. So, though, I did get personal with them, I could not totally give up this status. This relates to the suggestions made by Elliot (ibid), Ashcroft (1992), Dobbins (1996) and Thomas and Montemery (1997), among others, who point out that reflective coaches should not only be experts and reflective practitioners, but when necessary they should adopt partnership roles as facilitators and collaborative learners.

IMPLICATIONS

Though findings of the study cannot be generalized to teachers in Pakistan because of the small sample size, there are several important issues that the study illuminates and which I believe are of some significance to schooling and teacher education practices in Pakistan.

First and foremost, the study reveals that teachers can be reflective about their teaching if given the opportunity and equipped with the skills to do so. Prior to this study, the teachers in this study did not question their teaching or even think about improving it in any way. For example at our first meeting, Maryam told me, 'At the moment I don't have any difficulties handling my students or classroom. My teaching, I believe, is okay.' Similarly, Shafia told me, 'Maybe I need no improvement.' While for Razia, 'Everything went well, according to my satisfaction. I don't think there's any change that I should make to whatever I did in the classroom.' This attitude can probably be attributed to the fact that they never had the occasion to question their teaching; perhaps too, they were not used to talking about their teaching practices with others, especially if they were questionable. Cole (1997) suggests that teacher isolation in her or his own classroom works against reflection. To reflect, the teacher needs to communicate her or his private puzzles and insights, and test them against the views of her or his peers. This is supported by a well-known fact that teachers do not consult research findings when they encounter dilemmas in their professional practice; they prefer instead to consult their colleagues or invent solutions themselves. However, once the teachers in the study were exposed to reflective dialogue, they began to reflect. Indeed, the questioning was not limited to classroom teaching only, but was extended to the school structures and the larger society.

The above notwithstanding, we have to acknowledge that there are teachers who are likely to be uncomfortable with the process of reflection, as was the case with Razia during the study. Reflection is a demanding process that requires commitment on the part of practitioners, yet this commitment may be hard to come by among most teachers in Pakistan because school hours are structured to take into account the socio-cultural practices that are prevalent in the society. Most schools run for half the day, thereby enabling the female teachers to take up their familial duties at home, such as preparing the family meal, taking care of the young children amongst others, while the male teachers are able to teach privately to supplement the low income derived from teaching. Findings from the study indicate that the three teachers who actively engaged in reflective practice did so even after school hours, a task they found arduous indeed. This seems to suggest that if reflective dialogue is to be successful in schools then the school hours would have to be structured in ways that enable teachers to engage in these reflective activities while in school. In addition, those who help teachers to reflect need to be more aware of the personal lives of teachers and how this may impact on teacher practices. For example, Razia cited her marital status and family responsibilities as reasons for not engaging in reflective dialogue. Aliya too pointed out her family responsibilities as one of the factors that made it difficult for her to reflect through the reflective journal. Maryam found that too many things were happening at home and that she could not engage in reflective dialogue. She said, 'I was here physically but not mentally. I've been so busy at home...if you're disturbed, the lessons go, the students go. How can I even reflect?' In working with teachers like Razia and the others, I realized the importance of being cognizant of the fact that teachers' personal and professional lives are closely intertwined. As stated earlier, at the time of the study, Razia was not willing to engage in reflective dialogue because of her personal problems. Perhaps, the pace of my study was a drawback (given that the study had to be conducted within a limited period) in that Razia and I did not have time to reflect on her personal problems, which no doubt had an impact on the kind of teacher that she was. However, I strongly believe that reflective dialogue as a means of developing teachers is flexible enough to allow teachers to reflect on both their personal and professional lives. This would inevitably lead to teachers who have better control of their lives, both in and out of classrooms.

Secondly, the study findings suggest that the forms of reflective dialogue that would be more readily acceptable to teachers in this context are the one-to-one and group reflective sessions. Given that writing is usually geared towards passing examinations in this context and free writing is something that is not encouraged widely in schools, most teachers find it difficult to express themselves through writing. The teachers also found the reflective journal too time-consuming; encroaching on their free time after school when they had to tend to their other responsibilities. They preferred the one-to-one and group reflective sessions which could be done in school and not carried over to their homes. This is not to suggest that dialogue journals have no place in this context. On the contrary, the teachers did find the dialogue journal useful and the reflection it called for different from other forms of reflective dialogue. Perhaps, more work in terms of support, time, and effort is required of both the teachers and the reflective coach in order to make the dialogue journal a tool for reflecting on the teacher's teaching in this context.

One very significant finding from this study is that reflective dialogue represents an alternative approach by which teachers can develop their professional practice. The participant teachers felt that they had improved considerably, not only in the way they taught, but also in the way they viewed the entire teaching enterprise. Some of them even felt that the learning they had undergone as a result of their engagement in reflective dialogue was as good as, if not better than, attending in-service workshops. This view of reflective dialogue, no doubt, stems from the various activities described above that they and the reflective coach had to do in order for them (teachers) to become reflective. As Aliya remarked, 'I learnt a lot of things. As you know, I am very new in this school and I was having problems adjusting to the language and teaching used here. I had not been to any workshop but since I started reflecting with you, I've got new ideas, new techniques of teaching. Now, I'm even beginning to enjoy teaching.'

However, the above finding lends a different perspective to the role of the reflective coach in this context. Studies done elsewhere (Morrison, 1996; Thomas and Montemery, 1997 and Collier, 1999) show that teachers (both novice and experienced) took the central role in their reflective development. The reflective coaches gave the teachers opportunities to engage in activities on their own, playing a peripheral role of posing challenging questions to help the reflective process along or in the case of Thomas (ibid.), providing moral support to the teacher concerned. In this context, this kind of approach by the reflective coach would not be viewed as beneficial by the teachers. This is because currently teacher training in Pakistan is somewhat ineffective and therefore teachers have limited understanding of both subject content and pedagogical skills [UNESCO Principal Regional Office for Asia and the Pacific (UNESCO PROAP), 2000]. For a majority of these teachers, thinking of alternate ways of approaching their teaching, which is a natural and desired outcome of reflection, would be a near impossibility. Furthermore, the culture of questioning oneself or others is almost non-existent in this context because of the prevailing dominant norms of compliance and conformity (Warwick and Reimers, 1995). Therefore, teachers need to be helped in this direction. This would mean that the reflective coach in this context would need to be actively involved in helping teachers by suggesting and demonstrating alternatives; yet questioning the teachers' practice in an unassuming manner so as to develop a trusting and collaborative relationship, while at the same time helping teachers to develop the skill and art of questioning themselves and others without feeling threatened.

The above conditions suggest that if reflective dialogue is to be used as an alternative professional development strategy as suggested by the findings, then in the initial stages of the introduction of reflective dialogue, the reflective coach will have to play a dominant role and assume the status of the 'expert.' This is contrary to what Elliot (1991), Dobbins (1996), and Thomas and Montemery (1997) say about the role of the reflective coach. They suggest that the reflective coach needs to 'shed off' his or her 'expert' status in order to work collaboratively with the teachers. In this context, this would not be advisable because of the limitations mentioned above. The reflective coach can only assume the role suggested by Elliot and others after teachers become accustomed to reflecting on their teaching and are able to do so, on their own. Further to this, the reflective coach in this context would have to be a model teacher and quite informed of suitable teaching practices as well as be of sound content knowledge, because as mentioned earlier, the teachers in Pakistan need strong support in these two areas because of the prevalent inadequate teacher training practices.

Further to the above, certain conditions need to be in place in our schools to sustain reflective dialogue, especially if it is to be an effective alternate approach to teacher development. Gray (2002) describes schools as busy places in which little time or support is provided for reflection. Many schools in Pakistan do not support a reflective stance towards professional practice and the importance of 'mulling over' each lesson is often unrecognized. If teachers in Pakistan are to develop the ability to teach reflectively and even engage in reflective dialogue, their schools must provide a supportive environment. For example, reflection is inhibited by many structural features in our schools, such as heavy teaching loads and lack of resources that isolate teachers from one another, including the prescriptive nature of the curricula. Teachers here would need structural (institutional) and personal support in order to think reflectively about their teaching. Findings from the study suggest that this support may include teachers having significant influence over decisions related to instruction and curriculum, talking about teaching, observing and critiquing each other, and providing emotional and technical support for one another. By providing time and structural support for these activities, teachers would be encouraged to engage in activities that are essential for reflective teaching such as taking risks, viewing their own learning as important, engaging in group planning, and proposing alternative instructional strategies.

An additional characteristic of a supportive school would be the presence of a strong, supportive administrator. Wildman and Niles (1987) note that administrators who lack knowledge about and commitment to reflective teaching may create obstacles that limit teachers' reflective abilities. Many teachers would be unwilling to take the risks involved in reflective teaching if they lacked the appropriate administrative support. Given the nature of teacher education in Pakistan, it is likely that a majority of the heads of schools in Pakistan are not predisposed to being reflective practitioners, and therefore, in-service courses need to be put in place for heads of schools to enable them to be reflective about their practice. It is probable that in being reflective, the head teachers are likely to realize the importance of providing the same for their teachers, hence, providing an environment that supports teacher learning at their workplace and thereby leading to professional learning communities within the schools. More specifically, this would require heads of schools to encourage reflective practices within the school by providing time, and, if possible, leading the reflective dialogue sessions. For example, in this study, the teachers were able to engage in reflective dialogue because the school's administration was supportive of them. The support was evident in the interest they displayed in the teachers' activities as well as in their provision of time for the teachers to engage in reflective dialogue.

In this study, reflective dialogue addressed the teachers' practice problems. This, therefore, led the teachers, with the exception of Razia, to develop a positive attitude towards reflective dialogue. This suggests that teachers' professional development in Pakistan needs to have a reflective and practical approach arising from the actual classroom situations as experienced by the teachers. Currently, most in-service courses and workshops have become predominantly 'quick-fix' activities, done for short spans of time and are usually concerned with curriculum implementation or teachers' acquisition of teaching strategies that teachers barely understand as they are usually given in the abstract. Nor are they given the time to reflect on the worth and purpose of these strategies. If reflection is embedded in in-service courses and workshops, it is likely that teachers would develop the habit of 'mulling over' their actions and the ensuing consequences, thereby, making teaching a more thoughtful and innovative endeavour, rather than a series of mechanical actions as is currently the case in most classrooms.

Furthermore, the study suggests that any effort to promote reflective dialogue in our schools will benefit from any training teachers can be given that helps them develop sensitivity to their ways of looking at and talking about teaching and developing a positive attitude towards questioning their teaching skills. In other words, the training should develop in teachers the disposition to interrogate their unidentified knowledge about their practices. Without this, teachers are not likely to interrogate the ways they read and experience their practice. In a developing and changing society like Pakistan, children and parents are entitled to teaching which is based on reflection. Wells (1989) suggests that if classrooms are to become communities of active and inquiring learners, teachers who provide the leadership and guidance in such classrooms must themselves have professional development that is inquiry-oriented and collaborative.

CONCLUSION

From the foregoing, it can be seen that though the teachers found reflective dialogue beneficial; given the nature of schools and schooling practices in Pakistan, the most viable form of reflective dialogue would seem to be the group and one-to-one reflections. Nonetheless, since it is widely accepted that reflective teachers are now an essential requirement in our schools, it is imperative that appropriate forms need to be found to encourage teachers to adopt the practice of reflection. However, we (educators) need to be aware that reflection is a demanding process and reflection stimulated by dialogue is an even more complicated process. This notwithstanding, all teachers should be encouraged and supported to reflect on their teaching because this study has clearly shown a strong link between reflection, teacher development, and school improvement. By engaging in reflective dialogue, improvement in classroom practice is a natural outcome of teachers' professional development. In addition, the opportunity to step out of the classroom and reflect on more than just classroom practice is an essential part of enabling teachers to understand the educational and socio-cultural contexts in which they operate and thereby respond appropriately to the complexity of their teaching situations.

NOTE

1. This study was conducted as part of the M.Ed programme at AKU-IED.

4

Mentoring for Teacher Development: Experiences from In-service Setting

Haji Karim Khan and Anjum Halai

INTRODUCTION

Mentoring has a long history of success, beginning with Odysseus' decision to entrust the education of his son Telemachus to a wise and learned man called 'Mentor' some 3500 years ago and continuing to present times in the development of nurses, psychologists, scientists, teachers, and educational administrators (Gray and Gray, 1985). The concept of mentoring has come to the field of education from business and entails supporting learning to teach in teachers' workplace. Mentoring has been implemented in teacher education and induction programmes for the last two decades (Carter and Francis, 2001).

Literature on mentoring shows that mentors play a variety of roles to support teachers' learning. They play the roles of situational leaders, role-models, instructors, promoters of thinking skills, promoters of realistic values, demonstrators, supervisors, and counsellors (Gray and Gray, 1985). In teacher education, mentoring is mostly used in pre-service teacher education where a nominated school-based experienced teacher looks after the professional development of prospective teachers in a school setting (Burn, Hagger, Mutton, and Everton, 2000; Hagger, Burn, and McIntyre, 1993). The role of a mentor in such situations is that of a mediator and a liaison between the school and the university. In such situations, the relationship of the mentor and mentee portrays an asymmetry which was also noted by Randall and Thornton (2001), who maintain that, 'it clearly involves an asymmetrical knowledge relationship between the mentor and the mentee, but the relationship portrayed is largely informal, a relationship which is reinforced by the long time scale involved in such partnerships' (p. 14).

In Pakistan, in the pioneering work in teacher education being undertaken at AKU-IED, the process of mentoring has generally been employed as a strategy for in-service professional development of teachers (Ali, 2000; Halai, 2006; 1998; Chembere, 1995). The roles that mentors have played in the in-service context have been quite varied. For example, in a study of secondary school mathematics teachers in Pakistan, Halai (1998), found her role as co-planner, co-teacher, and as a subject expert to guide teachers' learning in a school. Similarly, Halai (2006) argues that in the context of in-service teacher education in mathematics, mentors work as expert coach, subject specialists, critical friends, and learners. The changes in the roles of a mentor are likely to arise due to the contextual needs and situations. For example, studies have shown that teachers' content knowledge (Ball, 2000; 1988; Feiman-Nemser and Parker, 1990) and pedagogical content knowledge (Shulman, 1987) are the most important and indispensable aspects of their knowledge. Studies in Pakistani schools have shown that teachers are not adequately prepared for their profession; therefore, lack of pedagogical knowledge and content knowledge is an issue (Hoodbhoy, 1998; Kizilbash, 1998; Saeed and Mahmood, 2002). Teachers need to enhance their understanding of subject matter and pedagogy; hence, mentors need to play their roles as facilitators of learning of content and pedagogy as well as learning to socialize and become a member of the school culture.

Mentor-mentee relationship is an important aspect in the process of mentoring. Successful mentoring relationships are built in an atmosphere of trust and mutual respect (Ballard, 2001; Wildman, Magliaro, Niles, and Niles, 1992). Perceiving the mentees as colleagues, respecting their ideas, and establishing collegial (Little, 1990), friendly, non-hierarchical, caring and nurturing relationships (Halai, 1998, 2006) are the fundamental aspects of mentoring.

THE STUDY[1]

The purpose of the study was to understand the process of mentoring and its contribution to teacher development in a setting where the teacher Maria[2] was a novice to the profession. She had started teaching about three years ago with no pre-service teacher preparation. She had an undergraduate degree (BA) and at the time of the study was preparing as a part-time student for her Master's study.

I adopted an action research approach to study and understand the process of mentoring as I worked as a mentor with my mentee Maria. As a mentor I engaged with Maria in a variety of ways which involved activities like co-planning, teaching, observing lessons, and conducting post-observation meetings. During co-planning I helped Maria to plan lessons with clear, observable objectives and appropriate activities. These lessons were mainly taught by Maria, while I observed and gave feedback. However, there were occasions where I taught a lesson and received feedback from Maria, who was an observer.

I took field notes of my observations in the classrooms which were used as tools for discussion during the post-observation conferences. Further data came from different sources: semi-structured interviews with the teacher, and my own reflective memos and documents, such as lesson plans. The interviews and post-observation conferences with the teacher were tape-recorded and later transcribed verbatim. These were mainly in English. I made sense of the data through critical discussions with the teacher, writing reflective memos, and ongoing analysis of data. After finishing the fieldwork I read the entire corpus of data to identify emerging themes and seek relationships. Presented below are the findings of the study which illustrate the process of mentoring, the changing role of the mentor and related issues.

The Process of Mentoring

'Lesson planning' was the initial focus of my work with Maria because Maria told me that she needed help only in lesson planning. For example, she said, 'Sir, I think the most difficult area for me is lesson planning. I need help only in it, nothing else. This is the only area that I need to focus on' (10 January 2002).

From my conversations with her about issues in lesson planning and looking at the lesson plans, I found out that she needed help in setting observable objectives in a lesson plan with activities appropriate to those objectives. In the initial week Maria and I met in three sessions to discuss the basic elements of lesson planning. Throughout the week, my role remained that of a coach or guide where I explained various aspects of lesson planning to her. I also gave her some handouts which explained the basic elements of a lesson plan. I assumed that she would read these handouts and we would discuss them in our next session. However, in the next session, I came to know that she had not read the handouts. She told me that she had been busy and could not go through those materials. Therefore, instead of giving her reading materials, I decided to have an analytic discussion with her on various aspects of lesson planning. The process of discussion and analysis of lesson plans appeared to help Maria understand the purpose of lesson planning. For example, Maria talked about setting objectives and said 'Sir, I was thinking that objectives were there just to guide, but now, it seems that these are the things that you want your students to achieve by the end of a lesson' (15 January 2002).

My reflections on the overall activities of the week suggested to me that my role was dominant in leading the discussion and a disadvantage of this was that Maria appeared to perceive me as an evaluator. For example, during the course of our work, she used to ask 'So, Sir, is this wrong?' or 'Shall I do it or not?' Her manner of asking was as if there was only one right way to do things, and as if I was an expert and knew the 'right answers'. This suggested to me that she perceived me as an evaluator or an expert, whose job was to make judgement on events rather than to support her in teaching. I recognized from my experience as a learner and from the literature on teacher learning that the fear of being evaluated often inhibits learning. Hence, I tried to address this issue by trying to develop a trust-based relationship with Maria. Initially this proved to be difficult as she seemed to be scared of sharing ideas and hesitated before speaking up. For example, whenever I asked a question during the discussion, Maria did not interpret my questions as invitations to reflect on her teaching. When I asked her to tell me how the lesson progressed in her view, she used to say 'Oh, sir, you were there yourself. You know better how the lesson went'. I conjectured that trust had not yet developed between us.

Hence, I looked for ways to establish a collegial and trusting relationship between us. I did a number of things in this regard; for example, I requested her to address me by my name and not by the formal title of 'sir'. I opened up to her personally by talking about my family, and myself, in particular myself as a learner. I introduced myself as a learner in her classroom; I reassured her that I would respect the confidentiality of the findings and would not report to her management. Finally, I made sure that I recognized her strengths as a professional, no matter how few they were, and appreciated her effort in learning to teach. Evidence shared in the course of this paper showed that my efforts paid off and there was a change in my relationship with Maria, who started to see me as a colleague, worthy of her trust; she opened up to me and began to share experiences and asked for help where needed.

Maria planned a lesson for the following day's teaching and agreed to share her reflections on the lesson with me. The next day I found that though she had prepared a written lesson plan, she did not teach according to that plan; in fact, she taught another topic. It seemed that she had planned the lesson to make me happy rather than for implementing it in her classroom. Therefore, I decided to co-plan with her and then to help her in executing the plan in her classroom. During the co-planning, I tried to take the role of a critical friend in terms of raising questions rather than leading the session. My purpose of restraining myself was to empower Maria to take decisions on her own. [Maria planned a lesson to teach 'Highest Common Factor'. She planned to select some questions from the textbook and to give one question to each of the groups so that they could solve it and then present their solutions in front of the whole class. The dialogue below provides a glimpse of the co-planning process].

> Maria: I want to give the task in groups.
> Haji Karim: Ok, so, what will you give in the group work?
> Maria: I think I will give these questions here from this exercise (points to an exercise in the textbook).
> Haji Karim: Do you think it is appropriate for group work?
> Maria: Yes, they can do it.
> Haji Karim: I mean, what if one of the students solves the questions and the rest of them do nothing.
> Maria: No, I don't think so.
> Haji Karim: Ok, let's try that and see how it works.
> (21 January 2002)

In the above dialogue, Maria seems to believe that selecting some questions from a textbook, primarily intended for individual work, and giving them to the students to solve in groups would work. As a critical friend, I tried to help Maria by pointing out that this might not necessarily be the outcome of her planning. However, in retrospect, when issues of classroom management appeared I realized that I should have explained to her more clearly that tasks for group work are not necessarily the same as those assigned for individual work.

The next day Maria implemented the plan. Observations revealed a number of issues. First was Maria's inadequate content and pedagogical knowledge. Classroom observation showed that Maria had limited skills in managing group work and giving instructions for the tasks. For example, when she asked the students to work in groups, the students were not sure what to do, which resulted in a lot of confusion for the students. As mentioned earlier, a key issue was that the tasks were essentially meant for individual work and not designed for group work. Second, when one of the students worked out 3 as the Highest Common Factor (HCF) of the numbers '12' and '18' instead of the correct answer '6', Maria accepted the incorrect answer as correct. In the post-observation conference, when I asked Maria to reflect upon her lesson she said, 'I feel.--err--, it was not bad, it was good' (22 January 2002). I wanted Maria to think about why she considered the lesson to be good. However, she found it difficult to articulate the reasons for her belief.

> Haji Karim: Ok, so, what else about the lesson?
> Maria: I think, I have told you, except for some noise from the students, the lesson was good.
> Haji Karim: Yes, true, but what about this question which they [the students] did and you accepted as a correct answer?
> Maria: I think they did very well…when one student faced difficulty in LCM, I helped and she understood.
> Haji Karim: Ok, what about the HCF? Did they do that correctly?
> Maria: Yes, they gave good answers.
> (22 January 2002)

The most difficult part for me was to come to the issue of an 'incorrect answer' being accepted as correct. I wanted to use an indirect approach to enable her to identify her own mistake without any embarrassment. The data extract shared above shows that Maria failed to realize her mistake. Hence, I decided to solve the same question again with her. I said, 'Some students were struggling with this question (I referred to the particular question 'What is the HCF of 12 and 18?'); let us see how it should be done.' Maria still perceived that to be an easy question and solved it in the same way as the students had done in the class. Then I showed her the correct way of solving the problem, but she remained defensive, and thus I did some more examples to support her understanding of the concept. Finally, she understood and said that she would clarify it to the students the next day.

Re-thinking the Mentoring Process

In the light of the issues of content knowledge and classroom management, I reflected on my role and decided not only to raise questions, but also to participate actively in planning, teaching, and doing mathematics with Maria. I recognized that without any professional qualification, she did not have the relevant skills to develop a lesson plan with specific objectives and implement it in her classroom. Maria requested me to teach in her class, so that she could observe my lesson. I agreed to do some demonstration teaching, as I recognized that teaching in Maria's class as a colleague and a learner might help me build rapport with her. I further recognized that Maria's only model for teaching mathematics was the way it was taught to her. Hence, observing me might add to her repertoire of strategies for teaching mathematics. At the same time, I was aware that there were some risks in teaching in Maria's class: she could perceive it as the only way to teach mathematics and model her lessons on the demonstration. Subsequently, if the lesson was not successful, Maria would perceive me as incapable of teaching well and mentoring her to enhance her teaching of mathematics. Teaching in Maria's class was also risky as I was not very familiar with her classroom context. In spite of all these concerns, I decided to go ahead with the teaching.

I invited Maria to co-plan the lesson with me. The topic was 'Common Fractions', where we had to teach the concept of representing fractions, parts of fractions (numerator and denominator) etc. During co-planning, Maria shared some good ideas. For example, she said, 'Mr Karim why don't you cut some apples and other fruits to show fractions' (28 January 2002). I was glad that she was offering suggestions. I respected her idea and decided to use apples as resources in teaching fractions.

The next day, I taught the lesson and Maria observed it. In the post-observation conference, when I appreciated her ideas of using concrete material as teaching resources, she responded, 'Actually, I had learnt it from you in a previous session'. Here, she was referring to an earlier discussion where I had advocated the use of resources from everyday life as teaching aids in the classrooms. This shows Maria's learning from the discussions in the pre- and post-observation conferences. During the post-observation conference, Maria talked a lot about my lesson. She talked about the wait time, involvement of the students in the lesson, use of resources, focusing on students' misconceptions, and my way of dealing with the students. She commented:

> And your friendly attitude towards the students was fantastic, because you set the pace in a way where the students remained disciplined as well as they enjoyed the lesson (29 January 2002).

She appreciated the lesson and said that she would like to implement some of these ideas in her own teaching. Talking about the use of resources she said,

> Your lesson showed me that resources can be used in mathematics lessons which I had never thought about. Before this, I thought that only the blackboard and chalk could be used (29 January 2002).

Furthermore, during the co-planning session for the next class she said,

> Motivational activities should be like that which motivate students to learn something...before this, what were we doing, we just asked them to open their books and just solve a question on the board (31 January 2002).

The above quotations show Maria's reflection on her action where she compared her past practice with her new learning experience. Thus, the opportunity to observe my lesson enabled her to reflect on her own lessons, make comparisons and learn from them to be able to enhance her teaching of mathematics.

Further Developments in the Mentoring Process

When I reflected on the process of mentoring so far, I found that my role was more active than hers. For example, I was taking a leading role in co-planning and also demonstrating lessons in Maria's class. Now I wanted Maria to take a lead role in her learning. Thus, I asked her to plan a lesson for the next week and to share it with me. She agreed, but asked for help in content to teach 'Equivalent Fractions'. This was the topic which she had decided to teach. Thus, at her request, I helped her strengthen her content knowledge in that area. I used paper strips as resources in order to give her the concept of equivalent fractions. She liked the idea and decided to use it in her class, which I agreed to observe.

On the appointed day, when I reached the school, I encountered a strange situation. Maria was very late for the pre-observation meeting and when she came, she informed me that she was not able to plan her lesson because of some reason. She requested me to wait so that she could prepare the plan and share it with me. I reflected on the situation, recognizing that she might have faced difficulty in planning the lesson. However, if I waited for her to plan the lesson in order to show it to me, then my role would be of an evaluator rather than a colleague and a co-planner. Thus, I decided to co-plan with her again. During co-planning I found that Maria had a problem in using the paper strips in her lesson. Although she had understood the concept herself, she faced difficulty in planning in order to implement it in her class. For example, she said, '…but, Karim, I don't know how to do the activities with the students and what to ask and tell them' (4 February 2002).

Therefore, I decided to demonstrate the activities again and helped her in recording all the instructions and questions that she was likely to ask during the activity. Thus, the plan was ready for being implemented in the classroom. During this co-planning my role and relationship once again remained active. I saw myself as a subject expert to support her in content, a coach to enhance her pedagogy, and a critical friend to make her reflect on her lessons.

Maria was pleased with the support and the next day she implemented the lesson in the classroom. During the lesson observation, I saw students showing great interest in the lesson. This was evident from the manner in which they were engaged in colouring and folding the strips, recording, and naming the next equivalent fraction. In the post-observation conference, Maria was very happy with her lesson and she talked a lot about it and about the resources she had used in the lesson. She reflected that the resources (paper strips) really helped the students to understand the concepts. Similarly, talking about involving students in learning process she said,

> I had seen you responding to the students' questions while putting the question back to the students and dealing with them during teaching in your lesson, so I tried to implement that in my class too (4 February 2002).

This also shows Maria's learning from observation of my lessons and that reinforces my role as a coach for her. At the end of the post-observation conference, Maria told me that she would try to plan a lesson for the next week and share it with me; I agreed and assured her of my support in case of any need.

The next week on the agreed day, Maria was absent from school. The following day she arrived without any plan. She explained that once again she was unable to plan a lesson for some reason. Maria's absence from school, and coming to school the next day without a lesson plan raised many questions for me as a mentor. For example, was Maria constrained to work with me? If yes, what were the constraining factors? Was I asking too much from her, in terms of time and effort? On the basis of the above questions, I changed my plan and decided to be more flexible in my approach and listen to Maria's perspective of being a mentee. In the meantime, co-planning and observation continued.

During the co-planning Maria asked me to help her in teaching the content on the topic 'Time'. Together, we prepared a model of a clock using cardboards. With the help of the model we discussed the concept of 'past', 'quarter to' 'quarter past', 'to' and 'past'. Maria was eager to use the model in her lesson. She decided to plan a lesson at home and to share that with me the next day, which she did as promised. During the lesson, she brought the students to the board and used the model of clock to demonstrate the time by setting its hands at certain positions. In the post-observation conference, she again reflected on the use of resources in teaching mathematics and the involvement of the students in the learning process. She also reflected on the importance of teacher's own content and pedagogical knowledge and said,

> Mr Karim, yesterday, you taught me about this 'to', 'past' and all that. At home I did it myself, I kept the clock in front. It was very helpful, and then I planned the lesson. (19 February 2002)

Examples like the above indicate that Maria learnt mathematics from her interactions with me and through her efforts in lesson preparation. In this case, my role again appeared to be that of a subject expert or a coach, who could help her in content, pedagogy, and in provision of resources. I recognized that unless improved systems were in place for teachers to develop content and pedagogical knowledge in in-service programmes, these core roles would continue to characterize a mentor's work in Pakistan and in similar contexts in other developing countries.

How Maria Experienced the Mentoring Process

In order to understand better how Maria saw the mentoring relationship, I discussed it with her at the end of the fieldwork. She said:

> You seem to be my colleague, teacher, friend and a normal person. Whenever you worked with us, you worked as a colleague. You did not perceive yourself better than us. You did not boast of doing Masters from AKU-IED. You did not think of keeping a distance between you and us. And if you would have done this then we would not have talked with you frankly, we would never ask you questions, never. We would fear you. So, these things were not there....You

have a good nature. Keep it up and just remain the way you are. (26 February 2002)

Here Maria has talked about some important aspects of mentoring in terms of the role of a mentor as well as the mentor-mentee relationship. A key feature of the relationship is the mentor not keeping a 'distance' with the mentee, and not portraying himself/herself as an expert based on better qualification. In other words, it shows the importance of a non-hierarchical relationship between the mentor and mentee, which is also collegial, friendly, and trustworthy. Maria further said:

> Another thing that I like about the process is that you did not come all of a sudden and tell us, 'Hey, you have to work'. No, never. [You did this]. You asked about our health. You said hello and hi, and talked [about] social things. You shared many things besides your planned work or things related to the schooling. You talked about things besides your planning. Really, you cooperated with us and helped us. You know, all the good people do this. (26 February 2002)

She has referred to the personal dimension of the relationship which helped in building a rapport between the mentor and mentee. Thus, Maria has invited the mentor community to think and reflect upon the philosophy of mentoring. It is about taking care of all aspects of a mentee as a human being, putting oneself into the mentee's shoes, and realizing his/her personal and professional needs, fears, emotions, and feelings as a member of the organization and the larger society.

Maria also liked the timing of the post-observation conference, as it was done just after the lesson observations. She said,

> You did it [observation] just after the lessons were over. In my opinion, if you would say, after observing the lesson, 'I will meet you tomorrow' or, 'We will talk tomorrow'. If this could be the case, then believe me, Karim, a fresh mind makes a big difference and if I ought to tell you the next day, I would tell you only fifty percent of

the things. So, when my mind is fresh, I tell you at once. And whenever I am telling you, I am listening to my words too. Thus, when I am listening then I say that 'Yes this was the fact'. (26 February 2002)

In the above extract, Maria has identified two key aspects of the coaching dimension of the mentoring process. First, the need for the post-observation conference to be immediately after the lesson observation; second, the role of teachers' talk in enabling them to reflect on their own practice and understand it better. Thus, a mentor has to create situations for reflection and listen to the mentee's voice.

Discussion of the Findings

The findings in the previous section shed light on the process of mentoring and its consequences for mentoring roles and relationships. In what follows, I discuss the key roles that emerged in the process of mentoring, the relationships that led to mentoring as a successful strategy for teacher development, and related issues and questions.

Mentor's Role as a Subject Expert

The story of the mentoring process shows that I had to work with Maria in the content area of mathematics. During the pre-conferences, my focus remained mainly on discussing the content and doing mathematics with Maria. It was because of the obvious gaps in her subject content knowledge. Several studies (Ball, 2000; Feiman-Nemser and Parker, 1990; Halai, 1998; 1999; Saeed and Mahmood, 2002; Shulman, 1987) have recognized the importance of teachers' content knowledge for effective teaching. In a similar mentoring situation, Halai (1998) preferred working with teachers to enhance their mathematical content knowledge; she said, 'I felt that by doing mathematics, teachers would practice their mathematical thinking skills, which was important if they wanted their pupils to think mathematically' (p. 311).

I argue that Maria's problems in choosing appropriate representations and activities and implementing them in her classroom were mainly because of her own limited understanding of mathematics. This finding is confirmed by Ball (2000) who mentioned that teachers' own understanding of mathematical concepts influences the kind of analogies, representations, interpretations and activities they come up with for their students. This raises the question of how should we, as mentors, support teachers to teach well. Should the mentor's role be that of a subject expert?

I would argue that in the context of Pakistan, where teachers' inadequate initial preparation for teaching is a major issue, mentors' knowing the subject matter is important; because, teachers also need to be supported in content in order to become effective and competent teachers. The role of a mentor becomes critical in supporting teachers' learning of the subject content and the pedagogy without damaging their self-esteem.

Mentor's Role as a Coach and a Critical Friend

The coaching cycle provided focused opportunities to the mentor and mentee to work together on specific areas of knowledge or skills. Ideas developed in the pre-conferences were practiced and refined in the real classroom. The post-observation conferences provided scope for analysis and reflection. Evidence shared throughout the paper shows that Maria benefited tremendously from the coaching cycle. For example, she enhanced her content knowledge in mathematics, enlarged her repertoire of teaching strategies, and learnt to be constructively critical of her practice.

I also played the role of a critical friend who encouraged, stimulated and gave support in planning and implementing lessons, and prompted Maria to reflect on her actions (Cubin, Featherstone and Russel, 1997; Schon, 1983). Initially, being a critical friend was very difficult for me; because this role required me to engage my mentee in discussions about her practice which were analytical in nature. However, to most of my questions my mentee gave one word answers or became defensive. I also learnt that engaging in critical discussions required a variety of strategies such as providing examples, demonstrations, and asking open questions.

This experience raised several questions. For example, why did Maria find it difficult to engage in critical conversation? Was it because she was culturally not prepared for it? Were my expectations too high? Or too unrealistic? These questions alerted me to the fact that mentoring interactions are situated in a culture and context and their efficacy depends on taking account of cultural and contextual sensitivity.

Mentor–Mentee Relationships

Mutual trust and understanding are the indispensable aspects of mentoring. Without establishing a trustful relationship, one cannot successfully work with others. In the beginning Maria did not ask me for support in content knowledge, but with the passage of time she started consulting me in content matters. The reason could be that I was a new person for her and she did not know much about me in the initial days. She could assume that sharing her needs with me might label her as a poor and incompetent teacher. Thus, these assumptions restrained her from sharing content-related issues with me. Therefore, I was facing problems in understanding her needs and enabling her to work in a fear-free environment. Mentor–mentee relationship became more problematic when Maria had issues in her own content knowledge, but could not realize them. However, as a mentor, I wanted her to realize the issues and improve her content knowledge. The problem was that I could not tell her so directly because of the fear that she might feel inferior which may affect my efforts to build a trustworthy relationship with her. Therefore, I had to look for other indirect ways and strategies in order to balance the relationship. With the passage of time, I tried to reduce this hierarchy through talking to her informally, discussing social matters, asking her to call me by my name, inviting her to observe my lesson and give feedback. All this resulted in a friendly and collegial relationship between Maria and me.

I found that establishing a collegial relationship with Maria was an important part of the process; because, without a sense of collegiality, professional learning might not have occurred properly. Little (1990), talking about the influence of collegiality on professional relations, says that, 'the various forms of teacher exchange that pass as collegiality comprise fundamentally different conceptions of teachers' professional relations. 'Weak' and 'strong' versions of collegial relations plausibly produce or sustain quite different conditions of teacher performance and commitment' (p. 531). Collegial relationship was an aspect that seemed to be most influential in my process of mentoring. Co-planning, co-teaching, narrating what Maria did during the lesson, inviting her to observe my lessons, and helping her in the development of teaching aids and resources are illustrative examples of collegial relationship between Maria and me. The relationship in terms of being a 'humble friend and colleague', and behaving like an 'ordinary person' helped Maria to share her problems and learn from the mentoring process. If the environment had been hierarchical, mutual trust might not have been established properly.

BECOMING A MENTOR: QUESTIONS, ISSUES AND RECOMMENDATIONS

On the basis of the findings of the study, I state that mentoring is a useful process for school-based professional development of teachers. It is a voluntary and collegial relationship between an experienced or expert teacher and a less experienced or novice teacher. Mentors should not enjoy the official position of appraisers; rather they should focus only on the professional and personal development of the practicing teachers. They should guide, help, create situations, teach, and enable novice or less experienced teachers to make sense of teaching in their classrooms. Mentors need to possess a good knowledge of content, pedagogy, adult learning, and reflective skills in order to be able to facilitate mentees' learning in schools.

This study was situated in the in-service context of a school in Pakistan. Hence, by giving an account of the mentoring process in a school, the study has raised a number of questions and implications for mentoring as an approach to teachers' professional development. The major question that has emerged is 'Should a mentor be a subject specialist or generalist?' If a subject specialist, as there seems to be a need to develop teachers' content knowledge also, this would have implications for teacher development programmes. For example, programmes such as the M. Ed offered by AKU-IED, which is not focused on specific curricular areas, would need to look carefully at their content and focus. The core content would need to change to include a deeper focus on certain subject areas. Similarly, the entry criteria for the programmes would need to change to include participants who have experiences of and aspirations for working in specific subject areas. On the other hand, if the mentor is seen as a generalist as is the case in the current Master's programme at AKU-IED, how would the need for support in content knowledge be addressed? This is an issue that graduates of AKU-IED called Professional Development Teachers are already beginning to face in their schools.

Similarly, in both the cases, school structures will need support in terms of availability of time and space for mentors and mentees to work together. This raises further questions of whether or not schools and school systems would accept the responsibilities of managing such facilities for school-based teacher development. There are also implications and questions for school structure and the roles that current Heads of Department (HODs) and Subject Coordinators (SCs) appear to play in their work with other teachers. Could HODs be mentors? If yes, then the question arises about the performance evaluation of teachers, because these teacher leaders usually do this job, and if the mentor starts evaluating the teachers, would there be a collegial, trustworthy, and professional relationship between the mentor and the mentee? Therefore, if the schools expect the

HODs and SCs to be mentors then their role as performance evaluator would need to be reconsidered.

CONCLUSION

The study confirms the evidence that mentoring is a robust strategy for teacher development in the context of developing countries like Pakistan. Besides being an expert in pedagogy, it was found that in Pakistan, a mentor needs to have subject matter knowledge in order to support teachers in their classrooms. A mentor teacher, as a subject expert, a coach and a critical friend, supports teachers while teaching them content and pedagogy, as well as creating situations for their reflective practice.

I found that being a mentor required, more than technical and discipline-based knowledge and skills, the ability to touch the mentees' mind and heart; putting myself into her shoes, respecting her as a human being, and listening to her voice as a humble and caring friend was as essential, if not more, than providing her support in content knowledge and pedagogy. Thus, I conclude that being patient, talking to mentees at their level, being a true and helpful colleague, as well as having appropriate content and pedagogical content knowledge are some of the challenging but important characteristics of a mentor.

ACKNOWLEDGEMENTS

I would like to acknowledge and thank the teacher and the children who participated in the study.

NOTES

1. The study reported in this chapter was undertaken by the first author as part of the requirements of the M.Ed programme at AKU-IED.
2. Pseudonyms are used.

5

Action Research: In Search of an Effective Teacher Professional Development Strategy

Bernadette L. Dean

INTRODUCTION

One of the key factors responsible for a decline in the quality of education in Pakistan is the quality of teaching (Warwick and Reimers, 1995; Hoodbhoy, 1998; Chancellor's Commission Report, 1994). Research indicates that good teaching requires students' active participation in constructing knowledge and learning to use knowledge for problem-solving and decision-making; instead teachers transmit textbook content to students expecting them to rote memorize for examinations. The gap between the theory and practice of teaching has led to a growing emphasis on teacher education. Research, however, shows that traditional teacher education programmes are not making a difference as relatively few teachers apply learning from these programmes in their classrooms (Groundwater-Smith and Dadds, 2004; Joyce, Calhoun and Hopkins, 1999; Elliot, 1981). A mode of teacher professional development that could address this issue and improve the quality of teaching and learning is that of action research.

What is action research? Action research is a process of investigating one's practice to understand and improve it. Kemmis, McTaggart, and Retallick (2004) define action research as 'a form of collective self-reflective enquiry undertaken by participants in social situations in order to improve the rationality and justice of their own social or educational practices, as well as their understanding of these practices and the situations in which these practices are carried out'. For them action research is not about finding technical solutions to problems of practice but an ethical commitment to change practice based on educational values that are rational and just.

Most forms of action research use a cyclic process of planning, implementing, observing, and reflecting on the action. Modifications to the plan are made in the light of findings and a new cycle begins. The constant alternating between action and reflection allows the researcher to continually refine methods, data, and interpretation in the light of understanding developed in earlier cycles.

Action research is also participatory. Involvement of co-researchers facilitates critical reflection, making it easier for individuals to improve practice and influence change in institutional policies and practices. Collaboration also facilitates validation as others are able to judge authenticity of claims and relevance of the research to a professional context. The publication of the research serves to convince others of the validity of the claims.

THE RESEARCH METHODOLOGY

In order to understand the teachers' ideas of democracy and education for democratic citizenship, I engaged them in conversations. To improve their practice, I used the process of action research.

My own experience as a social studies teacher educator gave rise to the question, 'How can we realize the potential of social studies education for democratic citizenship?' I had developed an eight-week in-service social studies education programme to improve teachers' ability to educate for democratic citizenship. I thought that in conversation with programme graduates and in observation of their practice I would find the answer to the question. I chose three teachers (from different cohorts) all of whom agreed to work with me. I conducted three conversations with them, each of approximately one hour. In the conversations the teachers expressed difficulty in converting their desires into effective classroom practices. They sought my help in realizing their desires; I reflected on their request and suggested action research as a way forward. I continued conversations with them individually during the action research process and at the end of the study had two joint conversations.

Action Research

I suggested action research for the following reason: Teaching is a complex and idiosyncratic activity. Moreover, the material conditions of Pakistani schools differ greatly; what is applicable in one classroom may not be applicable in other classrooms. I believed that the process of action research would help teachers better understand their practice and to improve it.

Teachers used action research over a period of four months to teach a syllabus topic and an aspect necessary for democratic citizenship. My role in the action research process was twofold—facilitator and researcher. As a facilitator, I helped teachers plan their lessons, observed the implementation, and facilitated critical reflection through reflective conversations. As a researcher, I documented the process, critically reflected on it, and wrote it up to disseminate learning.

In this paper I share parts of the conversations with the teachers and one action research project.[1] The conversations are presented to situate the action research project undertaken by the teachers. Follow-up reflective conversations with the teachers helped in seeing the benefits of the action research experience for the participating teachers.

Partners in Conversation and Action Research

Following the notion of conversation and action research outlined, I entered into conversation and action research with three teachers.

Anila[2]

Anila started teaching in 1992 after completing a Masters in Economics from Karachi University. The only formal teacher training she had received was the eight-week social studies education programme at AKU-IED in 1995. She teaches in both shifts of a private school. She teaches economics and commercial geography in the morning and social studies in the afternoon.

Malik

Malik began teaching in 1992 with a Bachelor of Education from Karachi University in Urdu and Pakistan Studies. He teaches social studies in a government middle school (classes 6–8). Just prior to participating in the research he had attended the eight-week social studies education programme.

Salma

Salma started teaching in 1991 with a Bachelor of Education from Karachi University. Salma teaches history and geography in the Cambridge Section of a private school in the morning and social studies in the Matric Section of the same school in the afternoon. She attended the social studies education programme in 1997.

DEMOCRACY AND DEMOCRATIC CITIZENSHIP EDUCATION: TEACHERS' VIEWS

Our initial conversation revolved around democracy in Pakistan, the teachers' vision of Pakistan and how they might educate for democratic citizenship.

Teachers' Understanding of Democracy

At first, our conversation focused on the purely structural features of democracy, what Barber (1984) might call 'thin democracy' in which citizens' participation is limited to voting. The teachers expressed dissatisfaction with this system, desiring greater participation in decision-making and freedom of thought.

This led to a discussion of the failure of democracy which the teachers attributed to the inequality in gender, religion, class, and ethnicity in Pakistani society. They believed democracy required citizens 'to live democratically [then] democracy will follow.'

Envisioning an Egalitarian and Just Society

I felt it was important for the teachers to envision a desired and possible future that they would work to realize. The long thoughtful silence to my question was broken by Salma, who said she wanted 'a peaceful society'. Anila argued that peace could only be attained if there were equality and justice. This required that the feudal system—the taken-for-granted belief that people are unequal because of the circumstances of their birth—be brought to an end and people be given their rights and performed their duties. She said,

> Nothing will change, we have to get rid of the *jagirdari nizam* [feudal system] and the *jagirdari* [feudal] mentality. Economic, social and political power are in the hands of the *jagirdars* [feudal lords]....
> We have to do away with this system. They had this system in India also but after Independence they finished it. In Pakistan there have been land reforms but none has been effective because of the power of the *jagirdars*....People should get their rights...and they must be held accountable for the performance of their duties....

Malik agreed with Anila and stressed the right to freedom of expression:

> I think citizens must have the right to freely express their point of view without any pressure. If there is pressure, there is no democracy. When people cannot exercise their right of freedom of expression they lose their ability to think and are unable to differentiate between right and wrong.

Implicit in the teachers' vision for Pakistani society was the desire for a democratic society based on freedom, equality, and social justice for all.

Education for Democratic Citizenship

The teachers believed that democratic citizens must have the knowledge and skills to understand and address the problems of society. Malik stressed the need for students to know their rights and make informed decisions. Anila felt students should undertake a comparative study of political, economic and social systems to identify strengths and limitations in the present system and improve it. Salma thought students should learn to cooperate and creatively address societal problems.

The conversations indicate that the teachers were aware of the knowledge, skills, and dispositions needed for democratic citizenship. Action research helped them to translate this vision into education for democratic citizenship.

ACTION RESEARCH ON TEACHING FOR DEMOCRATIC CITIZENSHIP

Malik's Action Research Project

During our conversations, Malik expressed the belief that citizens in a democracy must know their rights and responsibilities. For him an important right was freedom of expression or what Barber (1984) calls 'strong democratic talk'. It entails thinking, expressing one's ideas, listening to the ideas of others, presenting counter arguments, and making decisions.

Freedom of Expression

Malik decided to teach students about their rights and responsibilities through whole class discussion to encourage students to express their views. However, the lesson proved to be unsuccessful because instead of discussion Malik got monosyllabic replies. Malik, however, expressed satisfaction that a few students had responded and planned to continue teaching this way, interpreting students' lack of response as the result of 'shyness' and lack of 'familiar[ity] with the style of teaching.' He expected their participation to improve the next day. I suggested that another reason may be students' lack of knowledge about the topic. Malik thought the suggestion plausible, but wondered where he would get the information required.

I provided copies of 'The Convention on the Rights of the Child' (CRC). They were in English so Malik said he could not use them. We proceeded to translate each of the rights. Malik decided to teach the rights of the child and discuss three questions: What did the right entail? To what extent are children receiving these rights? and Whose responsibility is it to ensure children their rights? In keeping with his belief that the right to express oneself entailed the responsibility to listen, Malik wanted students to learn the social skill of 'listening attentively.' Unsure of his ability to teach a skill learned during the course, he invited me to teach it, which I did on his request.

The next day Malik negotiated a change from his classroom to the science laboratory to facilitate discussion. Following the teaching of the social skill, Malik again tried to elicit the rights through questions. Receiving no response, he explained each right as planned. The following day he arranged the chairs in a circle and started what became a very animated discussion about the best interests of the child and entitlement to rights. Students argued that they were not receiving their entitlement because the government built schools but did not ensure quality education, built hospitals but did not supply medicines. Malik asked, 'Who is the government?' followed by 'What is our role as citizens in a democracy?' Students responded, 'to vote' and 'vote for the candidate most likely to win'.

In the next lesson, students developed criteria for the selection of a candidate and used it to vote. Malik asked students what helped them make their decision. On a response that, 'education helped people learn to make good decisions,' he discussed their right to education. During the discussion, Malik followed my example and raised questions, asked students to clarify their ideas, and moved the discussion forward.

Malik found it difficult to engage in self-critical reflection on his teaching. He described what occurred in the classroom and his success in promoting students' learning. We, therefore, engaged in reflective conversations.

During our first conversation I asked Malik why he continued to question the students rather than teach as planned. He said:

> I wanted to teach the topic like I saw...during the...I faced problems while teaching this topic because I did not have information about this topic. I did not know that students needed information, I thought they were shy and not familiar with this style of teaching and that in a day or two they would start answering well. (Post-lesson conversation, 1 January 1999)

During the professional development programme Malik had attended, he saw teacher educators eliciting participants' ideas through questioning and this experience informed his practice. He did not realize that this model presupposed students' and teachers' prior knowledge about the topic. He was aware that he did not have the knowledge to teach the topic, but he took it up, relying on his questions to provoke discussion.

Malik believed that democracy required citizens to make informed decisions. In a representative democracy like Pakistan, the main decision citizens make is who to vote for. Malik was very concerned when a student expressed the idea that one should vote for the person most likely to win. He believed this lack of conscious choice by citizens during elections was responsible for the political crises in Pakistan:

> The *waderas* [feudal landlords] rule the people under them. They order the people to vote for them and the people do because they have taken money from them. The *waderas* stand in the elections and are given tickets by the political parties because the political parties know they will win because they have a hold over the people of their area....The lack of careful selection by the people is the

reason for the political instability in Pakistan. (Post-lesson conversation, 1 January 1999)

This concern resulted in Malik digressing to teach students the importance of their vote and the need to choose judiciously. Willingness to digress was an indication that Malik had the research question uppermost in his mind and was developing flexibility.

During the end-of-the-cycle conversation, Malik was ecstatic about his lessons. He had met his objectives as students understood their rights and were able to express their ideas.

> Children found it very easy to understand their rights and responsibilities because it concerned their personal life, because it is part of their reality....When they were asked to give their opinions they replied very well. That's how I concluded the children understood very well what I taught them. (Post-lesson conversation, 14 January 1999)

Freedom of expression, as Malik had pointed out, is more than speaking: it entails listening as well as reflecting on what others say. I modelled attentive listening, raised thoughtful questions, and challenged ideas presented. Subsequent lesson observations indicated that Malik had taken over this role. Malik was pleased I had observed how fast he and the students were learning.

Creating a Cooperative Classroom Environment

When Malik finished teaching the topic on rights and responsibilities in January, he felt pressured to teach for the exams scheduled for late February. Faced with the dilemma of preparing students for the exams and teaching for democratic citizenship, he decided to teach for the exams. He chose the textbook chapter 'Pakistan and the Muslim World,' incorporating map skills learned in the social studies teacher education programme. Acknowledging the importance of preparing students for the exams, I asked Malik to consider how he could also prepare students for democratic citizenship. He suggested he spend four days a week teaching the chapter and Saturdays discussing a social issue. Accepting it as a way of dealing with the dilemma, I challenged him again. Annoyed, he reminded me 'everyone has to study the same content for the examinations' but finally decided to use cooperative learning so that students learn teamwork. We spent an entire day planning. We revised the concepts and skills, ways to create a cooperative learning environment, and prepared lessons accordingly. Malik expressed a number of concerns:

> How do I deal with the weaker students? How will they learn?.... How do I teach so many students? Can you teach half and I teach half?....There is no large map of Pakistan, no world map in the school, how will I explain?....Can you help me identify the Muslim countries on the map?....(22 January 1999)

The enriched content, hands-on activities, and the teacher's role in creating a cooperative learning environment, required Malik to make radical changes to the way he taught and to question the assumptions underlying his teaching. He believed that students who did not learn quickly were weak and knowledge transmission was the only way to deal with large classes, lack of resources, curriculum and examination demands. He now had to confront these beliefs about teaching to change his practice.

Malik's lack of content knowledge had become evident when he stopped relying on the textbook. Therefore, he returned to it. Teaching from it gave him a sense of security, but he had doubts about his ability to teach map skills to his class of sixty-three students. As I acknowledged his concerns, discussed his assumptions, and shared ways to teach, Malik's anxiety decreased.

Malik began by asking students to draw a map from their home to school, followed by teaching compass directions and conventional symbols. Students learned to draw the map of Pakistan freehand, indicate directions and use conventional symbols on it. They learned how to locate Pakistan and other

Muslim countries on the world map. They also studied the importance of some Muslim countries. Malik also created a cooperative classroom environment. Students learned interpersonal skills and worked cooperatively in groups. Malik observed, explained to, and encouraged the students during this process.

The environment in Malik's classroom was electrifying. The enthusiasm of the students towards this cooperative, student-centered, hands-on approach to learning excited and encouraged Malik to challenge himself and his students even further. The roles of teacher and student blurred and the Freirean classroom of 'teacher-students' with 'student-teachers' emerged (Freire, 1970: 67). Reflecting later on his lessons he said:

> The work that seemed very difficult before we started became easy with your help and the help of the students. The students enjoyed this method of teaching way beyond my expectations. I think it is because we adopted the method of cooperative learning which is in accord with our way of life in Pakistan. They could see that what they were learning was useful and related to their daily life, therefore, it had a greater impact on them.... I also learned a lot during this time...to recognize the different continents, identify the Muslim countries....(Post-lesson conversation, 5 February 1999)

Malik made some important observations: the teaching method was effective because it was related to the way children learn (active engagement) and the way they live their lives (in community). In addition, students learned useful content. Pakistan is a Muslim country. Pakistan's relationship with and events in Muslim countries are regularly highlighted in the news. Knowledge of these countries would help students better understand the news and make thoughtful rather than emotional judgments.

Malik recognized that a cooperative learning environment led to a more open and equal relationship between the student and teacher. He confronted the myths of the teacher as sole authority and disciplinarian:

If we want to teach for democratic citizenship, teachers have to modify the traditional teacher-student relationship. It is commonly believed that teachers should be strict, should keep a distance from their students. I think there is too much distance between teachers and students....I think teachers should talk politely, treat their students equally, cooperate with them but must retain their respect....To change my own behaviour I have had to work hard. In fact, in these five to six weeks, I have come very close to the students. The change started when I encouraged the students to speak, when I accepted what they were saying and when I showed I had confidence in them....Now in creating a caring and cooperative environment I have seen what a difference the environment has made on me and my students. (Conversation 22 February 1999)

Looking through lesson observations, we found that Malik's interactions with the students showed his care and concern for them. His verbal behaviour was largely commendatory and accepting. He encouraged hesitant students to participate in discussions, to address the class, not him; and he asked more vocal students to give others a chance to speak. We also noted that students called absent colleagues to join their group, included them in group activities, and taught them what they had missed.

Discussing Social Problems

Malik decided to teach a social problem on Saturday to enhance students' understanding of the problem and suggest ways to address it because, 'citizens in a democracy need to be informed about the problems in society and see their role in solving them.' Malik decided to show the video *Der na ho jiya* (Before It's Too Late) which depicts environmental problems of Pakistan and people's actions to address them, and follow it with a discussion of problems and their solutions.

I suggested students take action to address the problems. 'What action?' he asked. I pointed out that the best solutions if not implemented are useless. Malik was surprised at my suggestion. It was not part of his experience as student or teacher.

Even in the teacher development programme from where he got the idea to teach social issues, they only discussed possible actions. Why was I suggesting taking action?

On Saturday, succumbing to pressure from the principal, Malik agreed to another class viewing and discussing the video. The students watched the video keeping in mind two questions: What are the environmental problems facing Pakistan? What solutions are suggested to these problems? Malik elicited the problems but managing both classes was difficult.

The next day he decided against combining the classes and volunteered to teach the other class later. In subsequent lessons, students discussed the effects of the environmental problems and possible solutions. Malik asked students to write down each environmental problem, its causes, effects, and possible solutions.

Following the sharing, Malik discussed possible actions and suggested students could pick up the garbage themselves. A student said, 'We have a sweeper who collects our garbage in the morning and evening. We do not have garbage in front of our house.' Malik responded, 'Can't we pick up the garbage ourselves? From today, why don't you start by keeping your classroom clean? Pick up the garbage on the floor.' Malik had intentionally thrown garbage on the floor. The students picked up the garbage, walked to the window, and threw it outside, there being no bin in the classroom. The students' behaviour disappointed Malik and he ended the lesson by telling students to act on their learning.

Malik realized that students acquired knowledge from the video; and when they related it to their own local problems, they were constructing knowledge. Knowledge resulted in increased participation in discussion and students supported their ideas and challenged those of others. His work had borne fruit, students were learning discussion and deliberation skills:

> I wanted to improve students' speaking power and their confidence to speak out....Before, they would only speak about what they were taught but now they talked about the environmental problems of Pakistan as well as the problems they are facing in their

surroundings....This means they got a lot of knowledge from the video but from the discussion I see they have knowledge also. The reason there was noise in the class was because students had ideas and were eager to share them. Due to their eagerness they were not waiting for their turn but were rushing to share their ideas. I feel in the last two months I have succeeded in making the students speak, listen, and ask questions....(Conversation, 2 February 1999)

Lesson observations revealed that practically the whole class had participated in the discussions. It also revealed that students were supporting their ideas, asking questions, challenging others' ideas, identifying limitations in proposed solutions, and suggesting alternatives. Moreover, some students had seen interconnections between problems and had moved from the national to the local level, seeing effects on their health and well-being. Furthermore, analysis of their written assignment indicated improvement in their writing. Malik believed there was such a difference because

This topic was not from their textbooks, it was new and challenging. It was challenging because they had to find solutions to the problems. Students themselves saw how national problems were related to their daily life, therefore, it had a greater impact on them. It is also because students are sharing ideas and learning from each other. (Conversation, 2 February 1999)

Malik was reluctant to go into any critical discussion of the action. I interpreted this behaviour of Malik in two ways. He was concerned about implications of challenging sedimented cultural beliefs and practices regarding garbage collection, a job reserved for poor religious minorities, or resistance to the authority of the expert. If it was resistance, it indicated Malik was not just accepting my suggestions, thus, opening up possibilities for his own agency.

REFLECTIVE GROUP CONVERSATIONS ON ACTION RESEARCH OUTCOMES

Group reflective conversations were held with all the three study participants, following the completion of their action research projects. During one such session, Malik noted that he had discussed environmental issues to prepare students to make informed decisions. He, however, wondered how he would continue to teach social issues and motivate students to act given that 'the textbook contained no information related to the issues affecting our life'. He then himself suggested a way.

> I think we must have students compare the content of the textbook with what is happening around them. They will ask why the difference and realize that to eliminate the difference they will have to make some efforts. We have to develop in them the desire to find out why things are the way they are and think of what can be done to change them....We must make them aware of injustice and the need to bring people together to unite and raise their voice for justice.

The conversation then moved to the instructional strategies that facilitated the development of the knowledge, skills, and attitudes required of democratic citizens. Malik found discussion helped students learn to express themselves and their confidence to speak is developed by encouraging them to speak before focusing on the content of their speech.

> I wanted to improve their speaking power. I wanted to build students' confidence to speak....That is why I didn't stop any student during our initial discussions. Even if he was saying something wrong, I allowed him to speak which encouraged him.

All the teachers found that cooperative learning facilitated students working together but more importantly it served to develop a democratic classroom environment in which teachers shared their authority with their students.

Through the research the teachers realized they had agency, they could enrich the curriculum, use different teaching methodologies, and create a democratic classroom; at each step they faced constraints which they addressed to move forward. For example, Anila said,

> When I first started all I could see were the difficulties. I was worried about how I would complete everything planned. I had to complete the syllabus as the exams were coming....Resources were unavailable to teach for democratic citizenship. When I got the resources there was no time, I had to borrow time from other teachers to complete what I had planned, complete the syllabus, and check students' copies....But because it was the end of term and many teachers had completed their syllabus I asked to take their periods and used them. There was too much work but it was satisfying. I have learned a lot and so have the students.

Malik lamented the lack of learning resources, especially their availability in Urdu, which made it difficult for him to acquire information:

> My problem is resources. There are no libraries in government schools to get information from other sources and it is very difficult to find resources in Urdu....Teachers lack awareness of local, national, and global issues because they do not have access to information.

The teachers then discussed the constraints of space and time. Salma and Malik acknowledged the support of the school head in addressing these constraints. However, all the teachers expressed the need for time for preparation and reflection to be timetabled.

The teachers moved from school level constraints to observing how the curriculum and examination system constrained their desires and the required changes. Anila realized that one way to address the issue of the curriculum was to enrich it. This required the support of colleagues in her own school as well as from other schools.

The syllabus that we are presently using provides very little opportunity for students to think, let alone think in a democratic way....Because there is so much lacking in the available syllabus, I am planning to prepare a syllabus with teachers in my school with the goal of educating for democratic citizenship. I think social issues should be part of the syllabus so I want to start by writing some materials on social issues during the summer holidays in a language that will be easy for students to understand. Malik, Salma, would you be willing to work with me?

The teachers' reflections then turned inwards as they reflected on how their assumptions and beliefs had been challenged through systematic action and reflection. They explained that changes in their teaching made them realize that they had underestimated students' knowledge and abilities. They found students were not 'dull' but had a 'lot of potential'. They also acknowledged that prior to the research they had been 'very strict' because they thought it was the best way to maintain control of the class but now even though they created a caring and cooperative environment the students were 'learning well' and 'not sitting on my head.'

Discussion of Findings

The study revealed that through action research the teachers, including Malik, developed their knowledge, skills, and dispositions, changed their beliefs and practice, leading to enhanced student learning outcomes and changes in the material conditions of school. The exclusive focus on examinations and the extent of expert support required for effective action research, however, posed challenges.

The Possibilities

As the teachers began their efforts to educate for democratic citizenship they found that the textbook content was limited and irrelevant to students' lives. It did not facilitate the development of skills and dispositions important for citizens in a democracy.

They addressed these limitations by enriching the content, using a variety of instructional strategies, and designing intellectually engaging activities. The pedagogy led to the teachers and students discovering a whole new way of being in the classroom. The traditional, distant and often antagonistic relationship between teacher and students was replaced by a thoughtful and caring relationship. The passive and bored students became active, cooperative, and independent participants in learning as they engaged with challenging, meaningful, and relevant tasks. This helped students not only develop a good understanding of the content studied but also learn a number of skills (interpersonal, communication, and problem-solving), values, and dispositions (cooperation, respect for others, and commitment to participation in civic life).

As teachers shared their authority with the students and became less controlling, their assumptions of 'weak' students and fear of 'losing control' were challenged. Furthermore, the teachers' understanding of knowledge—what is knowledge, who produces knowledge, what is official knowledge—also changed. The teachers had seen the textbook as the source of knowledge and their students as consumers of knowledge. Now they recognized that their students were also producers of knowledge. Anila realized that what she had accepted as 'school knowledge' was only one way of selecting and organizing knowledge to meet curriculum goals and that it included certain interests which did not serve democracy.

The teachers found that changes in their practice required changes in institutional structures and practices forcing them into negotiations with their school heads. This interaction resulted in changes in structure (longer periods for social studies) and practices (allowing students to participate in a signature campaign) of the school that opened up possibilities for more democratic ways of teaching. The students, recognizing the more democratic environment, in turn opened up their schools to new practices. In Malik's school, other students demanded they be taught like his students which resulted in the head teacher freeing another teacher to work with us and encouraging Malik to teach another class. Similarly, Anila's students used the democratic process to organize themselves and insist on taking concrete action on their learnings. This led to the teachers and students recognizing they had agency and could become change agents.

The Challenges

Understanding of Teaching and the Work of Teachers

Two major constraints to improving the quality of teaching repeatedly identified in the literature also constrained teaching in this study: coverage of the prescribed textbook and preparation of students for examinations. For teachers, the textbook is the curriculum and the goal of teaching, completion of the textbook. All teachers are expected to do is transmit textbook knowledge to students and ensure they memorize it for examinations. Since there are often two to three sections of the same class, all class teachers are expected to cover the syllabus at the same rate. In addition, teachers must ensure that students have the answers to all possible examination questions in their copies. Teachers spend their non-teaching time diligently correcting copies to ensure the answers are right. Thus, teaching has come to be seen as the transmission of textbook content and learning the consumption and reproduction of immutable truths. Enriching the curriculum took time away from teaching textbook content, a great concern to the teachers who feared students would not fare well in examinations which call for regurgitation of textbook information. In Pakistan, this is particularly important as examination results determine the stream (science, commerce, general) students can opt for and the quality of the college they will be admitted to. Examination results are also seen to reflect teachers' and schools' performance. Therefore, as teachers educated for democratic citizenship they simultaneously had to ensure students were prepared for examinations, which put enormous pressure on them.

Furthermore, to successfully enrich textbook content and change their pedagogy, the teachers had to access, review and translate materials, develop detailed lesson plans and reflect on their teaching. Present understandings of teaching do not allow time for planning and reflection so that the teachers continuously expressed concern with regard to time. The issue of time was compounded as the teachers could not access resources to improve teaching and learning. In government schools lack of resources is especially problematic as it is difficult to access resources in Urdu, even on the Internet.

Expert Support Required for Action Research

Given the present understanding of teaching and the fact that most teachers are untrained or inadequately trained, the teachers in the study required intensive expert support. This raises the question of whether it is viable to use action research for teacher professional development in resource-deprived contexts like Pakistan. I believe the support required must be weighed against benefits. In this case a university faculty worked with three teachers over four months. The benefits that accrued were of teacher learning and empowerment, and improved student learning outcomes and changes in some school structures and practices. Teacher professional development activity that facilitates learning while teaching addresses a myriad of problems facing Pakistan's education system—poor quality of teaching, poor student learning outcomes, high cost of in-service teacher education, and the low status of teachers. However, if action research is to become an alternative means to the professional development done in the setting of short in-service programmes in centralized locations away from teachers' workplace, I believe we will require the development of university-school partnerships to undertake action research as a collaborative endeavour and acknowledge teacher education as taking place both at schools and universities.

All the three teachers in the study were from schools that are in partnership with a university because they want to improve.

As part of the partnership, the teachers had all participated in an eight-week social studies education programme offered at the university but with no follow-up support. Malik had just finished the programme. The action research with him could be seen as the follow-up support built into the programme. (See also chapter 6) Furthermore, if we conceptualize the present study as a collaborative study then the same university faculty instead of working with one teacher would work with a group of teachers in each of the three schools. The teachers would collaboratively plan and reflect on their teaching. As teachers hone their skills they would take over the role of the university faculty.

IMPLICATIONS AND RECOMMENDATIONS

There is no doubt that action research facilitates teachers' professional development and improves student learning outcomes but if the benefits demonstrated in this study are to accrue and be further enhanced then the work of teachers must be reconceptualized and effective school-university partnerships developed.

Creating Enabling Institutional Structures and Practices for Teachers to Engage in Professional Development through Action Research

In this study the teachers demonstrated the possibility of teachers becoming curriculum leaders. They enriched textbook content, chose innovative instructional strategies and activities, and engaged in alternative assessment practices to realize the goal of educating for democratic citizenship. In order to do this within present understandings of teaching and school practices they had to make enormous personal commitments in terms of time and energy. Changes like this are not sustainable as they depend on teachers' willingness to volunteer and high motivation. What is required are changes in the structure and practices of schools to enable teachers to make quality improvements at the classroom and school level.

One such change is related to time for teachers to reflect on their teaching and student learning. Non-teaching time could be allocated for planning, reflecting, and correcting students' work. Timetables could be developed so that teachers teaching a year group can come together for two periods a week. Better still is to provide a half day each week for teachers to come together to plan and reflect on their teaching. Students of the senior year could teach classes or volunteer parents could work with students in areas not covered by the curriculum. Alternatively, the setting aside of a professional development day for teachers once a month has also proved to be very useful. These strategies will require schools to explain to parents the need for teachers to have this time and seek their support in such efforts. Providing time for teachers to plan and reflect within the present set-up are often used simply to fulfil institutional requirements. Planning and reflecting can become meaningful activities if teachers actively participate in the identification of an area of concern for improvement. This would give teachers a sense of purpose and direction to change as demonstrated in this research study. Moreover, if schools are to become sites of teacher education then schools must be adequately resourced. A variety of strategies will be required given the diversity of contexts in Pakistan. In urban areas, teachers could access university or public libraries, and a few computers with Internet connections could become a valuable resource for teachers. In areas where Internet connections are not available, material can be downloaded on CDs and made available to schools. The teaching and learning resource centres can provide access to conventional and, where possible, Internet facilities. Mobile libraries for teachers could also be developed. Furthermore, successful use of action research to address concerns or implement innovations will require school leaders to not only generate time and resources for staff development, but also to provide ongoing expert support to assist with the implementation. In addition, school leaders must become familiar with the knowledge base, ensure implementation, and study learning outcomes. Research has shown that changes, especially complex ones, require at least two to three years for institutionalization (Fullan, 1991); so school leaders must be willing to provide support from initiation through to institutionalization.

University–School Partnerships

To realize the possibilities of action research for teachers' professional development, we will require the creation of effective university-schools partnerships by drawing on each other's strengths. University faculties could play a number of facilitation roles in action research projects being undertaken in schools. University courses can be designed to take place at university and schools. At university, teachers learn content, pedagogy, and action research. At schools, they use action research to improve their practice under the guidance of university faculty. Well-written action research reports could satisfy thesis requirements for university award-bearing courses as is currently done at the Institutes for Educational Development of the Aga Khan University in Karachi and Dar-es-Salaam. Alternatively, schools could identify an area of concern or university faculty could facilitate schools in thoughtfully considering practice to identify an area of concern. University faculty and teachers review the professional knowledge base about content, pedagogy, and school practices required to develop in the focus area. Teachers in each school engage in a reconnaissance to get a clear picture of where the school is with respect to the focus area. Based on the data, teachers design a plan of action, engage in action research, and study outcomes. Schools receive expert advice and support while university faculty gain through opportunity for research with teachers in a situational context.

CONCLUSION

Research shows that traditional forms of teacher education have resulted in little change in classroom practice as few teachers use their learning from these courses. In the present study, as the teachers engaged in the action research process of planning, acting, reflecting and modifying plans to address issues that constrained their efforts, they came to see teaching not as a repetition of monological performances but as a continually evolving and deeply satisfying process in which teachers both teach and learn and through which student learning outcomes are improved and schools revitalized. It made them realize that democracy, like teaching, is not an 'ideal state' to be realized but is 'built through their continual efforts at making a difference' (Apple and Beane, 1995, p. 13).

NOTES

1. This is part of a larger study completed in 2000. Following conversations with three participating teachers, they were supported to do an action research project each, on selected topics for teaching democratic citizenship to secondary school students in different school settings in Pakistan.
2. Pseudonyms are used.

6

Contexts and Conditions for Action Research as a Tool

Razia Fakir Mohammad and Roshni Kumari

INTRODUCTION

This chapter presents our findings from a research initiated to support teachers' continuous development through action research in the rural context of a developing country (Pakistan). The study was designed as a follow-up on an in-service teacher education programme to provide support to the participants in their efforts for bringing reform in the teaching and learning situation in a rural context, and to simultaneously study and understand the processes involved in terms of identifying outcomes, opportunities, and issues of continuing professional growth in such contexts.

The findings suggest that as part of their action research plans, and through the facilitators' support in the context, the participants were able to initiate change and introduce innovative ideas in the classroom. The participants' engagement in this experience provided them with the opportunity and motivation to think about the actions that may improve their practice. However, going beyond the initial level of effort in terms of being able to influence their teaching or teacher learning practices or to improve the learning experiences of students in classroom on a long-term basis was still difficult. Various constraints restricted the possibility of engaging in action research as a self-initiated and self-sustained process of an individual's learning and growth. The participants, on their own, were not able to understand and address the complex issues related to teaching or teacher learning. This restricted the use of action research as a strategy for ongoing professional development of teachers in the rural context of Pakistan.

This chapter provides a discussion on how action research was redefined in the context of a developing country. More specifically, it will focus on the opportunities that facilitated the process of participants' learning and growth, the constraints that hindered, and the conditions that were/are necessary for teachers to engage in action research as an effective way to promote self-learning and self-growth.

Action Research for CPD: Theoretical Perspective

The notion of teachers' action research is built on the foundation that, 'Practice is a form of power—a dynamic force both for social continuity and for social change' (Carr, 1995). Action research has been seen as an attempt for a teacher committed to fundamental change in teaching practice, to make impact on classrooms as well as on the larger society, through analysis of own actions, its outcomes, and limitations resulting in taking new actions (for example, Elliot, 1978; Kemmis and McTaggart, 1988).

According to Kemmis and Wilkinson (1998):

> Through action research, people can come to understand their social and educational practices more richly by locating their practices, as concretely and precisely as possible, in the particular material, social, and historical circumstances within which their practices were produced, developed, and evolved—so that their real practice becomes accessible to reflection, discussion, and reconstruction as products of past circumstances which are capable of being modified in and for present and future circumstances. (p. 25)

Teachers' actions have rationales but also room for further improvement, and improvement requires involvement in the process of inquiry. Action research therefore aims to investigate reality in order to change it and at the same time, it aims to change the reality in order to investigate it.

The linking of the terms 'action' and 'research' highlights the essential feature of the method: trying out ideas in practice as a means of improvement and as a means of increasing knowledge about school leadership, curriculum, teaching and learning. The result is improvement in what happens in the classroom and school, and better articulation and justification of the educational rationale for what goes on. (Kemmis, McTaggart and Retallick, 2004, p. 1)

Action research is also viewed as a systematic approach to introducing innovations in teaching and learning which, in turn, results in improved teaching practices and contributes towards the overall aim of school improvement. The claim is well-supported by the argument that since teachers have the knowledge of the context as well as the practical knowledge built through years of experience, they could use new knowledge in a better way to identify and address issues concerning them directly through taking a self-inquiry approach (Cochran-Smith and Lytle, 1993; Ponte, Ax, Beijaard and Wubbels, 2004). A number of research studies in the western context and also in the urban context of Pakistan provide evidence that engaging practitioners/teachers in action research had, to some extent, transformed their thinking and practice—enough to confirm the potential of action research as a vehicle for teacher learning and educational reform (for example, Halai, Ali, Kirmani and Mohammad, 2003; Retallick and Mithani, 2003; Ponte et al., 2004). Thus teachers as researchers learn and create knowledge by critically reflecting on their own actions, developing concepts and theories about their experiences as a result of their reflections and thereby becoming responsible for their own learning. In this way, learning becomes an on-going process. Educational research has been defined by Carr and Kemmis (1986) as 'a form of research which places control over processes of educational reform in the hands of those involved in the actions' (p. 189).

Teachers' participation in research encourages them to be decision-makers and constructors of professional knowledge, as 'involvement' and 'improvement' are key factors. As a result, the participants develop new theories of teaching and learning and a practical understanding of the research process and outcomes.

Based on the above discussion, 'Action Research' in our research project was defined as a tool for continuing professional development—a tool that provides opportunity for teachers to engage in the process of improving their practices through implementation of new ideas, learnt in a teacher education programme, as well as reflection on the actions and outcomes. However, we found that despite its potential as a tool for continuous professional development, it was not simple to create conditions that support teachers' growth through action research. In fact, major obstacles constrained this activity in rural schools in Pakistan and teachers agreed that it would be difficult to sustain their learning through the use of action research. The facilitators' presence and approach during the research process enabled them to take some initiatives for improvement; however, there were various constraints that hindered their taking ownership of their learning. The question for most of the participants towards the end of the research study, therefore, remained, 'What would happen when the facilitators won't be there?' This, in turn, raises an important question for us: 'Now that the inquiry is over, how can the study participants, i.e. teachers and teacher educators, be enabled to continue?' Thus, although the chapter provides a discussion on the opportunities and outcomes of action research for teachers in a developing country context, the major thrust of our findings and, therefore, of this chapter, remains on highlighting factors that hindered teachers in their growth in terms of their thinking as well as practice. Based on the discussion, it also attempts to make some recommendations for future teacher education initiatives, highlighting conditions that are necessary for teachers to bring about change in their practice.

CONTEXT OF THE STUDY

The findings presented in this chapter are based on a study that investigated the experiences of seven teachers and teacher educators from the rural context of two provinces in Pakistan—Sindh and Balochistan. The participants spent nearly six months undertaking action research projects following a university-based teacher education programme titled 'Certificate in Education: Teacher Education'. The course intended to develop a core group of teachers and potential teacher educators who, on their return, would play a key role in improving the teaching and learning situation in schools in rural Sindh and Balochistan. The overall aim of this programme was to enable the participants to become reflective practitioners and life-long learners. Therefore, the participants were introduced to various tools to help them continue their professional growth process after the end of the programme. Action research was introduced as one of the strategies to achieve this important aim.

Altogether, thirty-four teachers and teacher educators from the public sector and working in the rural context participated in the course. All the course participants had developed their action research plans during the course as part of the course requirement and were encouraged to implement these plans in their context after their return. However, only seven selected participants were part of the research initiated by the course facilitators due to the reasons discussed below.

Participants' involvement and participation in the study was mainly based on their consent and motivation to be part of this research. 'Willingness' was one important criterion that we began with. However, the people who volunteered to participate in the research were too many and too scattered in terms of physical distance and the number available in one particular district. Thus, the sample needed to be reduced for practical and logistic reasons (which included our capacity in terms of human resource, time commitment, and logistics etc.). More importantly, expanding our sample in terms of number of participants as well as geographical boundaries would not have allowed us the depth and insight into the processes, context, and conditions for the professional growth of the participants, which was the aim of the study. Thus, the participants were selected on the basis of maximum representation, i.e., selecting the district on the basis of maximum number of participants as well as ensuring that the districts were selected in such a way that both the provinces got equal representation. Consequently, we had seven research participants in our study (including two females), three from Sindh and four from Balochistan. The study was conducted after the completion of the university-based programme, when the participants had gone back to their respective institutions and were expected to initiate action research projects in order to implement their new learning.

These teachers and teacher educators came from schools where they had limited resources, especially for teaching and learning. For example, in some cases, the children would be seated on the floor due to non-availability of furniture. Frequently, two or three grades were combined in one small room due to shortage of space, furniture and/or teachers. Children in this context would mostly travel several miles on foot to reach their schools. They had very limited exposure and access to any resources other than the textbook. In certain cases even the basic living facilities were not available, such as electricity, telephone, newspaper, etc. An extreme example is that of a context where the community/residents did not even have the notion of 'toilet'. The availability and provision of resources, however, varied from one context to another, both in Sindh and Balochistan.

Researchers' Role in the Participants' Research

Our role in this research was a dual one; we played the role of a facilitator as well as a researcher. As facilitator, we provided follow-up support to the participants in order to help them improve their practice, which was done mainly through our monthly field visits to their context. These visits would normally include observation of their lessons and pre- and post-conference discussion sessions with the participants. In the discussion sessions, we would facilitate the participants in reflecting on their practice, helping them identify, understand, and improve their roles and practices in order to bring reform in the teaching and learning situation in their context. However, we had kept our role flexible so as to be able to respond to the emerging needs of the situation. For example, in some cases, we had to take on a more leading role, where we would either make direct input or guide our participants in their decision-making so as to help them take decisions that were more ethically appropriate and justified. The need for this change in the role was justified because although the course included intensive input sessions to help the participants understand action research, we realized that the participants would still need ongoing follow-up support to be able to carry out action research on their own, once they returned to their context. Our findings and analysis further elaborate the possible impact of university tutors' presence and support as one important factor in the participants' completing their action research projects following their training programme.

In addition to this facilitative role, we were also studying the process of participants' growth and learning, in particular, the issues, challenges, and opportunities related to their learning in varied contexts. We were engaged in the process of research— collecting and analysing data, as well as reflecting on the emerging issues during the fieldwork. The research was conducted in the qualitative paradigm to help us understand the processes of continuous professional development in depth. The study design involved frequent visits (approximately three to four) to each research site. The initial visits were part of the entry negotiations process, which involved researchers' spending time on the site in order to develop an understanding of the participants' context (their work places); negotiating their action research plans and implementation, defining roles, etc. In addition to the entry negotiation visits, the researchers had approximately three to four discussion sessions with each participant. These sessions were audio-recorded with the permission of the participants. In addition to the discussions, in-depth interviews were also conducted with the participants. We also observed the activities that the participants engaged in as part of their action research. This included the implementation of new strategies such as group work in a multi-grade classroom and mentoring sessions with teacher colleagues. The purpose of these observations was to gain some understanding of the implementation process of their action research plans. In addition, these observations also provided concrete examples for generating and enriching post-observation discussion sessions; the observation also served the purpose of data validation. In order to record these observations, field notes were maintained.

CONTINUOUS PROFESSIONAL DEVELOPMENT: EVIDENCE OF PARTICIPANTS' EFFORTS

In this section, we will present two case studies including the participants' background information, their action research plans, and the outcomes of their new practice. Out of a total of seven cases, these two case studies have been selected to represent the two groups of participants, i.e. teachers and teacher educators. The first case study involves a teacher's efforts to bring reform at the level of his own classroom, whereas, the second case study presents a scenario of a teacher educator working with a teacher/ mentee to improve his role as a mentor. Based on the analysis of these case studies, the following section would present our synthesis and conclusion—examining conditions that facilitate or hinder teachers in implementing new knowledge to improve existing practice in the rural context in Pakistan. Issues related to sustainability of teachers' learning within these constraints are also discussed. While two cases have been selected to provide elaborate examples, the final discussion involves a synthesis of the overall findings from the seven cases studied.

Case Study 1: Hayat Khan

Hayat was a Head Master in a middle school, having 15 years of teaching experience. He started his teaching career as a Junior

School Teacher (JST) in 1990. After the completion of B.Ed., he was promoted as a Senior School Teacher (SST). Along with his responsibility as a head teacher, he taught all the subjects to lower secondary classes. There were only two other teachers in the school; however, they did not have sufficient knowledge of the subject or of teaching in general. The main responsibility for teaching fell on Hayat. Hayat's school was very far from his hometown. Therefore, he usually took a week or ten days off from the school to visit his family. In his absence, the school would remain closed unofficially. He had applied for a transfer to his hometown since he had been living far from his family for many years and it was difficult for him to commute between his hometown and school on a regular basis. However, he had not been very successful in getting transferred since, according to him, 'the system of government does not make appropriate or justified decisions'.

Prior to Hayat's participation in the teacher education certificate programme at AKU-IED, he used to focus on teaching only one class at a time in the multi-grade setting (classes 6 and 7), while the students of the other class sat silently or were sent outside the classroom. He did not engage both the classes simultaneously in the learning activities. Therefore, in his action research plan, he aimed to use 'Group Learning' as a strategy to maximize students' learning time as well as engage both classes at the same time. He wanted to understand how group work could help the students of two different levels learn more effectively from each other and with each other. He planned lessons to allow all the students of varying levels to participate in group activities. Hayat also maintained his reflective journal on a weekly basis.

Hayat's participation in the action research process resulted in an enhanced understanding of group work and his role as a facilitator.

Our work with Hayat provides evidence of significant changes in his understanding of the use of group work in a multi-grade setting. It was evident that he had conceptualized group work as a strategy that could be used for different purposes in a multi-grade setting; he learnt to plan the lessons in such a way as to achieve different aims and objectives for different levels. For example:

- Engaging both the classes simultaneously in a classroom setting of small groups aiming to achieve different purposes: serving as a revision lesson for one grade level whereas providing new knowledge to children in the other grade
- Teaching common topics related to both classes such as use of language, learning about sentence structure, discussion on problems, professions, issues regarding health, education etc.
- Teaching one class while the other class engaged in solving problems or tasks specific to their respective level
- Teaching them 'learning from each other': combining groups of varying levels for the purpose of sharing ideas/learning from each other.

In his planning, he considered how a lesson could be designed in such a way that if the students of class 6 learned new things, then students of class 7 could do a revision of their previous learning. For example, for teaching 'Fractions', he divided the class into groups according to their respective levels. He had planned some problem-solving tasks and the same worksheet was provided to each group; however, the purpose of the task was to teach a new topic to class 6 and engage class 7 in solving problems or tasks based on their previous learning. On another occasion, he taught an English lesson where he aimed to teach one class and engage the other in revision, thus, aiming to achieve different purposes for different levels.

> ...they [these words] were not new for class 7—they were new for class 6. For class 7, these terms, 'might', 'right', 'light'—they have been studying in their lesson...but for class 6, they were not....I had decided that it should be easy for 6 as well as 7, so that both of them could learn and revise these words together (post-lesson reflection).

Similarly, sometimes, he would prepare tasks specific to the group levels. This was done to teach them according to their grade level syllabus. For example he said,

> If it's Maths period, then I teach Maths. For example, I ask one class to do these questions that these sums are for class 6 and these are for class 7. Class 6 is doing its own work and 7 is doing its own. When I'm explaining to class 6, then 7 is doing its own work. That is, in a way, both are doing their own work (post-lesson reflection).

In other instances, he would try to identify the topics in the textbook that could relate to both the classes and plan them in such a way that all the students could learn together and remain involved.

> The lesson that I have planned today in class 6 is an English lesson in which children are to be told what 'I' means and what 'you' means…and this is a bit easy for class 7 and [but] for class 6, it is suitable. I have planned this for both the classes (post-lesson conference with university tutor).

Group work was also used to build the confidence of shy students. For this purpose, he would make mixed ability groups so that the active students could encourage the shy ones to participate effectively. He viewed this kind of grouping as helpful in promoting self-learning attitude in the students as well as providing them with a diverse experience of learning with one another and from each other.

Hayat realized that his role was not only in planning the lessons, rationalizing objectives and designing the relevant tasks, but also in providing appropriate facilitation that includes on-going assessment for taking actions to further enhance their learning.

> In group work, a teacher should facilitate each group and explain to them. He should help them a little and see [monitor] how the children are working and also encourage each student [within the group]….I took the role that if the children were hesitant or not

participating, then I encouraged them to take part, or participate in writing...(post-lesson reflection).

He had also come to the conclusion that reflection on the lesson's outcomes was very important for a teacher to be able to analyse practice. His effort to plan lessons according to the purpose, level, and expected outcomes was evident throughout the duration of his fieldwork. In the feedback sessions with the facilitators, he would critique his planned tasks and reflect on the nature of the tasks and their outcomes. This experience also helped him realize how to improve group participation and what should be the nature of tasks designed so as to increase participation. For example, while teaching about the various 'Professions and Occupations' in one of the lessons, Hayat did all the explanation himself rather than involving the students to initiate or engage in any genuine discussion. Later, he assigned a task to the students to discuss different occupations and relate them to their own experiences. In the feedback session, however, he reflected on the nature of participation and realized that he could have invited the students in the beginning to promote meaningful discussion since the students, in their discussions, had not moved beyond what the teacher had already explained to them. As a result of his reflection on the lesson, he decided that in the following lesson on 'the qualities of a teacher/doctor/nurse', he would invite the students to first share their opinions and views before he made any input. On another occasion, he realized that his own instructions were not clear enough to generate rigorous discussion amongst the children.

His analysis and follow-up actions helped him move beyond his traditional practice, as reflected in his comments below on his own learning and its outcomes:

What I had planned that when [earlier] I used to teach one class [level], then the other [level] would remain quiet, get bored, start making noise or they would simply go outside. But when I started working on my research [action research] according to the plan— that I have to take both the classes together and that I have to select such topic that is of interest for both and both could get involved in it at the same time—so, the benefit was that both [levels] did not remain quiet, both classes were being taught, they were both reading, were involved in the lesson, giving responses as well, they were listening as well (post-lesson conference with university tutor).

He further commented,

Today, I saw that to prepare any lesson, for any teacher, it's necessary—that to prepare his lesson, a lot of preparation needs to be done. Before today, we just used to go like that. We used to teach by looking at the text. However, in this teaching method [referring to the current one], even to prepare a small thing [activity], we need to think a lot, to go into such depth. That means that, in a way, it's my development, the development of my teaching.

Thus, as a result of his participation in this research, he was able to articulate and refine his theoretical assumptions about using 'group work' as a strategy for multi-grade classroom in the practicality of his context.

Case Study 2: Nabi Buksh Khan

Nabi Buksh was a Learning Coordinator (LC). He was initially appointed as a Primary School Teacher (PST) in 1987, but was currently given the post of a Learning Coordinator (LC) on the basis of seniority, i.e., number of years of service. However, this did not entail any change in terms of salary benefits. His current role as an LC involved visiting schools to monitor teachers' and students' attendance, assess regularity in the conduct of examinations and other school activities. According to Nabi Bukhsh, his role as an LC did not involve working with the teachers for their professional development. His main responsibility was to monitor routine school activities. On the basis of school visits, he would prepare a report of the school activities and submit it to the ADO (Assistant District Officer). There were nearly 250 schools in that district with approximately 1000 teachers; these schools were divided equally among nine officials in the district office. Nabi Buksh was responsible for monitoring more than 100 teachers in ten schools. In addition, he was assigned the responsibility of dealing with documentation and financial matters in the ADO office, such as matters related to school budgets, professional expenses, teachers' salary bills, etc., due to shortage of clerical staff. Nabi also looked after his family lands and agriculture, since this was a major source of his income and financial support.

Nabi Buksh's action research focused on 'Improving teaching and learning through collaborative teaching (co-teaching)'. He wanted to improve his role as an LC and take on the role of a mentor to provide classroom-based support to the teachers. He aimed to use 'group work' as a strategy to promote child-centered learning. He viewed the experience of action research as very helpful for improving his future work with the teachers in the schools assigned to him. As part of his research, Nabi Buksh selected one teacher to work with whom he met twice a month. His action research plan involved planning sessions with the teacher, classroom observations and/or co-teaching sessions as well as post-conferencing sessions.

Our findings indicate that Nabi's involvement in the process of action research helped him develop a reflective stance and analyse and review his practice. Although his earlier role was mostly administrative in nature (office work and documentation), he made efforts to provide academic support to the teacher in the classroom. Initially, he could not move beyond his traditional role of giving orders and, therefore, asked the teacher to follow the lesson plan prepared by him. However, later he gave the teacher space and freedom to initiate lesson planning. He would also encourage the teacher to facilitate group discussion, whole group presentation, and teach through innovative materials. The findings suggest the following outcomes of his learning:

Change in his Thinking and Approach as a 'Teacher Educator'

Nabi came from a culture where he was accustomed to receiving and following orders from his superiors. He, in turn, used the same approach with his subordinates or teachers. However, during the process of action research, we noticed a change in him: he began to question his own decisions and actions, and tried to find out the rationale for his decisions and their implications. Commenting on the change, he mentioned,

> There has been some change in me, Madam. Earlier, whatever we did, we did it without thinking, but now we have to think before doing anything that what is the nature of the work/task. So, this has been a change in thinking.

He referred to the examples of his earlier work with the teacher when he imposed his planning, whereas, now the teacher had been given the freedom to plan on his own and discuss the planning with Nabi for input. He realized that without encouraging the teacher to initiate planning, it would have been difficult for them to work together in the long term. He realized that such freedom to think about lesson planning would reduce teacher-dependence as well as his own workload. Moreover, initially, the selection of the topic was based on Nabi's own needs and agenda; for example, he had developed a unit plan on the topic of 'Matter' and, therefore, expected the teacher to follow the plan as it was given to him. However, later, he realized that some of the lessons in the unit were very basic and not meant for Class 5, and that the teacher needed to teach the topics that had not been taught before. He, therefore, asked the teacher to follow the syllabus for planning his lessons. He realized that since the teacher was closer to the children, he was in a better position to take decisions about classroom-related activities appropriate to the level of the students.

Similarly, in the post-conference meeting with the teacher, Nabi would initially tell the teacher directly what went wrong in his lesson and how he could improve it. However, later, he changed his practice as a result of his reflections on his discussion sessions with the facilitators. He reflected on the nature of our interaction, the kind of questions asked that encouraged him to reflect on his actions, the nature and level of his own engagement in the discussion, and compared it to his own discussion with the teacher. This reflection and self-analysis made him realize the need for improvement in his post-lesson discussion sessions with the teacher. We noticed a change during the process of action research; he would now invite the teacher to share his perspective and feelings about the lesson rather than imposing his own thoughts on the teacher.

Thus, we observed a change in his role as a teacher educator in various ways: the nature of his feedback sessions changed to make the sessions more interactive, reflective, and less mentor-centered; he started probing the teacher instead of using a list of pre-identified questions based on what he considered were the teacher's shortcomings while teaching the lesson. Similarly, in the feedback sessions, we initially observed a one-way interaction, where the teacher did not have any role in the discussion. Nabi would identify the strong and weak points of the lesson taught by the teacher and then ask him to add anything if he wanted. In the later meetings, however, we observed progression in Nabi's role; he would invite and encourage the teacher to talk about his feelings, learning, and challenges in the lesson by asking questions such as: 'What did you learn today? How did you feel? What were the successes of the lesson?', etc. The questions were then followed by specific probes so as to understand the teacher's perspective as well as help him reflect on the classroom teaching and learning processes. Although, the teacher did not take on a very active role—he would merely respond to the questions or sometimes ask a question or two—Nabi made visible efforts to make the meetings interactive. He would analyse and summarize the teacher's responses to help him understand and reflect on children's learning. Likewise, initially, Nabi's focus during observation seemed to be on whether the teacher had conducted the session according to the lesson plan or not. However, in the later meetings, he was able to focus on teacher learning and teacher's perspective on the lesson's outcomes and challenges.

ACTION RESEARCH FOR CONTINUOUS PROFESSIONAL DEVELOPMENT: ISSUES AND CONSTRAINTS

It was evident from our analysis of the cases discussed in the previous section that the participants were able to change their practices and beliefs to some extent due to their positive attitude and the follow-up support provided to them by the facilitators. However, there were various factors that seemed to constrain the participants' continuous professional development and its consequent impact on students' learning outcomes. The participants' engagement in this experience provided them with the opportunity and motivation to think about some continuity or follow-up on the course after returning to the context. However, it was evident that the participants, on their own, were not able to understand and address the complex issues related to teaching or teacher learning. The issues and constraints that the findings of the study identified fall into the following two broad categories:

1. Personal constraints
2. Administrative/organizational constraints

Personal Constraints

These were evident in terms of:

- Limited understanding of the new approaches, strategies, and subject knowledge
- Limited perspective of moral and ethical dimensions of teaching
- Lack of commitment to the improvement of their learning.

Limited Understanding of New Approaches, Strategies and Subject Knowledge

There are examples from our wider set of data that the participants, in their various capacities (teachers or teacher educators), aimed to encourage students' participation in their own learning; therefore, they adapted relevant strategies accordingly. However, it was difficult for them to promote participation due to their limited understanding of the essence of these new methods and their use for promoting meaningful learning. Their limited understanding of the strategies in terms of the clarity of purpose, need, and rationale hindered them in implementing these strategies effectively. Therefore, they made use of these strategies in a mechanical way; for example, asking students to sit in groups and repeat what the teacher had already explained to them rather than giving them a more meaningful task for group work. Consequently, they frequently organized and reorganized students in groups without any real purpose or rationale for doing so. The group tasks did not require any involvement on the part of the children to generate meaningful discussion or bring their own understanding or perspective to the discussion. Often, students sitting in groups were required to listen to the teacher and re-write his verbal explanation.

The participants' engagement in action research required making an effort to use their intellectual capabilities in planning, teaching, and evaluating their lessons, something different from their routine practice. However, in some cases, they appeared to be highly routine-bound. They did not seem to have any clarity about the purpose, objectives, and outcomes of innovative instructional strategies and their implications for student learning outcomes. Although, they sometimes managed to design group tasks for students or changed their seating arrangement, it was still difficult for them to create a real context for group learning. The focus of the reflection sessions was also on the identification of contextual constraints rather than on their limited role as a facilitator in encouraging group interaction or in promoting child-centred learning. Due to limited understanding, it was difficult for them to reflect on the lessons in terms of identification of outcomes, successes as well as the constraints, in order to improve their teaching and learning practice. During the post-conferencing session, it was evident that although they tried to identify various factors responsible for the limited outcomes of the new methodology used, they could not relate it to the issues of their own understanding and role. Some of them were able to reflect on their conceptual constraints but did not have any resources available to them to fill in their knowledge gaps, especially, the gaps related to the subject content knowledge.

Moreover, the content knowledge provided to the students in most cases was also inadequate or incorrect. For example, in Nabi's case, the teacher teaching a lesson on 'Matter' informed the students that sand is an example of liquid since it changes its shape when poured in different containers. He also proved his explanation through demonstration by filling in sand in containers of varying shapes. Thus, the participants' own lack of adequate content knowledge and limited understanding of pedagogy did not allow them to promote child-centred learning environment in the classroom or work effectively with the teachers. It was difficult for them to plan or teach the lessons in a way that focused on the students' understanding, and not just on the delivery of the textbook content, which was also being done inadequately.

Shulman (1986; 1987), Borko and Putnam (1995) suggest that good knowledge of the subject is needed by teachers when designing curricula, lesson plans, and related instructional strategies that could address the learning needs of students. Teachers do not need to know only general aspects of classroom teaching and techniques of teaching but also the methods that are specific to the subjects. This, in turn, requires teachers to have a deeper perspective of the subject, both from the point of view of content as well as pedagogy. Our study also confirms that in order to transform the personal subject matter knowledge into something meaningful and purposeful in order to promote students' thinking, teachers' first and foremost need is to have a strong, basic conceptual understanding of the subject matter knowledge.

Limited Perspective of Moral and Ethical Dimensions of Teaching

As discussed, the participants' positive attitude was a crucial element in supporting their professional development. However, their limited moral and ethical perspective restricted them from analysing their actions in terms of the moral and ethical implications of their decisions. This had the following implications:

- Implications for teachers' learning
- Implications for students' learning

Our findings reveal that the teacher educators, working as mentors, spent a major chunk of their time on planning and feedback sessions with teachers. However, it seemed that this collaboration did not result in any significant outcome for the teachers. In most cases, it was noticed that the aim of the discussion during post-conferencing sessions was to provide a superficial perspective on how the lesson went and what outcomes were observed. Similarly, the discussion between the mentors and teachers did not involve any identification of or reflection on genuine issues related to teaching and learning in general, and new teaching strategies in particular. This could be due to the teacher educators' own limited understanding of their new roles or their lack of interest and commitment towards their own learning and children's learning outcomes. However, this had serious implications for the teachers' time and motivation. It was very obvious in some cases that although the participants wanted to take on new roles, they were not able to move out of the constraints of their traditional role characterized by the hierarchy of relationship between a supervisor and supervisee.

Similarly, it was evident that due to the participants' inadequate knowledge and incomplete understanding of a strategy, e.g. group work, the students were asked to sit in groups but there was a lack of clarity regarding the task for the students. This had implications for students' time and their learning outcomes. On the surface, the teachers had designed group tasks for children; however, in actual practice, they still expected the learners to reproduce on paper what they had already told them rather than encouraging them to engage in genuine and purposeful discussion or knowledge generation activity.

It was also observed that the students' work, which they were asked to do on separate sheets, was not required for any real purpose of evaluation or assessment of their learning. Hence, no feedback was ever provided by the teacher on such written assignments. For example, in Nabi's case, the participant teacher told us that he neither had the time nor any reason to check and give feedback on students' written work. The students were asked to tear off papers from their notebooks, which for us, raises an ethical question: What was the purpose of this exercise? More important, the way in which pages were being torn from children's notebooks is highly questionable, particularly in a resource limited context.

Similarly, we found that, in some cases, sometimes, the teacher would do a revision lesson to prepare the students for observation by the facilitators. What are the implications of this practice for children's time? Why was the whole exercise (action research) being done—was it being done for the sake of the observer only? What kind of message were the children getting? It was evident that despite researchers' attempt to clarify their role as 'not evaluators', it was difficult for the participants to view their role as 'facilitators' in a context where traditionally classrooms were observed for inspection only.

The participants' limited moral and ethical perspective regarding teaching and learning restrained them from reflecting on the enormity of the implications of their decisions for the teachers as well as the learners. This, in turn, resulted in limited learning outcomes for all.

Lack of Commitment towards their Learning

Participants' own interest and motivation towards bringing reform in their context served as a major facilitating factor. This encouraged them to create time for planning and reflection despite the contextual constraints. In cases where the participants lacked a professional attitude, they did not make a real attempt to create time for planning, reflection or follow-up actions for improvement. Rather, it seemed that they were engaged in action research to oblige the tutors for their own personal reasons or as part of the local, cultural norms of giving respect to the teachers.

Administrative/Organizational Constraints

The administrative/organizational constraints included

* Lack of role clarity
* Contextual constraints

Lack of Role Clarity

Role clarity was another factor that supported action research; where such role clarity was missing, action research was seen as a short-term activity, being done as an obligation or a compulsory task related to the training programme they had attended. There were cases where the participants had clarity regarding their job responsibilities, i.e. teaching but there was a lack of commitment that, in turn, resulted in their making limited efforts towards their continuous professional development. Due to various reasons including personal priorities, career opportunities etc., they did not create time or/and put in efforts to learn from their practice. In fact, even access to these participants proved difficult after the initial field visits; for example, one of the female participants went on leave due to personal reasons. The other female participant was mainly interested in getting transferred to her hometown; therefore, her 'efforts' mostly revolved around this objective. Another participant's priorities changed when he was selected for an international training programme. It is important to note here that the issues facing the participants cannot be identified as gender-specific. Lack of commitment and preoccupation with personal issues was equally evident in both male and female participants.

In cases where there was evidence of lack of role clarity, the participants who had commitment succeeded in creating time for their professional growth (action research) but it was seen as a short-term activity due to their role ambiguity and lack of incentives and motivation from the government for their continuous professional development. For example, Nabi was a very committed professional, and highly motivated to try out new ideas; however, despite his being a Learning Coordinator, the reality of his work situation neither required nor encouraged him to work closely with the teachers or provide them support and guidance for their professional development. Thus, he did not see any possibility of continuing his work with the teachers on an on-going basis. In fact, he often raised questions about the conflict between his job requirements and the expectations of the course.

Thus, we conclude that commitment, both to one's own continuous professional development and improving students' learning outcomes, is a key factor required for adjusting to new roles, reform or improved practice. People grow intellectually and professionally only when they have the necessary desire, intent, and motivation to do so. Without this, a professional may not be able to grow in terms of thinking and practice despite the availability of follow-up support.

Contextual Constraints

Teachers' work setting and the overall environment, undoubtedly, has a very strong influence on teacher education initiatives. In addition to the factors identified above, the participants' growth process was also affected by various contextual constraints. Teachers and teacher educators were working in conditions where mostly they did not have any authority or decision-making power. Moreover, their efforts for reform were neither appreciated nor acknowledged. In addition, they were not provided with any practical or moral support for implementation of their new knowledge after their return from the teacher education course. In most cases, there was not even an expectation for them to improve their practices in the light of their new learning.

Mostly, all the participants worked in poor environments not conducive for continuous professional development. For example, since Hayat's village lacked basic necessities, he was isolated from the outer world after his teaching time; he did not have any activity or entertainment to keep him busy after the school hours. Lack of availability of like-minded people in the locality further constrained his opportunities to discuss teaching or related issues and, therefore, increased his sense of isolation. Additionally, his workplace was at a great distance from his hometown. As mentioned earlier, he had been trying to get transferred to a school closer to his home for many years but his application had not been considered due to corrupt practices prevalent in the government system. Thus, his sense of complete isolation created mental and emotional barriers, which constrained his professional growth. This kind of situation was very common in some other cases also and became an additional source of demotivation and frustration for the participants. The question that they raised is a pertinent one, which has implications for teacher education initiatives: Why do we always think about the children and their improvement when teachers' concerns, even if they are genuine, are neglected by the government?

Some additional constraints were the limited availability of human and physical resources in many schools. For example, due to shortage of teachers in the school, Ghulam (one of the seven participants) had to take on a major teaching load in addition to his responsibility as a head teacher. Similarly, in Nabi's case, he was engaged in clerical and administrative work due to the lack of clerical staff. Moreover, his efforts for his own as well as teachers' professional development were neither appreciated nor valued by the senior officials. It is evident from our findings that there was no motivation or incentive for the participants to work for their professional growth and development.

Although, as a result of decentralization, different government officials were assigned responsibilities for teachers' professional development, the ground reality was found to be entirely different. It was reported that many schools had never been visited by the designated government officials; similarly there was no response to requests made for provision of resources (for example, provision of the necessary furniture or teachers) which caused great frustration amongst the participants working in such far-flung and remote areas.

It is evident from our findings that institutional values, expectations, and practices influence and dominate the participants' practices and professional growth. A number of writers (cf. Ball, 1987; Burgess, 1988; Helsby, 1999; Day, 1999) have written about teachers' feeling of powerlessness within the structural organization of schools or systems. The situation is exacerbated by the fact that teachers work under severe pressure, having to comply with demands to 'complete the syllabus', to do regular and frequent assessment, and to teach in ways that accord with the existing policy. This, together with their minimal involvement in policy and decision-making, increases the divisions between teachers and school managers, whom teachers regard as isolated from the world of the classroom and preoccupied mainly with financial and managerial matters. Therefore, professional development is often a remarkably low-intensity enterprise. Our findings also confirmed that the enormity of contextual constraints made it extremely difficult for this group of teachers to implement their learning from an in-service teacher education programme.

ACTION RESEARCH AS A TOOL FOR 'CONTINUOUS PROFESSIONAL DEVELOPMENT' IN A RURAL CONTEXT

The discussion above raises a very important question: What are the possibilities of continuous professional development in the rural context in Pakistan? To what extent can action research be used as a tool of professional development in a context characterized by teachers' professional isolation, lack of incentives and rewards for continuing professional development, and no support for implementing new learning from their teacher education course? Despite these constraints some participants benefited from their experience of action research and their engagement in the process of implementing their learning in the field. This could be seen as an important step in beginning the process of their professional development. However, our findings suggest professional development through action research can only be sustained if the teachers' context and conditions provide the necessary impetus and support to the teachers.

The discussion in the previous sections identifies a number of conditions that can influence action research and the continuity of participants' professional development. Some of these are:

- Clarity of role and responsibilities, and their consistency with the activities expected by the teacher education programme
- Knowledge, understanding, and skills for implementing innovative strategies
- Emotional support from colleagues to cope with the anxiety and uncertainty induced by change endeavours
- Availability of time to implement the change processes
- Integration of action research in teachers' routine plans and workload
- Availability of facilitators' support to help them develop their reflective skills to critique their own and others' practice
- Feeling of empowerment through reflection and research, to identify and address contextual constraints and dilemmas.

The facilitators' presence made some of these conditions available to the participants. For example, in the presence of the facilitators and their support, the participants were ready to take risks in the implementation of innovative classroom strategies. Now that the inquiry is over, we wonder if in the absence of the above conditions they would be able to continue with their professional development. There is no simple answer. In a few cases, the participants did express their willingness and commitment to continue the process of their growth; however, in the majority of cases, the answer was a plain 'No!' The participants clearly stated that they did not feel competent to continue this process, despite their realization and acknowledgement that the outcome of action research would be *learning* for them, as well as for their learners.

The issues, faced by the teachers in public sector schools in general (for example, see Mohammad, 2004; 2006) get further compounded and create additional constraints for teachers serving in the rural and remote areas.

The participants' involvement in their action research enabled them to experience possibilities of continuous professional development—to provide a basis on which they could build as they develop their vision of change in their classrooms, schools, and communities. This leads to the assumption that teachers come to see the purpose of action research by doing it and they start to do it when they start to understand the purpose. Thus, at a conceptual or theoretical level, everyone had this understanding and belief that action research is a means for continuous professional development—seeking to understand and acting on the best we know. However, for real outcomes in terms of improved practice, the participants required motivation (both intrinsic and extrinsic), commitment towards their profession as well as reform initiatives to improve the teaching and learning situation, emotional attachment, and a moral and ethical perspective of teaching and education.

The essence of the notion of action research, as discussed in the literature, is the simultaneous development and application of knowledge by teachers. This implies that development and application of professional knowledge are aspects of a cyclical process that teachers are themselves responsible for—they apply knowledge to achieve certain goals and based on their application of knowledge they develop new knowledge, which they then apply again, and so on. However, in the context of this study, it was not possible for the participants to engage in this process on their own: due to the enormity of the teachers' constraints, they required continued and long-term support.

CONCLUSION AND RECOMMENDATIONS

Thus, there is no doubt that action research does have the potential to serve as a tool for teachers' professional development in a rural context. However, to plan action research projects for such contexts, there is a need to build in more time, support, and resources to help teachers initiate and engage in the process at the initial level. The facilitators' support provided some support; however, for continuity of efforts on the part of the teachers and for their efforts to result in positive learning outcomes, there is a need for a lot more input and investment at various levels. What follows are some recommendations to help increase the utility and impact of action research in the rural context of Pakistan.

In consistence with the findings from research (e.g. Nicol, Moore, Zappa, Yusyp and Sasges, 2004), our study strongly suggests that for continuous professional development, there must be a collaborative setting involving like-minded professionals where teachers, who encounter the same situation, work together to help one another in designing and investigating the situation. This implies that there are better chances of sustainability of teachers' efforts if they engage in collaborative action research projects/activities rather than undertaking action research as an individual task. Working in a 'community of action researchers', it is envisaged, would provide them on-going support and the necessary impetus to continue with their efforts. 'Support' implies on-going opportunities of interaction with colleagues for discussion of issues, sharing of ideas and/or findings from their research as well as opportunities for shared reflections. The knowledge that 'you are not alone on this journey', we believe, would also serve as a strong motivation and emotional support for teachers. Therefore, an important recommendation that this chapter puts forward is to initiate action research projects in settings where there are possibilities for teachers to interact and engage in professional dialogue or to invest in creating such settings before initiating action research projects to decrease the possibilities of teacher efforts resulting in frustration or discontinuity. University–based facilitators can provide the initial impetus and necessary facilitation to help initiate such collaborative projects. The need for outsider facilitation, it is envisaged, would decrease with increased collaboration and participation within the collaborative networks. However, before any such assumptions are made, there is a need for further studies in this area. It would be a worthwhile experience to design and study the outcomes of such models of professional development in the rural context of Pakistan.

In addition, as the discussion above has already pointed out, changing the contexts and conditions cannot be done without the support and participation of the management at the system's level. The system needs to provide facilitative conditions to the teachers to help them in the implementation of their new learning. These conditions include first, the availability of time and necessary resources; second, some incentives and rewards or at least some form of acknowledgement and appreciation of teachers' efforts. In addition, clarity of expectations is required from the training as well as their expected roles on return. Therefore, it is imperative that the teacher education institutes form stronger partnerships with the government system to dialogue and negotiate the need and future utilization of the training provided.

7

Becoming a Teacher Educator through Action Research

Rahat Joldoshalieva

INTRODUCTION

Action research ' is widely used in a range of courses and research studies particularly concerning school improvement, teacher development, new teaching-learning strategies and curriculum enrichment' (Kemmis, McTaggart and Retallick, 2004, p. 2). Due to its strengths in bringing about change and improvement, action research is encouraged in most AKU-IED's initiatives and programmes. The explicit expectation from action research in AKU-IED programmes is to enable teachers and school heads to improve their professional practice and bridge the gap between educational theory and practice. Several action research studies have been undertaken by its faculty. Teachers learn action research in certificate and advanced diploma courses. In the M.Ed programme, the action research method is explicitly taught in subject specialization areas and the research methods course, which has resulted in many graduates choosing this research method for their Master's thesis.

My desire to improve my own teacher education practices led me to select action research for my research study in the Master's programme. My research question was: *How can I improve my practice of facilitating two social studies teachers to improve their understanding of curriculum enrichment?* Similar to many beginning action researchers, my inquiry happened to fit well in what Carr and Kemmis (1986) defined as, 'a form of self-reflective inquiry undertaken by participants in social situations in order to improve the rationality and justice of their own social or educational practices, their understanding of these practices, and the situation in which the practices are carried out (p. 162). I realized that by engaging in action research, I could bring about change and improvement in my own knowledge and practice of teacher education as well as enhance teachers' understanding about curriculum enrichment. Action research allowed me to conduct my inquiry with scientific rigour to study and solve my practical problems in learning to become a teacher educator. More important, my experience of working with Fatma and Samira taught me a lot about myself as a novice teacher educator. Engaging in action research allowed me to test my accumulated theoretical knowledge about teacher education and curriculum enrichment in real practice and taught me more than I could ever have learnt by just sitting in the university classrooms. The study indicates that action research on the development of teacher educators through working closely with teachers in the school contexts could be a powerful strategy in the preparation of teacher educators.

THE METHOD OF THE STUDY

According to Feldman and Atkin (1995), 'As with many expanding movements, action research is beginning to take a variety of forms as people adapt the basic concept of inquiry by teachers to their own views of desirable educational research or approaches to teacher education' (p. 127). Action research, termed as 'insider research' (McNiff, Lomax and Whitehead, 1996) allows for the researcher's professional and personal development. Lately, some researchers have called for re-conceptualizing the notion of action research as research of one's own lived practice (Carson and Sumara, 1997).

There were two reasons for my selection of this research method. Firstly, action research allowed me to study the process of becoming a teacher educator while attempting to improve my own practices and beliefs. Secondly, continuous reflection enabled me to alter my actions in accordance with emergent issues.

I executed my research plan in a school setting by adopting a strategy of discussion with the participating teachers on the subject (curriculum enrichment) and by drawing examples from real classroom practices. The duration of each session varied from 1 to 2 hours within a four-week period.

The data was collected at three research stages, i.e., the reconnaissance, intervention, and post-intervention stages, through semi-structured individual interviews with teachers, lesson observations, and audio-recording of the sessions with teachers, researcher diary, and teachers' reflective journals.

RESEARCH LOCATION AND PROFILE OF THE PARTICIPANTS

This study was conducted in a community-owned secondary school in Karachi, a large metropolitan city in Pakistan. I selected two beginning social studies teachers as participants of the study. I chose to work with social studies teachers as I had specialized in Social Studies education during the M.Ed. programme. I wanted to work with a limited number of teachers due to my inexperience as a teacher educator. Also, I wanted to make the research manageable within the limited timeframe of a Masters dissertation. The teacher-participants, Fatma and Samira (pseudonyms) were relatively inexperienced in teaching but differed in age and subject specialization backgrounds. In the first meetings, I attempted to get to know these teachers better which helped me greatly in my future work with them.

Fatma was young and, single, with two years of teaching experience at this school. She was teaching English, Math, and Social Studies in different grade levels. She was in her last year of MA in International Relations at a local university. Her formal professional development was limited to occasional participation in workshops at a local teacher training institute. The second teacher, Samira, was middle-aged, married, and a mother of two children, with only one-year teaching experience. Though Samira had a Master's degree in Science she had been assigned to teach

Social Studies ever since she had joined this school. Samira had not participated in any formal professional development programmes till the time of the study.

Starting the Action Research Project: Reconnaissance Stage

In action research, the reconnaissance stage is important as it describes and explains the people and context prior to any actions that are carried out. Provided that the focus of research was my own understanding and practice of teacher education, I started reconnaissance of myself and moved on to studying the context. In this section, I will share my own understanding of curriculum enrichment and the existing knowledge and practices of the two teachers about curriculum enrichment prior to taking any action.

Self: My Knowledge about Curriculum Enrichment and Teacher Learning

My knowledge of curriculum came mainly from the curriculum course in my Master's programme, prior to which the term itself was unknown to me. Reading widely in the area of curriculum, I realized that the notion of curriculum is contested. I learnt that curriculum means the 'series of studies required' (Barrow, 1989) and was usually equated to the content of programme. However, the concept became more confusing when I came across the debate about curriculum which went beyond the programme of study to the 'totality of the experiences the pupil has as a result of the provision made' (Kelly, 1999, p. 7). From further readings, I explored classifications of curriculum, which mystified and complicated further my understanding of a curriculum. Each type such as planned, obvious and intentional purpose of a curriculum and intended as well as unintended outcomes (Kelly, 1999; Connelly and Clandinin, 1988) was a vast area to explore.

I realized that at the heart of curriculum enrichment was the attempt to convert the learning process to an exciting journey for the students. Thus curriculum enrichment was considered as 'enlarging horizons, tackling problems whose solutions give rise to further problems, experimenting with new materials, processes and ideas' (Eyre and Marjoram, 1990, p. 9). Further, my readings opened up the limitations of the work produced in this area. I discovered that most of the suggested enrichment activities were targeted to support the most able or talented children (Renzulli, 1977; Renzulli and Reis, 1997, Eyre and Marjoram, 1990). However, I believed in the inclusion of all students into any enrichment activities carried out inside and/or outside the classroom. In addition, I wanted to propose that enrichment activities should become an everyday teaching-learning practice rather than be considered as add-on activities. Working within the inclusion and social justice framework, teachers need to enrich the curriculum for all children. I was firm in my belief that in a developing country context such as Pakistan, where the learning opportunities are inadequate, the curriculum content is narrow and examination-oriented teaching is predominant, curriculum enrichment is a requirement rather than a luxury for improving the quality of children's education.

With this thinking, I adopted curriculum enrichment strategies (material, organizational, and pedagogical) shared by Eyre and Marjoram (1990) to introduce the concept of enrichment as addressing all students irrespective of their achievement or ability level. I conceptualized material enrichment as a process of enriching the content with additional, up-to-date information and use of graphs and diagrammes to facilitate students' detailed study of a topic. This strategy was thought to enable the teachers to critically analyse the textbooks in use and identify their limitations. Teachers could implement organizational enrichment strategy through field visits and inviting guest speakers/subject specialists. I strongly believed that enrichment activities would fail to achieve their objectives if teachers' pedagogical enrichment was missed out. By this enrichment, I meant that teachers' own pedagogical expertise in providing good instructional activities and creating a challenging environment affect teaching-learning more than any additional provisions (Eyre and Marjoram, 1990). In my study, I rated this aspect in enrichment high because teachers play a central role in the curriculum implementation process. However, I was conscious that teachers' pedagogical expertise depends on their knowledge and skills of several instructional strategies as well as their ability and commitment to constantly learning new strategies to enrich their existing repertoire.

Others: My Teacher-Participants' Knowledge and Practice of Curriculum Enrichment

Studying these teachers' classrooms and views about teaching enriched my own understanding of social studies education. I found out that the National Curriculum did not reach the school; instead, the teachers developed their syllabus relying on the prescribed textbooks. Teachers acknowledged that for them the notion of a curriculum was something new. Their conception of the curriculum was limited to the textbooks. In fact, the textbook served as the 'surrogate' curriculum (Venezky, 1996). Teachers' objectives of teaching social studies were oriented towards preparing students for examinations, hence, excluding the broad social studies education goals of preparning students for informed and participatory citizenry. With these narrow objectives of teaching, the teachers planned substantial time for revision of the textbook content in order to prepare the students for examinations. They rarely used any additional information. Moreover, they believed that it was the teacher only who could impart knowledge to students and excluded any idea of encouraging students' independent learning ability.

What was my Plan of Action?

To develop my general plan of action, I familiarized myself with the staff development models shared by Joyce, Calhoun, and Hopkins (1999) and adopted some of their strategies as a framework for my training model. I held strong beliefs about teachers' need for a broader theoretical conception of curriculum, its goals, and enrichment strategies in order to bring about changes in their classroom practices. In this I agreed with Joyce et al. (1999) that, 'It is difficult to imagine practice without prior awareness and knowledge; that is we have to know what it is we are to practice' (ibid., p. 118). I planned to challenge teachers' perceptions and beliefs of teaching and create an opportunity to subject their practice to critical reflection. However, I envisaged the danger of pure theoretical discourse which could make the sessions too abstract and irrelevant to teachers' classroom experiences. I realized that discourse on curricular theory may not necessarily bring about changes in teachers' classroom practices. Thus I pondered over the ways to enable teachers to practice their learning. The following major activities were outlined in my initial plan of action:

- Firstly, I planned to develop teachers' understanding about curriculum and curriculum enrichment strategies (content, pedagogical, and organizational) through group discussions
- Secondly, I planned to support teachers in lesson planning for using enrichment strategies and co-teaching with them, if required. During this stage, I wanted to work with each teacher individually.

Each major activity, however, was split into several stages and followed the process of planning, acting, observing and reflecting, and re-planning. Given the limited time, unavailability of the teachers for the research and difficulty of striking a balance between the scope of discussion on curriculum and enrichment, I could cover only the first major activity and the second was limited to a session with one teacher only.

My Teacher Education Strategies

I used the following strategies to educate the teachers about notions of curriculum, curriculum enrichment, goals and objectives of education, and strategies of curriculum enrichment in both group and individual settings.

Working with Teachers in a Group Setting

To begin with, I identified teachers' conceptions of curriculum, the goals of school curriculum, in general, and the goals of social studies in particular, through 'eliciting existing views' technique. I recorded teachers' responses on a chart so that teachers could compare and identify any changes that may occur in their own understanding about curriculum as the sessions proceeded. By recording teachers' views in this way, I could map what Eraut (1994) described as the '...relationship between existing and new conceptual knowledge' (p. 90) about curriculum. I used a sample Social Studies curriculum document to introduce the teachers to the notion of a broad curricular document as opposed to their experience of considering the textbook as syllabus only. Unsurprisingly, the teachers found it difficult to believe that a curriculum could exist in a written form. Fatma stated, 'No it is not a curriculum, curriculum cannot be compiled in a book like this', whereas Samira tried to make sense of it in a different way, 'These are the ideas to prepare students for detailed knowledge' (Transcript 1). I realized that the teachers defined curriculum as content bodies of different disciplines coming together. As there were different disciplines in Social Studies, according to them, it was impossible to make a written document as such. To clarify these misconceptions, I presented two definitions of curriculum to challenge the teachers' conceptions and asked them to compare these definitions. Soon I realized that their discomfort was related to the comprehension of new concepts in these definitions. Quickly realizing this, I started to share some examples to relate to those concepts. For example, to explain what a hidden curriculum was, I shared the example of gender stereotyping, which was perpetuated by teachers' practices and curriculum materials like textbooks and favouritism on the teachers' part and its effects on the students' overall learning. Though teachers could reflect and broaden their own definitions, including different aspects such as hidden curriculum, from this exercise, they still emphasized content as of paramount importance in the notion of curriculum. Samira for instance shared her definition, as 'Curriculum is the knowledge of any topic, subject or any field of study. It is vast knowledge of subjects or topics planned in specific direction to make a person socially fit in the society' (Transcript 2). For her, it seemed that the purpose of education was to prepare students to fit into the existing society, but excluded the opportunity for equipping students with knowledge and skills to change the society.

As a learner, I realized that I learn better when the theory is categorized and explained according to classifications. Hereby, I believed that my way of learning was generic to all the teachers and introduced teachers to the types of curriculum, such as intended, taught, and learned (Cuban, 1996). My intention was to enable teachers to view their role in bringing about change within their own classroom teaching and schools. I wanted them to realize that teaching was not confined to teaching the textbooks only. In fact it included developing the ability to bring about changes in society. With teachers' permission, I brought examples from their own practices to unpack the meaning of types of curriculum. Implicitly, I intended to challenge the way they taught through their own reflections. From their reflections, I noted that teachers openly acknowledged the limitations of their practices. Teachers stated that they implemented some activities without rationalizing their objectives and linking them with broader curricular goals. Hence, I challenged teachers to become more reflective practitioners who could think more deeply about their practices.

After a few discussion sessions on what a curriculum is, I noted some conceptual changes in teachers' understanding of curriculum. The improved understanding was indicated by their shared definition which was 'Curriculum is a series of activities which have educational intentions for developing students mentally, physically, ethically and socially under the school's guidance' (Transcript 3). In addition, the teachers realized that the notion of curriculum was very complex as it had both hidden and overt aspects. Fatma acknowledged her growing understanding about the curriculum thus: 'I think this is not the last definition;

rather the definition seems evolutionary. I believe we will develop it further with our discussions' (Transcript 3). As teacher educator, I was pleased with small improvements in teachers' understanding of curriculum which could further help the teachers become better informed practitioners. However, I was deeply concerned about their limited teaching objectives. To bring about a change in their objectives of teaching Social Studies, I encouraged teachers to share their thoughts on why they wanted to teach social studies.

> Samira: We teach Social Studies because it [social studies] gives the knowledge of environment. It gives the knowledge of current affairs. It gives the knowledge of our own world: Earth, relationship between countries, between people...their economic progress, how the world is divided geographically.
>
> Fatma: My objectives changed gradually when I started using activities. I have seen visible change in my students' learning. They became more interested, lively and active. And my objective of teaching is to enable the students to acquire more knowledge, unknown things and search for them. I want students to create thirst to learn more by themselves.

Though generally both teachers' objectives were confined to develop students' content knowledge, slight differences in their perspectives could be noted. Fatma's objectives seemed wider as compared to Samira's purpose of teaching because Fatma extended her objective to prepare inquisitive learners with a thirst for knowledge. Samira wanted her students to learn about the world they lived in.

Reflecting on the process so far and its outcomes, firstly, I did not expect quick changes in teachers' beliefs but realized that it would be a gradual process. I was fully aware that change in their beliefs would not necessarily come from theoretical discourse; in fact change in practice can also lead to the change in their beliefs. In addition, to make a case for curriculum enrichment, I realized that it was important for teachers to link their objectives to broader curricular goals or goals of education, which would show them the gaps in their current practice.

Secondly, I noted a difference in teachers' individual contribution to discussions. Fatma seemed more articulate and open to sharing her ideas without any hesitation and mostly she was the one who talked. Moreover, she demonstrated self critico-reflective ability to examine her previous experiences in the light of new information provided. In contrast, Samira was relatively shy. She found it difficult to be questioned by her peer. My attempt to draw Samira into discussions resulted in her short statements 'I agree with Fatma' (Transcript 2). 'I have similar experience' (Transcript 3). Samira's limited participation in the discussion sessions worried me as I was unable to find out the extent to which Samira was developing her knowledge of curriculum from these sessions. With limited practical knowledge as a teacher educator, I struggled to solve this emerging problem. After considerable reflection, I changed group discussions into individual sessions to create a comfortable environment for each teacher to share their experiences and understanding without being intimidated by the presence of their peers.

Introducing Curriculum Enrichment Strategies: Individual Sessions with the Teachers

Different from the group discussion setting, I tried to address the individual needs of the teachers in one-to-one meetings. For instance, in Samira's case, I reviewed conceptions of curriculum initially, but with Fatma, I decided to allow her to compare her own objective of teaching with broader Social Studies curriculum goals. I wanted both of them to reflect on their objectives on the basis of what they wanted to achieve and what they could do to achieve those objectives. This would, I hoped, naturally lead to the notion of curriculum enrichment which, in turn, would allow me to introduce enrichment strategies.

Samira recognizes the need for Learning Instructional Strategies

I planned to encourage Samira to wrap up the discussion about curriculum notions and goals and then move to curriculum enrichment. Soon after I introduced Samira to curriculum enrichment, she related the notion to the incident when her own daughter was involved in project work. She stated, 'My daughter prepared presentation of city planning of Moen-jo-Daro using mud for houses and other buildings, straws for canal system. I also learned many things while helping her out in this project' (Transcript 5). Availing this opportunity, I highlighted the importance of curriculum enrichment in students' learning, which was contrary to short-lived memorization and acquisition of information approach. However, my concern was Samira's view which again emphasized that curriculum enrichment could enable students develop their understanding of the content.

To move her from her sole emphasis on content acquisition, I encouraged Samira to think whether and to what extent textbooks could help her to achieve the broader curriculum goals. In reply to this, Samira shared her dissatisfaction with the textbooks-in-use, stating 'The textbooks which I use do not give any guideline for me how to teach' (pre-session interview). For me it was important to enable Samira to realize that as a teacher she could enrich her textbook with other available literature and resources to make her teaching more meaningful to her students. However, soon after, Samira noted that she needed more support in learning new instructional strategies to enrich the curriculum. I realized that the reason for Samira's reluctance to enrich the curriculum was related to her lack of pedagogical expertise. Additionally, Samira's lack of formal teacher training hindered her in articulating her concerns related to enrichment with relevant vocabulary. Unfortunately, soon after, Samira withdrew from study due to her family circumstances.

Fatma's Progress towards Lesson Planning

In individual sessions, I found Fatma's keenness to better understand the broader goals of the curriculum as an encouraging factor. From extensive discussions about curriculum, Fatma realized the lack of communication between curriculum developers and teachers as implementers:

> Curriculum Board and teacher should come up to certain conclusions as possible [sic]. Board developed curriculum and teachers implemented curriculum in classrooms, so curriculum developers should keep in mind how the teacher will be taking it to the classroom (Transcript 6).

My questions led her towards a critical analysis of the existing school system. This provided her the opportunity to identify the issue of exam-oriented approach in school education. In the discussion, Fatma highlighted certain limitations of textbooks: the textbooks continue to give distorted information to the young generation; they exclude students' daily life experiences from their school learning. When I led Fatma to reflect on her role as teacher of social studies, she shared the view that her role should be to provide students with more inclusive teaching, irrespective of religion, sect, and social class, encouraging them to value their diversity and learn from each other. This belief was evident when Fatma shared the recent incident of sectarian clashes in the city. From this, Fatma gleaned her objectives of teaching towards development of tolerance in her students. I recognized that teachers' own experiences in the society could influence their goals of teaching.

Acknowledging the teachers' embedded belief of teaching content and school expectations of the same, I began to introduce content enrichment first as an enrichment strategy. In that, I emphasized that teachers' core role in curriculum enrichment was to relate curriculum to students' experiences. Fatma admitted that although she was able to enrich the content of textbooks in her teaching, there were several factors which hindered effective planning and implementation. The school's tight schedule, emphasis on curriculum coverage, and teachers' lack of time for lesson planning were some of her concerns. Cultural practices also impeded the effective implementation of curriculum enrichment:

> This school is for girls only and belongs to a community. I have ideas of taking students on field trips but parents will not allow them as they are girls. The parents will disagree also because the students are still young (Transcript 7).

Being a foreigner, I had not anticipated this as a hindrance for curriculum enrichment. I realized that Fatma, a local female educator, could better understand the restrictions over girls' freedom to move in the Pakistani context. I also realized that none of the curriculum enrichment readings had noted this as a challenge. This made me question my selection of readings, which were mainly from Western country contexts, in terms of the applicability of suggested enrichment strategies in Islamic cultural contexts. It also enabled me to ponder on whether and how the strategies, which I had mainly learnt from books, could be adapted to suit the Pakistani context.

I organized for Fatma to plan a lesson with any enrichment strategy to demonstrate her improved and changed understanding. Prior to this, I introduced her to simple enrichment activities such as teaching students to conduct interviews, organizing debates in the classroom, and inviting guest speakers for specific topics. Fatma chose the topic, 'Citizen's Rights and Responsibilities' for enrichment purpose in the forthcoming textbook unit to teach. In her lesson plan, Fatma shared, 'I will invite a guest speaker so that he or she will talk about rights and responsibilities of a citizen. I can find a person from our community who is involved in social work. He/she will come and take a session on it' (Transcript 8). Her above statement concerned me because it appeared that Fatma happened to plan an enrichment activity simply for the sake of doing it. However, I wanted her to realize that she had to state her objective in teaching first and then align the enrichment with that objective. To attain this end, I further questioned Fatma in discussion,

> Rahat: Fatma, why should that person come if you and your students can get this information from the textbook? What extra information can the person tell which students will not get from their textbooks? How will you arrange his or her coming?'
>
> Fatma: I think I have to prepare some points for the guest speaker to cover then. May I ask his or her own practice of rights and responsibilities as a citizen?

Similarly, Fatma planned a lesson based on Cinderella's story to teach rights and responsibilities, an idea she had got from the Internet. I found this encouraging in terms of an attempt to search for materials on her own; however, I was concerned about her ability to contextualize the activity especially when Pakistani children may not necessarily relate to the story of Cinderella. Moreover, the link between the curricular goals, her own objective of teaching and students' learning seemed to have been missed once again during planning her lesson.

LESSONS LEARNT AS A TEACHER EDUCATOR

From this small scale action research study, I improved my understanding of how to be a teacher of teachers (teacher educator) which was in agreement with what Mawdsley (1992) experienced, 'Offering professional learning support to others had the effect of producing a corresponding growth and development of skills for me' (p. 90). Below I share the major lessons learnt about teacher education practices from the process of educating two teachers to enrich their Social Studies curriculum in a school setting in Pakistan.

Lesson 1: Teachers prefer 'to see' rather than 'be told' about enrichment strategy

By the end of the study, I noted some improvement in the teachers' understanding of curriculum enrichment and they also acknowledged their enhanced learning. However, I realized that the teachers' priority was application of these understandings in their teaching practices, 'In order to be successful in using enrichment activities, you need to help us plan and introduce new ideas, observe or teach with us, and then discuss the lessons' (Fatma). Similarly, Samira, asked for help in the implementation of her new learning: 'We learned many things, but it is very difficult for me to do them because I am new in teaching. I think teachers like me need more help in planning for lessons with enrichment activities and in implementing.' They viewed the support of teacher educator in their immediate classrooms as more valuable than in leading theoretical discourses about curriculum enrichment. Analysing our discourse on curriculum enrichment, I discovered that teachers' ability to enrich their curriculum depended on their pedagogical expertise. This was evident when I instructed teachers to think about plans to enrich their forthcoming units for teaching and found that teachers had few ideas about instructional strategies. For example, when asked to enrich her unit on citizens' rights, Fatma could only repeat the same pattern in teaching that was relying on textbook information. Realizing her limited pedagogical expertise, Fatma extended her eagerness to contact me for further support on her enrichment activities. Fatma had genuine concerns over initial support in implementing enrichment in teaching. She not only required the knowledge about instructional strategies but also support in translating this knowledge into practice in the classroom.

From this experience, I learnt that with a few sessions on teaching teachers how to help students learn to conduct interviews, how to prepare for guest speaker, how to conduct inquiry, how to integrate content of English language and how to use additional readings, I had only succeeded in helping teachers recognize the variety of opportunities for curriculum enrichment. In doing so, I had not deliberately taught those ideas in greater detail. However, I had overlooked that development of any teaching skill was gradual and teachers required support in their classroom application attempts. In addition, I recognized that each idea, shared above, needed both deliberate teaching of the idea and helping the teacher to implement it in the classroom. Having joined the school without any formal teacher training, Samira and Fatma were only familiar with teaching practices that focused on transmitting the textbook information in the schools. Thus, it was learnt that demonstration of any innovative instructional strategies, enrichment strategies in this case, can make a difference in teachers' ability to apply it in their classrooms.

Lesson 2: Teachers' objectives of teaching dictate what they will enrich in their curriculum

Both teachers claimed that they had learnt about ways to enrich their curriculum. However, I found that each teacher's understanding of curriculum enrichment differed due to their own beliefs and goals of teaching. Samira believed that the goal of education was to teach more knowledge 'to make a person healthy, thoughtful, a good citizen with good personality and good behaviour to fit into the society' (post-session interview). From this belief, her enrichment strategy preference focused on the content area:

> At the beginning, we knew that whatever is in the textbook, we should teach that to students and students should understand it well. But after the discussions on curriculum, I realized that we should teach more about the topics, we can enrich the content with more information so that students can learn more (post-session interview).

Fatma acknowledged that she did not have any familiarity with curriculum enrichment prior to this research project. However she realized that as a teacher she had a potential role in enriching her existing curriculum. Unlike Samira, Fatma believed that her students should be proactive in bringing some changes in society and should be given a chance to learn to do this.

To enrich curriculum I want to organize some learning beyond the classroom activities. I can organize so that students can acquire more information from sources other than textbook such as use of legal documents or their surroundings. Students should learn and develop their understanding by working with different sources. I may invite someone who can make the topic more interesting to students. By using different strategies, I should make the lesson more involving. My students can go out to study some issues which the community have and then try to share their ideas on how to solve those. (Post-session interview)

Thus, I learnt that the *teachers' chosen strategies to enrich were in resonance with their beliefs about teaching*. As a teacher educator, I noted the need for these beliefs to be subjected to further critical scrutiny. As for how to do it, I needed to think further about ways of encouraging teachers to reflect on the relationship between their objectives and curriculum enrichment strategies. Thus, teacher educators should work with teachers to identify and challenge teachers' beliefs for any new initiative or idea to be embraced by them. Unless teachers believe in new ideas, they may only stay as echoes of trainings.

Lesson 3: Teachers have different learning styles and motivation to learn

As Nias and Groundwater-Smith (1988) noted, 'the uniqueness of teachers is similar to uniqueness of a child' (p. 208). I identified each teacher's unique personality and learning styles. Fatma had a confident and outspoken personality, whereas Samira was covert and preferred to be asked to answer. My extensive attempt of encouragement was directed towards Samira. She had to be constantly encouraged to share her ideas. The teachers also differed in their preference for social setting. I came to know that Fatma appeared positive about both individual and group discussions. She once mentioned, 'Two heads are better than one. I can learn from listening to Ms Samira and you' (Transcript 5). On the contrary, Samira expressed her preference for individual sessions:

> I think we should sit separately. I presumed you realized also that that's why you separated individual sessions later. Because we can speak more in individual sessions, there is more time for me to express ideas. At times I felt Fatma and I had different ideas. In this [individual] session we can discuss whatever we have in mind and feel freer. (Post-session interview)

I realized that individual sessions provided Samira the opportunity to participate more in the discussions. She took full advantage of this situation. Unlike Samira, Fatma felt that a blend of group and individual sessions would increase their opportunity to learn from each other, 'When I was in individual sessions, I had your full attention for me. I had to prepare what you have asked me to read or write because I was the only one. But when Ms Samira was with me, her ideas helped me think and add more ideas about curriculum'. Due to this, I unintentionally felt more comfortable in working with Fatma who seemed to need little effort or encouragement to talk.

> I am quite [a] confident person. I don't hesitate speaking in front of many people and I can learn in the groups by sharing but also I can be assigned individual tasks after the discussions. But I also prefer other teachers' and trainers' openness and encouragement for ideas without feeling embarrassed. In this sense, your approach to ask me and clarify my understanding by questioning my own ideas helped me more. (Post-session interview, Fatma)

Following Dean's (1991) classification of teachers' learning styles, I could identify both teachers' learning styles. Fatma was a reflector as she was more comfortable to reflect on her practices critically, whereas Samira was close to the style of a pragmatist as she indicated her intentions to learn through applying her 'new' knowledge in her forthcoming teaching. Consequently, I realized that teacher educators should allow for teachers to learn new practices *on their own terms*. In addition, teacher professional programmes should be tailored to address varied learning styles for increased impact on teachers.

Moreover, as a teacher educator, I learnt that *teachers' motivation to learn affects their intake from training sessions.* Although, both teachers were identified by the school principal as participants for my study, each of them came with differing levels of motivation. Fatma was enthusiastic to attend the discussion sessions from the beginning of the study. As far as Samira was concerned, she looked reluctant in coming to these sessions, providing different reasons to be 'released' from them. This experience revealed that in the absence of any other incentives and rewards for professional development, a teacher educator should be able to motivate the teachers and increase their interest in learning.

THE ROLE OF ACTION RESEARCH IN DEVELOPING TEACHER EDUCATORS

Classes at the university provided me theoretical knowledge about teacher education and school improvement and helped me develop an understanding of what it means to be a teacher of teachers. Thus, while I accumulated the relevant theoretical knowledge about teacher education, I had little opportunity to implement my theoretical knowledge and study the process of my own development as a teacher educator.

This action research study forced me not only to reconsider my strategies for teacher development but more importantly to critically examine my own beliefs and practices of teacher education. Thus, action research played a very productive role in my becoming a teacher educator in several ways. Foremost, following the cyclic process, action research compelled me to systematically observe and research my own strategies of teacher education. My actions were not spontaneous and hasty; rather, they were based on reflection, as was my planning. For instance, I did not simply start educating teachers about curriculum enrichment. Instead, I spent a substantial amount of time analysing my own knowledge and teachers' existing beliefs and practices of curriculum enrichment. After this, I took time to plan strategically and relate my plan to the teachers' teaching-learning context. Furthermore, my reflections on group discussions revealed that Samira's participation in the discussion was limited to short, often monosyllabic replies to questions asked of her specifically. This led me to reassess my strategy and change from group to individual sessions with each teacher. Thus, the interactive process of action research enabled me to base my actions on my reflections so as to bring about change and improvement in my knowledge and skills for teacher education.

Use of literature in action research is continuous and contextual and not predetermined. The practitioner's consultation of literature is based on emerging issues. I had to persistently consult relevant literature on the basis of my reflections. The literature, for instance, informed me about teachers' different learning styles (Randall and Thornton, 2001) and their motivation for professional development (Dean, 1991), which then supported me in changing my strategy of educating teachers. Analysing and identifying both teachers' learning styles, I took the decision to hold separate sessions for each teacher. I learnt that teachers' learning styles rested on their personality styles and teachers' motivation affected their intake from the discussions. In general, it is through action research that I improved my knowledge about content (curriculum enrichment) and research focus (teacher education). At the beginning I found searching for, selecting, and reading relevant literature an extremely demanding activity. However, I gradually developed the ability to do so. Thus, reading the relevant literature helped me in critically thinking about my next actions.

Action research leads to transformation in the practitioner, and this makes it a valuable strategy in becoming a teacher educator. The very beliefs about teacher learning which I religiously held were transformed as a result of reflections during the process of action research. It is the action research experience which challenged my assumptions about the change process in teacher learning. At the beginning of the study, I strongly believed that teachers' conceptual change would lead to change in their practice of curriculum enrichment. I presumed that from theoretical discourse sessions, teachers would conceptualize their implementation of curriculum in broader terms and critically examine and change their own practices and objectives of teaching. However, through the action research process, I realized that a blend of theory and application about a new idea or strategy may influence the change in teachers' beliefs and actions simultaneously. In addition, through action research, I recognized that teachers preferred 'seeing' to 'being told' about enrichment strategies. At the initial stage of the action research process, I presumed that teachers would know different ways to enrich, but later in the discussion with them and reflecting on those discussions, I realized their need for demonstration sessions or being shown how to do something practically in the clasroom. This was probably due to the fact that both teachers did not have any formal teacher training.

CONCLUSION

Through this action research, I learnt what it means to be a teacher of teachers. Action research served as a useful strategy to enhance my understanding about school-based teacher education. For aspiring teacher educators the lessons I have drawn from this study may echo the familiar 'lyrics' from their university classes. However, experiencing teacher education theories in the real context of school-based teacher education could open novice teacher educators' eyes to new possibilities and development and use of contextually appropriate strategies for school-based teacher education. Though in recent years, action research on beginning teachers has been conducted in several contexts, this study is significant in terms of creating new knowledge about the use of action research for becoming a teacher educator in a developing country context. This could open new avenues for further research. Prior to educating the teachers, it is the effective preparation of teacher educators which matters.

Part II
Leadership and School Improvement Practices

Introduction to Part II

Leadership is the capacity to translate vision into reality.
(Warren Bennis)

The importance of effective leadership as a key factor for school improvement is widely recognized (Harris, 2002). However, in Pakistan the educational landscape is not homogeneous and neither are the aspects of leadership for quality schooling. On one hand, there is a large public sector which serves the majority of the population in both rural and urban areas (Khan, 2005). Most of the public sector schools use national and/or regional languages as medium of instruction and try to reach out to all income groups especially lower income and lower middle income groups (Rahman, 2004). On the other hand, private school systems, based mainly in the urban areas (Bergman and Mohammad, 1998) serve the upper middle class and elite sections of society. These schools mostly use English as their medium of instruction. In addition, faith-based and community schools are also catering to the needs of different socio-economic sections of Pakistani society. This variety of schools in the rural and urban areas and affiliated with different systems, present diverse prospects, potentials, and problems for leadership and change with implications for improving the quality of schooling in Pakistan. The three chapters in Section II present the possibilities and challenges for leadership roles at different levels, in different school systems and locales in Pakistan.

In chapter eight Abdalla and Qureshi present the findings of a field research that explored the leadership roles of a Subject Coordinator in an urban private school in Karachi. In the educational leadership hierarchy Subject Coordinators are considered to be the middle managers (Mercer and Ri, 2006; Leask and Terrel, 1997). The authors explore the multiplicity of roles a subject coordinator is expected to play in the school and the challenges faced by him. The study in particular highlights the leadership role of a Subject Coordinator as a promoter of school-based professional development of fellow teachers thus suggesting that middle managers can be co-leaders. This suggestion is in line with the globally emerging sense of both the need of and the room for distributed leadership for school improvement. At the same time it draws attention to the challenges for school improvement which are 'local' thus requiring contextually appropriate strategies and skills to overcome these challenges. For example, the study reveals that the personal abilities and interpersonal skills of a subject coordinator could compensate for the lack of proper training in leadership skills for middle managers in the school. This finding has important implications for the utility (or perhaps futility?) of the global orientation of the educational leadership and management courses being conducted at various teacher education institutes.

The importance of personal abilities and interpersonal skills as a resource is also highlighted by John Retallick's research findings reported in chapter nine. Retallick analyses the management practices and strategies in three successful schools in Pakistan. The most important amongst the factors found to contribute to the success of these schools were the, 'personal qualities of the people who are to be principals of the schools' (Retallick, Rarieya, Safdar, Mithani Babur and Sewani, 2004). The study findings also suggest that leadership is contextual. Sosik (2006) points out that, 'Leadership is a social process that is accomplished through human relationships' (p. 102); therefore, the roles, challenges, and coping strategies are constantly negotiated and renegotiated. This finding again questions the suitability of global training for preparing different levels of educational leaders whose expected roles are contextually determined.

The final chapter, chapter eleven, describes the experiences of, and lessons learnt from a whole school improvement programme

(WSIP) based on a locally developed model in the Northern Areas of Pakistan. This cross-case analysis by Fauzia Shamim provides a deeper understanding of the nature of challenges faced by the variety of schools affiliated with different systems in the Northern Areas of Pakistan. The WSIP was found to be potentially positive for the three major school systems, i.e., public, private, and NGO schools. Nonetheless, the lack of sustainability of the programme's impact was found to be a common issue across all school systems. The major factors influencing the level of impact of the whole school improvement programme during the intervention stage included the individual capacity building of teachers and heads, head teacher's personal and professional characteristics and support from the community and the school systems. More importantly, it was found that changes introduced by WSIP during the intervention year were sustained only in those schools where the head teacher and/or the system provided intended or unintended support for school improvement to the teachers. The study findings bring out the need for contextually relevant 'maintenance' strategies in addition to development strategies for sustainability of school reform efforts for improving schools in Pakistan and similar settings elsewhere.

Rashida Qureshi

8

Teacher Leadership for School-based Professional Development: A Case Study

Muhammad Jumma Abdalla[1]
and Rashida Qureshi

Teacher leadership is 'the process by which teachers, individually or collectively, influence their colleagues, principals and other members of school communities to improve teaching and learning practices with the aim of increased student learning and achievement' (York-Barr and Duke, 2004; pp. 287-288). Teacher leaders 'influence others through formal leadership roles such as the traditional department chairperson' (Moller, 2006:524). Subject coordinator is one such formal position in schools and subject coordinators influence their colleagues through their role as an instructional leader whereby they engage in 'the process of increasing or extending the capacity of staff for performance of various duties' (Lodiaga, cited in Wanzare and Ward, 2000, p. 265). This role involves building the capacity of teachers in a specific subject area and, consequently, the school's capacity to meet the needs of school improvement programmes (Mangin, 2005).

In Pakistan, similar to many other developing contexts, the leadership roles in schools have remained an uncharted area. There is a small body of emerging research studies that have explored school leadership with a focus on the role of head teachers, (Khan, 2005; Khan, S.T, 2005; Khan, G. 2005; Shah, 2005; Begum, 2004; Fraidonov, 2004; Oluga, 2004; Khan, 2003; Shah, 2003; Simikins, Sisum and Memon, 2003; Swai, 2002;

Abdulalshoev, 2000; Ishmatov, 2000; Maksutova, 1999; Yousafi, 1998). These studies tend to create an impression that head teachers can improve schools single-handedly whereas Hopkins, Ainscow and West (1994) have pointed out 'that a school which looks to the head teacher as the single source of direction and inspiration is severely constrained. It is dependent on a single individual's supply of intellectual, emotional and physical energy...it is restricted by a single imagination' (p. 154), thus pointing out the need for and importance of distributed leadership for school improvement. However, there exists a gap in research literature in Pakistan and other developing countries on teacher leadership which includes subject coordinators. Hence, there is a need to explore the subject coordinators' leadership roles for school improvement in these contexts. The present chapter is based on a research study that examines the leadership roles of subject coordinators for school improvement, in general, and for leading teachers' professional development, in particular, in the context of a private community-based school in Pakistan. Keeping in mind that 'the actual way they [teacher leaders] practice their participation in leadership activities is dependent on the particular context of a school' (Brooks, Scribner and Eferakorho, 2004: p. 246), the contextual challenges in playing this role are also highlighted.

CONCEPTUAL CONTEXT OF THE STUDY

Until the 90s, the leadership literature separated leadership from management (Snowden and Gorton 1998), the argument being that leadership is solely concerned with change or the developmental aspect of an organization, whereas management is concerned with maintenance and stability of the structures of an organization. This distinction was challenged by those who maintain that in its broader sense leadership includes management functions (Gregory, 1996; Kekale, 1998). The present study concurs with the notion of leadership as inclusive of management functions and adopts the definition of leadership by Stogdill cited in Snowden and Gorton (1998): leadership is 'those activities engaged in by an individual or members of a group that contribute significantly to the...development and maintenance of role structure and goal direction, necessary for effective group performance' (p. 65). This definition has two strengths. First, it has used the broader meaning of leadership which includes both developmental and maintenance activities. Both of these functions are important for school improvement. Second, it considers leadership as not merely the province of one individual but something which can be shared with other members of a group or organization—a leadership approach which is now regarded essential for bringing about and sustaining school improvement (Crowther, Ferguson, Kaagan and Hann, 2002; Jackson, 2000). The relevance of this definition to the present research is that it presents the possibility of extending the role of subject coordinators to include both development and maintenance functions for leadership. Following this definition, the position of the subject coordinator can be defined as more of a leadership position than a managerial position in school organization. This is similar to the position taken by Leask and Terrel (1997) who place the middle managers at the centre of leadership for school improvement because of 'the complexity of the organization and curriculum, the need for all teams to be fully involved in realizing the school vision and in creating conditions for school improvement' (p. 2). For complex organizations to function smoothly and implement the school vision and policies, subject coordinators as 'middle managers' need to work with other departments and the head teachers to make the whole school operate as one unit. Hopkins, Ainscow and West (1994) state that commitment to staff development, involvement of all stakeholders in decision making, transformational leadership, attention to the benefit of enquiry and reflection, effective coordination and commitment to collaborative planning are essential conditions at school and classroom level which support and sustain improvement. These essential conditions are developed as much through leadership and organization of the department as they are through the whole school management (Leask and Terrel, 1997).

Williams (2002) identifies three levels of leadership namely: strategic, operational, and individual levels. The strategic level is concerned with providing a sense of direction for the whole organization, planning how to reach there and ensuring that the plan is put into practice. Subject coordinators may have little contribution at this level though the possibility of their contribution for strategic planning cannot be ruled out. As stated by Early (2003) for school improvement a 'strategy must be worked out in partnership...' (p. 356).

The second level, i.e., operational, is about interpretation of the school policies or strategic planning into workable procedures whereas the final level, i.e., individual, is about inspiring team members and raising their morale for the implementation of the plan. Subject coordinators at the last two levels have a major role to play both as formal leaders as well as during informal interaction with colleagues. It must be noted that all these three levels of leadership are not always exclusive to the top organizational or school level. They all come into play at one time or another at the departmental level too (Williams, 2002). Thus subject coordinators can play a leadership role at all these three levels in their department.

Glover, Gleeson, Gough and Johnson (1998) in their study of seven schools in West Midlands identify four dimensions of subject leaders' roles. The first one is to translate the school policies or changes introduced by senior management into classroom practices. This requires such roles as managing and allocating resources. The second dimension is promoting and maintaining group identity. This involves such roles as promoting shared vision, values, collaboration, and collegiality. The third dimension is improving the staff and students' performance. This involves promoting teacher professional development and improving teaching and learning in the classroom. This instructional leadership (Moller, 2006) or educational leadership (Fidler, 1997) also includes monitoring and supervising teaching and learning both of students and teachers. The fourth and final role of middle managers, identified by Glover et al., is the representative role. Subject leaders can be representatives of their departments to other stakeholders including other departments, schools, parents, community, and/or senior management.

The above mentioned four dimensions of the role of a subject coordinator are closely interlinked. For example, making contact with other departments can be a liaison role. It can also be seen as translating the policy of the senior management into action. At the same time it can be considered a role for promoting staff and students' development. More important still, a subject coordinator's roles in all the four dimensions can fall within the scope of school improvement depending on how they are executed. Monitoring role, for example, can be for school improvement, if it is conducted in a way and with the intent to help teachers or students' learning. These four dimensions identified by Glover et al., have been used as a broad framework for analysing the leadership roles of a subject coordinator in the context of a private community-based school in Pakistan. The main focus of this chapter, however, is on how a subject coordinator provides leadership for promoting teachers' professional development and improving teaching and learning in the classroom.

PHYSICAL CONTEXT OF THE STUDY

This study was conducted in a school in Karachi run by an NGO. The school, part of a large network of schools in Pakistan, had recently introduced several school improvement initiatives including setting up the formal position of subject coordinators for each learning area programme in the curriculum. Unlike the head teachers, subject coordinators spend most of their time working in classrooms, where the real school work, i.e., teaching and learning, takes place. More importantly, their focus is on the improvement of students' learning through supporting teachers' professional development which is at the heart of their school improvement programme. It was envisaged that these subject leaders would provide a link between the senior school leadership and the teaching staff.

The leadership hierarchy of the school includes a principal at the top, assisted by head teachers for each school section. The head teachers are the immediate supervisors of subject coordinators. Each school has got finance and students' affairs offices which deal with financial matters and students' affairs, respectively. Up and above the school level, there is the executive board. A central office acts as a coordinator and resource for the school system and supports schools and teachers in their school improvement initiatives.

According to the programme officer at the central office, there is no hierarchy in relationships between the office and the school. They work as partners for school improvement initiatives. While there are variations in implementation among different schools in the system, their overall efforts are coordinated. Also, there is a close working relation between different schools. The school where the present research was conducted was working closely and collaboratively with two other schools belonging to the same system. The purpose of this networking is to enhance each school's capabilities in dealing with the change process.

The school under study has two sections—pre-school and junior secondary—with about 4000 students. The junior secondary section has classes from 3 to 10 and is further divided into two sections—boys' and girls' sections. Each section has its own head teacher and seven subject coordinators. This study was conducted in the junior secondary boys' section.

PARTICIPANTS

The purpose of the study was to explore the leadership role of a subject coordinator in the professional development of fellow teachers. The research participant Muhammad (pseudonym) was identified through purposive sampling. He was an experienced teacher and had held the position of a subject coordinator for more than three years at the time of the study. He was the major informant on what roles a subject coordinator was expected to perform in that school and how he (as the incumbent of that position) enacted his role, the challenges he faced, and the strategies he used to surmount those challenges. In order to have both in-depth and a wider perspective of the leadership role of a subject coordinator, especially as the promoter of teachers' professional development, two teachers and the head teacher of the same school and a programme officer from the system's education office were also involved as research participants in the study.

The data was collected through semi-structured interviews, formal and informal conversations, observations, and document analysis. The emerging concepts and themes from transcribed interviews, conversations, and notes from observations and document analysis were then converted into interconnected statements (Jackson, 1995) in order to have an in-depth understanding of the leadership role of a subject coordinator in the professional development of fellow teachers.

MUHAMMAD'S LEADERSHIP FOR TEACHERS' PROFESSIONAL DEVELOPMENT

The head teacher described Muhammad as a mentor and a facilitator of teachers' learning on the job. One of the teachers described him as an exemplary teacher and a role model, 'He [Muhammad] is a good teacher. He is good at IT and at teaching. You know, he is a good human being as well, very supportive and hard working and always he is on time, I mean he finishes the syllabus in time. You want to be like him.' The study findings show that Muhammad provided support for the professional growth of teachers in his learning area by facilitating their professional learning through mentoring and exemplary teaching. This section examines how he enacted his role.

Mentoring is a powerful tool for teachers' professional growth as it facilitates and supports the growth of other members

(Beattie, 2002). It is also considered a teacher leadership role as 'the concept of learning by precept and example, of being instructed to develop certain practices and fine-tune a personal style of delivery, brings in the instructor, the coach, the advisor, and, of course what we now term the mentor' (Cullingford, 2006:1). Muhammad used 'the concept of learning by precept and example' to induct inexperienced teachers into the school culture. One of Muhammad's mentees elaborated on his role as follows:[2]

> I can say I am the least experienced here, and Muhammad has helped me a lot, I used to have sessions with him....You see, you can say the problem was not content. It is not that we don't know, for example, fractions, I know it, but how to deliver it, and how to have a good lesson planning. We sometimes need help in these areas.

'New teachers may have particularly unsettled feelings about their professional situations in the schools which, if not resolved, may cause some of them to abandon the profession or submit to its demands without a real sense of reward' (Avalos and Aylwin, 2007:521). Helping new teachers in 'the settling in' (Avalos and Aylwin, 2007:520) phase of their teaching career is an important step in the professional growth of novice teachers especially in Pakistan where pre-service teachers training is not an entry requirement. Muhammad opened up his classroom for other teachers and encouraged them to visit his classes to observe his teaching strategies:

> Any teacher can go to any class. Like my other staff say... you have an excellent class. Excellent class means whatever I teach in terms of disciplined class and most of the teachers face a problem of maintaining discipline in the class. They come into my class. They observe whatever I do. How I manage the class, how I maintain discipline in the class.

Muhammad also used his classroom teaching to pilot a programme of study that he was involved in preparing for his department.[3] He monitored its implementation and the final appraisal of its effectiveness. Moreover, Muhammad was also involved in developing a programme of study for the students who were underachievers in his department. These activities, in the context of leadership for school improvement, became means of translating the school improvement programme into a workable document (curriculum document). While the school improvement programme had set general goals and standards to be aimed at, the curriculum document translated these goals and standards into topics, sub-topics, activities, and strategies for teachers to implement in their classrooms. Thus, preparing a curriculum document was a way of facilitating others to implement school improvement programmes. And by implementing this curriculum document in his class, Muhammad acted as a role model for other teachers.

Muhammad helped experienced teachers in fine-tuning their 'personal style of delivery.' His colleagues consulted him about their problem areas; ['then] we sit together. I give my ideas... and we plan...whatever to do next.' He also encouraged teachers to do peer observations, so as to learn from each other. One of the teachers said:

> Muhammad wants us to have peer observations, and we sometimes observe each other, if we have time. There is little time for this. You see! We don't have much time, we have to plan and check the copies and sometimes we have to take arrangements [substitute teaching].

Other strategies Muhammad used for enhancing his colleagues' professional development included co-teaching and lesson observation. He co-taught with teachers he was mentoring: 'Sometimes I go and do co-teaching with the teachers. Sometimes I ask them to come into my class and co-teach with me. Even I am not an expert. I am also learning. We plan together and during the lesson we observe each other...and share our observations after the lesson.'

Lesson observation was yet another strategy used by Muhammad to promote the professional development of his colleagues. 'I observe teaching in classrooms. It is in my job description to see that teachers observe standards, that they teach according to the standards, and that they follow the curriculum.' Educational research suggests that middle managers are reluctant to enter their colleagues' classrooms for performing the monitoring and evaluation role (McGarvey, Marriot, Morgan and Abbot, 1997; Wise, 2001). The present research, however, does not indicate the existence of such attitudes. Muhammad did not report any hesitation in undertaking monitoring and evaluation of his colleagues. Likewise, the teachers who were interviewed claimed to have no bad feelings about being monitored through classroom observations by Muhammad. In addition, Muhammad also encouraged his fellow teachers to observe each others' classes for mutual learning. Muhammad followed a regular practice of observing teachers' lessons and giving feedback to them. It was verified by one of the teachers as, 'both the head and Muhammad observe us during classes. Then they share with us their feedback.' Wise (2001) states that some departmental staff has negative attitudes towards the practice of observing teachers' lessons for monitoring and evaluation purposes. The negative attitude can be attributed to the belief that the practice implies status differences (Smylie, 1992). However, while Muhammad held the formal position of a subject coordinator, the teachers in the study context acknowledged that Muhammad was more of a colleague and supported them professionally in different ways.

Park, Oliver, Johnson, Graham, and Oppong (2007) in their study of the role of colleagues in the professional development of teachers found that 'teacher interactions...helped one another's professional development in several ways: (a) enhancing reflection on teaching practice, (b) establishing a professional discourse community, (c) raising the standards for teaching performances, and (d) facilitating collaboration' (p. 368). Muhammad employed several strategies for facilitating teachers' professional interactions.

For example,

> I sent our two teachers to attend the summer session. It was a
> six-day session, and it was my request to the teachers to share each
> and everything they learnt.

By asking teachers to formally share their learning with
colleagues, Muhammad was actually facilitating his fellow
teachers' professional development and he did it within the
framework of existing school resources and structures. The
teachers who had received training from any external organization
were invited to share their 'new' learning with their colleagues
during the professional development activities on Fridays[4] or
during the summer learning sessions. Muhammad used both
these structures, i.e., Friday meetings and summer learning
sessions in the school to promote teachers' interaction for
professional development. This made teachers happy as they got
'new' information useful for their ongoing professional
development without having to spend 'extra' time at school.

Muhammad also helped teachers learn through co-planning
with them in the Friday meetings mentioned above. The same
sessions were used by Muhammad for encouraging collaborative
learning.

> You see, we discuss our planning, we share our valued reflections,
> whatever has happened in the classroom. If there was something
> very special, when they learnt something from the students, then
> they share whenever they feel like. There was a very difficult problem
> for the teacher to solve them, the teachers share that problem with
> other teachers…it is like we help and learn from each other.

Muhammad believed that reflection was one of the most
powerful tools for teachers' professional development. According
to him, reflection allowed teachers to make meaning of their
classroom experiences. In fact, without reflection on their
experiences, teachers can repeat the same mistakes over and over
again (see Rareiya, in this book). Thus, he used Friday sessions

for facilitating group reflection by teachers to help them improve their professional practice. One of the teachers, while commenting on Muhammad's role as the facilitator of the Fridays' sessions, said:

> He [Muhammad] is like a chairman, he chairs the session, or he is a facilitator you can say. He is the one who provides the things we use there, he observes the social skills in the group and he guides us during the whole process. You see, if there is no one to lead, every one will be doing his own thing, and it will be like impossible.

Although it was not impossible for Muhammad to perform his leadership role he was in a context where the position of a subject coordinator had been introduced fairly recently as a formal leadership position. Muhammad faced certain challenges in his role enactment and he devised various strategies to address those challenges. The coping strategies used by him in enacting his leadership roles can be classified at two levels, i.e., organizational and personal. The first type includes the role of the school system in providing supportive infrastructure and the second refers to his personal characteristics that had an impact on his performance as a subject coordinator. This section will look briefly at the challenges in role enactment at two levels—organizational and personal.

Organizational Challenges in Role Enactment

As mentioned earlier, the school had recently introduced the position of subject coordinator as a leadership position. Muhammad had a written job description which served as a point of reference for both the teachers and the senior management in terms of their expectations from a subject coordinator. For Muhammad, the written job description of his role and responsibilities reduced role ambiguity. As a result, the possibilities of conflict between him and the teachers, on one hand, and between him and the senior management, on the other, was reduced. For instance, he was required to be a mentor; therefore, Muhammad had about 50 per cent of his workload allocated to helping other teachers. He used this time to observe teachers' lessons and give them feedback as well as to develop and review programmes of study.

Muhammad's job description allocated him time for mentoring his colleagues. However, the workload of his mentees prevented him from enacting this role effectively.

> They [teachers] are very much burdened, working for 16 to 17 hours per week. They have to teach their own teaching load, but if someone is missing [absent], someone has to go to the classroom to take the arrangement [substitute teaching]. So most of the teachers I must say not 16 to 17 hours, they are taking 19 to 20 hours per week. ...so they usually complain about the teaching, when are they going to complete their work? I mean, they are going to check their copies, when will they find something for the students?

The teachers had little time to observe Muhammad's or each others' classes and work collaboratively and these were the strategies that Muhammad was trying to promote for teachers' professional development. The teachers felt that it was difficult for them to achieve the performance standards being role-modelled by Muhammad, 'You want to be like him [Muhammad] but for us it is difficult.' The teachers' feelings that their workloads (teaching) were much heavier than that of Muhammad indicate a potential source of tension between Muhammad and his colleagues.

Among the other organizational factors that enabled Muhammad to enact his role effectively were the existing school structures like the Friday meetings, and the finance and students' affairs offices. Muhammad used Friday meetings for collaborative planning and reflection; this provided him the space to meet with other teachers and encourage them to collaboratively reflect on their practices while helping them in their planning. The same sessions were also used to share teachers' learning from seminars and workshops which they attended elsewhere. These meetings provided avenues and time for Muhammad to perform his leadership role of supporting teachers and facilitating their professional development. However, one of the teachers felt that these meetings also took time away from teachers which was set aside for routine activities like checking students' written work, and discussing individual students' problems.

Two other school structures, i.e., finance and student affairs offices also helped Muhammad in playing his role in teachers' professional development. These offices were established as part of the restructuring of school organization for supporting the then recently introduced efforts for school improvement. By taking over financial and student counselling duties from teachers, the two offices helped in freeing up the time of teacher leaders, such as the subject coordinator, for leading professional development activities in the school.

Additionally, two other organizational structures outside the school also facilitated Muhammad's school-based professional activities. These were 'structured' opportunities for inter-school collaboration and central education office of the school system. Under the inter-school collaboration, most of the instructional and curriculum development activities took place in inter-school meetings which provided opportunities for sharing ideas and doing tasks collectively. It would have been difficult for Muhammad, for example, to produce his curriculum document alone thus jeopardizing his officially assigned role of a curriculum developer. By implementing this curriculum document in his class, Muhammad had the opportunity to try it out for himself in the context of a real classroom and thus guide his colleagues in implementing the same curriculum in their classes more effectively. Muhammad's involvement in monitoring and evaluating the effectiveness of both the document and its implementation by his fellow teachers, on one hand, made him a key player in translating the schools' goals and values into classroom practices. On the other, it reinforced his role as a mentor.

Lastly, the central education office of the school system also facilitated Muhammad's efforts towards supporting the professional development of his fellow teachers. The office, working both with and for the schools, within the school system was instrumental in providing, (a) structures, such as learning sessions and inter-school links; (b) resources, such as skilled personnel to conduct training sessions for teachers; and (c) support in curriculum development and more importantly, its successful implementation at classroom level. Hence, both the organizational structures at the level of the school and school system facilitated Muhammad in playing a leadership role for teachers' school-based professional development.

Personal Factors

Muhammad's job description spelt out his officially assigned roles and responsibilities as a subject coordinator, but his role enactment often went beyond the assigned leadership roles. For instance, Muhammad's role modelling was not limited to being an exemplary teacher or mentor; he was also looked upon for setting high performance standards through hard work. His fellow teachers described him as punctual, approachable, and easy to talk to because of his friendly attitude toward both teachers and students. Muhammad was observed spending most of his break time in discussions with groups of students in a very relaxed manner. His personal qualities seemed to facilitate his interaction with people around him thus enlarging the circle of his possible influence. Shaaban (2005) in her study of teachers' involvement in school development plans in Pakistan also found out that teachers were more creative when they knew that the leaders they were working with were both friendly and accessible. This finding is suggestive of the importance of personal characteristics of teacher leaders in facilitating teachers' professional growth, particularly in socio-cultural contexts such as Pakistan where there are no clear boundaries between the personal and official role particularly in working with colleagues.

Another personal trait that helped Muhammad perform his duties as a subject coordinator was his positive attitude toward learning. Muhammad was expected to be a role model by being a mentor and an exemplary teacher. However, he did not consider himself 'an expert'; instead he constantly looked for opportunities to learn from his fellow teachers. Although most of his interaction with teachers took place during the official meetings, the driving force behind these meetings was his personal interest and motivation for learning. Muhammad shared that a major source of his knowledge was his fellow teachers. He particularly appreciated opportunities for learning with and from them through co-teaching. He also welcomed their feedback when they observed his classes.

Muhammad's learning through interaction was not limited to teachers only. He also learnt from students both directly and indirectly. His direct interaction with students happened during his own classroom teaching and in informal discussions with them during the school recess. He also introduced the practice of asking for students' feedback at the end of every computer-based Maths session:

> It is mandatory for each and every teacher to go to the computer lab and integrate Math with IT, that prepare and teach some lessons with IT, and at the end of the lesson we take their [students'] feedback. They [students] write their feedback.

This practice helped him in increasing the effectiveness of his own teaching of Mathematics through integration of Information Technology (IT) which in turn, helped him to facilitate the professional learning of other teachers. By introducing the practice of getting students' feedback (reflections as he preferred to call them) in his subject area, Muhammad contributed, on one hand, to his own learning; on the other, getting student feedback provided learning opportunities to other teachers as well. In addition to learning from students' reflection, Muhammad used his own reflections for improving his practice. He maintained a reflective journal on his practice and also engaged in collaborative reflections with other teachers (cf. Rarieya, 2005).

Finally, Muhammad also learnt from a more formal and structured set-up of professional workshops and seminars organized both by his own school and other organizations. Muhammad recalled one such workshop where he had learnt something new: 'mental math was a new idea to us. So we had no idea about mental math; then our PDT [Professional Development Teacher], she gave us a demo lesson on how you are going to teach mental math.' He feels that all these formal and informal activities have helped him improve his practice:

> I think I have improved a lot. If I compare myself from the beginning, and whatever I am now because it was a new experience for me. Now, the things are very much clear in front of me, how to work, how to deal with the staff members, how to deal with the parents, with the students of mixed abilities.

Muhammad's continuous engagement in learning activities make him a true leader (cf. Beatie, 2002). He was engaged in two types of learning: learning about leadership skills, and ways of improving his own and his colleagues' practice. The former would be significant for the effective enactment of his role as a teacher leader. The latter to a certain extent compensated for a potential handicap, i.e, lack of formal leadership and management training to facilitate teachers' professional development. Muhammad was expected to play a leadership role without any formal training in leadership skills and practices. For instance, Muhammad regularly observed teachers' classes but the two important components of observation for professional development purposes, i.e., mutual agreement on focus and purpose of observation and giving formative feedback (Gunter, 2002; Bartlett, 1998), were missing from his practice. Although there was no separation between *observation for teacher development* and *observation for monitoring and teacher appraisal,* the lesson observations were done mainly for appraising teachers' performance thus making it 'essentially the process of collecting information on teachers' performance for the purpose of determining pay levels, disciplinary actions, dismissal, promotion and in-service training needs,' (Geraldine, 1997:206). Muhammad carried out classroom observations without prior sharing of the purpose of observation; his feedback focused mainly on weaknesses of the lessons, and therefore, was characterized by narrow-focussed suggestions for improvement, as one of the teachers commented; 'They [head-teacher and Muhammad] share with us whatever feedback, whatever is lacking. They give us and we are to follow the pattern, what they tell us.' The teachers indicated that the only sharing done was that of the lesson plan prior to the observations. More importantly, the feedback provided focused mainly on the shortcomings of the teachers' lessons. Teachers in the research study, however, acknowledged that they had benefited from the feedback given by Muhammad.

DISCUSSION

The purpose of this research study was to examine the leadership roles of a subject coordinator. Muhammad's role enactment facilitated both by organizational structures and his own personal traits highlighted the significant contribution of a subject coordinator in teachers' school-based professional development. By playing the twin roles of a teacher and a teacher leader, the subject coordinator appears to be in a powerful position to make a difference by being a role model for the teachers to follow. However, for a school-based teachers' professional development programme to bring about and sustain change for improvement, the level at which the leadership roles are performed is also important. There was no evidence of Muhammad playing any major role at the strategic level of leadership at the school or system level. Even at the departmental level his role in strategic planning and decision-making was minimal. The implication of this finding is that a subject coordinator, being closer to the teachers' life, is likely to have a major impact on the professional development of his/her fellow teachers; however, given the hierarchical and beauracratic structures of school systems in Pakistan (Simikins, Sisum and Memon, 2003), the key decisions for the professional development of teachers are likely to be more top-down than in collaboration with 'middle managers' like subject coordinators. Despite the fact that the school system (to which the school under study belongs to) has established the position of subject coordinator as a leadership position, all the roles that Muhammad performed for the most part corresponded to the operational level of leadership, e.g., his role in teachers' professional development and evaluation of teachers' and students' learning. Muhammad worked towards improving student outcomes both through supporting teachers in improving their classroom practices, and through designing and supervising programmes for underachieving students in his department. The school records showed that these interventions had had a significant impact on students' learning. Muhammad's main role as a staff and curriculum developer was to implement policies that were not made by him.

Muhammad was an exemplary teacher and a role model for his colleagues. He was also involved in articulating and helping teachers translate the school goals and values into practice through his roles performed at the operational level above. Muhammad, as a committed professional, promoted the culture of cooperation which is a pre-requisite for continuous professional development as well as a key component for school improvement. Yet all these roles correspond to the lower levels of leadership where room for leading the change at the strategic level of planning and decision-making is minimal.

The research findings also draw attention to the various strategies that can be used by the subject coordinators for teachers' school-based professional development. Muhammad, for instance, undertook mentoring of teachers through co-planning and/or co-teaching, classroom observation and feedback, and facilitation of collaborative reflection sessions. He also involved other staff members in sharing their learning with their colleagues through the provision of structured interaction opportunities. Muhammad was required to perform all these roles because of his formal position as a subject coordinator or 'departmental teacher leader' (Brooks, Scribner and Eferakorho, 2004) which included teaching and other roles like mentoring, and the institutional structures (such as teaching workload) allowed him to take on the role of a mentor for his fellow teachers. Although mentoring as a strategy for enhancing professional development of colleagues has been found useful even within the contextual constraints of Pakistan (Mohammad and Kumari; Karim and Halai in this volume; Kabylov, 2003; Haque, 2002; Khan, H.K., 2002; Lalwani, 1999; Mehta, 1995), how many teacher leaders would opt for it at an informal level? Although we hesitate to draw a conclusion that has implications beyond the context of this study, findings indicate that the effectiveness of teacher leaders could be increased through creating formal situations and opportunities for developing teacher leadership skills. The implications for policy-makers and school managers are that professional development being a continuous process needs certain enabling organizational structures including protected time for teachers to engage in professional development activities, and formal training for teacher leaders to play their role effectively in school-based teacher development.

One of the most peculiar findings of this research study is that neither the subject coordinator nor the teachers reported any feelings of discomfort that have traditionally been associated with observing teachers' lessons for monitoring and evaluation. One could argue that it was because the teachers were invited from time to time by Muhammad to observe his classes too. The limitation of this reasoning, however, is in the purposes of observations. The subject coordinator's lessons were for role modelling whereas out of six lesson observations conducted for each teacher, three observations were selected for appraisal. It was not clear what criteria were used for selecting observations for appraisal but the outcome almost always appeared to be the administrative decision to either grant a salary increment or to withhold it. This finding is particularly important for school leaders and school managers who may not realize that teachers' performance appraisal can be used to help teachers in identifying their strengths and weaknesses for planning their future development and thus making teaching and learning more effective (Khan, M.A., 2005; Piggott-Irvin, 2003).

CONCLUSION

This research study has revealed that a teacher leader can influence his/her colleagues' in-house professional development albeit not informally. In the context of bureaucratic organizational structures in schools in Pakistan, creating formal leadership positions for teachers with officially assigned roles may assist them in learning with and from one another. The formal position of subject coordinators at the department level will allow them opportunities to work with other teachers while their role as classroom teachers will help them keep their feet grounded firmly in the reality of a classroom. Playing the dual role of a leader and a teacher will also help subject coordinators to be easily accepted by teachers as one of their colleagues. This would enable the subject coordinators to scaffold teachers' professional development through strategies such as mentoring on an on-going basis.

NOTES

1. The research reported in this chapter was conducted by the first author as a graduate student at the Aga Khan University-Institute for Educational Development in 2004.
2. All direct quotes are original and unedited.
3. This was the syllabus document which the school currently follows. It has to be reviewed every year and this task is carried out by the subject coordinator.
4. Teachers met on the first and third Friday of every month for co-planning, preparing resources, and collaborative reflection on their practices. These meetings were facilitated by subject coordinators including Muhammad.

9

Successful Schools: What Can We Learn from Them?
John Retallick

INTRODUCTION

The focus of this chapter is successful schools in Pakistan. Whilst there remain significant problems with the overall quality of education in the country and there is a dire need to transform most schools (Retallick and Farah, 2005), there are, nevertheless, some good schools. The research project reported here set out to find three such schools and ascertain what makes them successful. The research team[1] felt that findings about the characteristics of successful schools would be useful knowledge for policy makers and practitioners who are concerned with improving schools in Pakistan and other countries.

The first step in the project was developing a set of criteria of 'successful schools' for use in selecting the research sites. To begin with, we had a brainstorming session to identify features of successful schools. We then analysed the responses and reduced the list to a manageable number. As a result, the following criteria of successful schools emerged (not in order of priority):

- A satisfied and motivated staff willing to go to school
- Students willing to go to school
- Flexibility and open to change
- Effective professional development of staff
- A moving school culture
- Curriculum has a view of the world beyond the classroom
- A stress-free atmosphere
- Increased life chances of students

We considered two other factors concerning school selection: the schools should represent a range of school systems and geographical spread across Pakistan. Taking account of all those points and accessibility in terms of travel, we decided upon an NGO school in Northern Areas, a government school in Lahore, and a private school in Karachi.[2] The research team was divided into pairs to spend four days at each school collecting data for later use in writing case studies. At each site there were three sources of data: interviews (audio tape-recorded and later transcribed), observations (general observations around the school and focused observations in classrooms), and documents (analysed for content relevant to the research).

What follows in this chapter are brief presentations of the three case studies (fictitious names) and the findings of the cross-case analysis. For interested readers, the complete case studies are available in the research report (see Retallick et al., 2004).

CASE STUDY 1: MOUNTAIN SCHOOL

Mountain School is located in a rural town in the Northern Areas of Pakistan. It is a diverse Muslim community with Broshaski and Shina as the main languages. Most adults in the community are illiterate and earn their living by farming and trading, though, because it is near a larger city and on the Karakoram Highway, it is a lively centre for business and trading from China.

Mountain School is a girls' school of the Aga Khan Education Service, Pakistan (AKES, P). It was established in 1953 as a co-education primary school up to class 3 and it grew year by year until it was upgraded to middle level in 1973. In 1982 the present building was occupied and in 1989 it was established as a high school with a single stream of Arts. From 1992 significant improvements were made. A school management committee was formed for the first time and a Science stream was introduced in 1994 in classes 9 and 10. Some additional land was purchased and an examination hall and library were built. The school became very popular and student numbers grew to 720 which made it overcrowded.

In 1995 it was changed to a girl's only school to relieve the overpopulation and a separate AKES, P boys' school was established. Additionally, at that time, some other schools were established in the town which meant that some students moved. For these reasons, the student numbers dropped quite considerably. In 2003, the school had classes from nursery to class 10 and 408 students in total.

Substantial improvement had occurred in the physical conditions of the school over the previous two to three years. A boundary wall had been constructed, grounds planted with grass (previously bare and dusty earth) and interiors painted and cleaned up. The principal's office had been extended and improved, the staffroom relocated and refurnished, and the examination hall made into a multi-purpose facility. Classrooms had been cleaned and moveable furniture installed to allow for group work. Classrooms were nicely decorated with charts and students' work (also displayed in the principal's office). However, the library was not in good condition and there was no computer laboratory. All subjects had a textbook provided which was also the syllabus for the teachers to follow. Not much other reading material was available due to lack of a proper library.

Class sizes were relatively small compared with most other schools in Pakistan (where classes can be 40+). This can be attributed to the fact that there are many AKES, P schools in Northern Areas and this school was for girls only. Classes were quite homogeneous in that they were all girls of similar age, all used Urdu language and the majority were Ismailis.[3] Learning time was 8 a.m. to 1.30 p.m. with one break of 30 minutes. There was 1x40 minute period (first each day) and 7x35 minute periods with real teaching time being about 30 minutes per period.

The school had twenty-one teachers (eight males, thirteen females) and in the principal's view it was understaffed by three to four trained teachers. The Head Office formula, based on a ratio of teachers to student numbers, did not allow for more teachers to be appointed. To counteract this, the principal had obtained funds to employ five community teachers. Involvement in the local community was very strong as all teachers lived nearby and most were leaders in social and community development work. For example, the principal was the local ITREB[4] chairperson, another was leader of the scouts' group and another was a leader of a women's organization.

What Makes this a Successful School?

The principal was asked what makes this a successful school. He identified teamwork and cohesion amongst the staff, building trust and quality relationships, shared decision-making, empowerment, and positive community involvement in the school as the major factors. He emphasized that the school has adopted a slogan of 'We sink or swim together' as part of the school vision statement. This means there is a shared sense of responsibility and accountability for the school and that everyone is expected to be a part of the team.

The principal tries to involve teachers in school management committee (SMC) meetings, so that they know the community people don't talk against them and are working for their benefit. Community involvement, especially of mothers, is very important. When the present principal first came to the school, he found that parents were invited to the school only to be told of the student's weaknesses. The parents didn't feel comfortable and they were often victimized; for example, they would be told in front of a school gathering that their child was not doing very well.

He felt that a change of strategy in dealing with parents was needed. He invited mothers to a meeting and made arrangements for eighty-four mothers, but only six attended. When he interviewed them they said that they feared that the new head would be harsh with them and tell them that their child was not doing well, so they would not feel comfortable. Instead of this, he asked them to share the problems that their children were facing at home and in school. Next, he involved the SMC in inviting the mothers; they made a list and took the responsibility to go to the people and invite them. They arranged a workshop for sixty mothers and everybody turned up. The workshop was for 3 hours and included group activities, discussions, and presentations that were quite helpful and the mothers' involvement was high.

Academic performance has improved and as a result for the last two years some Year 12 students have got admission in Islamabad Central College, a premier institution of higher education in the capital city, for the first time. Though, the Mountain school has been functioning since 1953, it is only in the last two years that students have got admission (two in total) to a premier quality institution of higher learning like Islamabad Central College. This is a matter of raising students' and parents' expectations about possibilities in the future.

The principal was asked what the school was like when he first took up the appointment and how it has changed. First, he mentioned the environment: 'the physical environment was not safe and not appropriate, different kinds of vehicles used to cross this area and even animals could be seen in the school premises'. Second, he referred to the teachers' attitude to students:

> Most of the teachers strongly believed in harsh, physical punishment and there was a definition of discipline, that if there was pin-drop silence in the classroom it meant it is a well-disciplined classroom but we had some sessions of professional development where we discussed it and we tried to modify that definition.

Third, he mentioned the staffroom and staffroom culture:

> That was also very much strange like the things which were displayed in the staffroom were vividly showing an environment where teachers were not very careful about things, such as the bookshelves on the back side, there were books inside but they were full of dust and everything was just jumbled inside … it was quite helpful for me to look at school culture and specially the classroom culture and that sort of thing we shared with the teachers and there has been a

change. So a kind of balkanization was there, teachers were divided in their own groups.

Finally, he mentioned the aspirations of the students:

> Students were not confident and I remember when I asked the students 'how many of you want to go to university', they used to say 'we are not those people who can go to the university'. That sort of remark they had about themselves but now if you ask, most of the students will raise their hands because encouragement has been given, the feeling has been given that you can also join universities, they are not for special people, you are the ones who can go there, so this is what has been done.

The perspective of the teachers confirmed the point about school improvement. One teacher said: 'Our physical environment has changed a lot. Initially we didn't have a boundary wall and that's why all the outsiders could pass through here, but now the boundary wall is constructed'. Another teacher commented:

> When he joined the school, a number of people, as parents and as guardians, they began taking interest about their children, before that they totally ignored the children. And the second step was he went to different community centres and met a number of community people, they were told of the situation, that work was happening in our school; that is why our results are good this year.

This view of the school was also shared by a member of the SMC:

> Yeah, it is very good according to the past. Like in the past, there was no involvement of VEC [Village Education Committee] and the community people as such. But now as you all see that the community people, the school, the staff, VEC, even the students, everyone is so involved and they participate in progressing the school day by day...everyone is giving their efforts, the school management, head teacher, community people, VEC, all the people are working hard, that's why all the people are satisfied that the school will develop more day by day.

Leadership and School Improvement

We noticed in the principal's office a prominent display of the School Action Plan (equivalent to a School Development Plan). We asked the principal to explain how the Action Plan was developed:

> All the teachers and some SMC members were involved in preparing this action plan. All SMC members were not involved because of their other commitments but, later on, it was shared with them so that they could give their input....We had discussion, brainstorming and group work and then finally we designed this action plan. So all the teachers were involved and where we felt that students should be involved they were also asked in different classes specially in senior classes that this is our plan and even that plan was shared with the student in the assembly as well like this is our school vision and this is our school development plan, so these were shared in the assembly.

An explanation for the success of this school, particularly over the past three years, must take into account the leadership of the present principal and his focus on school improvement. On a notice board in the principal's office was a statement about school leadership indicating that he was aware of literature on leadership and this, most likely, came from the various courses he had completed at AKU-IED and at the Professional Development Centre, North.[5] Fullan (2002) says 'School leaders with moral purpose seek to make a difference in the lives of students' (p. 17). It was clear that this was high on the principal's agenda and one of the ways that he expressed that agenda was through a statement of the school vision which was also prominently displayed on a notice board in his office. The notion of 'vision' is strongly featured in the literature and this, too, indicated that he had an understanding of leadership. The school vision was:

> *This almer mater is a learning organization where every individual is furnished with highly commendable opportunities and facilities to attain*

the optimal standards of academic results, social skills, moral and spiritual qualities and physical well being. A unique team spirit with a slogan 'sink or swim together' and a sense of strong collaboration among students, faculty and parents unifies this organization. Centre of excellence is its identity.
Our slogan 'committed to quality and merit'.

CASE STUDY 2: ROYAL SCHOOL

Royal School is located in Lahore, Pakistan, a city well-known for architecturally significant buildings and monuments, many dating from the Mughal priod (1526–1707). An educational and cultural centre, Lahore is the site of the University of the Punjab, the oldest university in Pakistan, and the University of Engineering and Technology as well as several other institutions well-known for imparting quality education in Pakistan.

Royal School is a remarkable and different kind of institution. It was established in 1908 for the daughters of the landed gentry. Initially a college for the rich and powerful, now it provides educational services to all sectors of the society. It operates under the Punjab Department of Education and provides education from class 1 to post-graduate (Master's) level. There are three sections (junior, senior, and college) with the principal as chief administrator. In 1998, Royal School was granted autonomous status with a board of governors appointed by the Punjab Government. Although, the board was the supreme authority for providing resources, to date they had always respected the principal's requests. Their approach was very professional. Some 3200 students were studying in the school (not including the college) with a combined teaching faculty of more than 240 members.

The school buildings, spread over more than 22 acres presented a picture of traditional architecture. It had well-equipped laboratories, spacious lecture halls and three libraries. The extensive grounds provided many sports opportunities and the college offered residential facilities to students. The two wings of the school and college were linked by a massive arched bridge built by the City Government of Lahore fulfilling a long-standing demand of the students.

The 'Young Queens of Royal School' mostly belonged to middle class families who spoke Punjabi and Urdu. The school placed a high emphasis on tradition and encouraged the students to display a strong sense of responsibility and observe high norms of ethics. The age of students was 5 years to 16 and they were very keen to attend school; there were very few absentees.

The normal work allotment of a teacher was five to six periods per day and there were five co-curriculum periods allocated. The size of classes was surprisingly large, ranging from seventy to ninety-four students per section due to the constant demand of the community to accommodate their daughters. Despite the large classes, the teachers were found to be quite up-to-date with the checking of notebooks that were selected at random for inspection.

The student-teacher relationship was very strong. In addition to regular classes, the teachers conducted remedial classes and often stayed at school working long hours to complete projects. Both teachers and students were willing to stay after school. The school hours were from 8 a.m. to 1.30 p.m. except on Fridays when it closed at 12.30 p.m. They had six periods each day and 29 hours of teaching per week.

The teachers were very polite and friendly with the students. The lessons we observed were well-planned but could have been more interactive. Regular homework was given to students. There was a strong emphasis on the handwriting of students, which was uniform and neat.

What Makes this a Successful School?

According to the principal, ample resources, but well-managed and properly accounted for, is one of the criteria for a successful school:

> Financial resources, no doubt, play a very pivotal role but if we want to utilize our resources we have to go through the budget, to the

board of governors and everything, you know it's not only the principal who can utilize it.

They have a vision and development committee with the prime objective of monitoring on a quarterly basis to keep the school focused on excellence. The principal delegates responsibility with enough flexibility to manage smoothly but she is informed of all the activities on the campus. She only intervenes in situations where there is a deadlock and she has to arbitrate. She said: 'I don't do anything until and unless my services are unavoidable and then I give the suggestion, otherwise, it's the staff that does the job'. The principal runs the school through a vice-principal and three heads. There is considerable dissemination of powers to the heads yet there is firm and strict control by the principal.

A teacher commented:

> It all depends not only on the teachers or the students, the parents are also cooperative and they cooperate with teachers. And our principal is also good; she knows how to manage the school administration from class 1 to post-graduate.

Another said: 'A teacher's conscience, if it is alive, we work. Secondly, devotion to our work and love for our profession, we love teaching and we love our profession.'

When asked to give an example of the working of a committee, the Principal gave the example of the discipline committee:

> It has six members. They come to college before the school is open and they check the uniforms of the students and the cleanliness of the school and then they also check the staff, whether they are in their classes or not. This will be their duty throughout the day till the last student has left the premises.

There were no formal associations between parents and school management. However, the relations were very cordial and contact with the parents was through parent-teacher meetings which could be scheduled any day from 12 noon to 1 p.m. There was no direct funding contribution by parents.

The principal had a high opinion of the school: 'I think Royal School is a good school, not only in Punjab but also in Pakistan.' She added: 'We are comparatively better than many other schools but we should strive to be better and better for which we are working day and night.'

The staff also acknowledged that. One teacher said: 'Our new principal works very hard. She would like our school to flourish as it did 20 to 25 years back. She works very hard to achieve that status'.

When the teachers were asked their opinion of a successful school they said it should have qualified staff, good administration, caring and supporting environment, good classes, good students from good backgrounds, good teaching and learning, fewer students in classes, and cooperation of the parents. All this together makes a school successful. When it was pointed out that there were more than fifty to sixty students in a class, the teachers said that their credibility and fame had made it impossible to refuse admissions. But at the same time, their love for this institution had bound them to 'go that extra mile' and they worked very hard, staying late in the evenings, checking copies, and maintaining the standard of the institution. Their love for the institution and tradition seemed to overcome whatever challenges they were facing.

Initiatives by the Principal

Although the principal had joined the school only recently, her previous experience in the school had given her an advantage and she started many new initiatives. It is part of her personality for she is quite dynamic and as she acknowledged: 'I always look for good opportunities. I always struggle for them and, fortunately, I am successful.' She had started 'O' level classes and 'A' level was to begin soon. A four-year B.Sc. Computer Science course had been initiated and the college had been upgraded to a Master's level.

Keeping in mind the traditions of her school in developing the students holistically, she was keen to introduce drawing and music:

> I am also about to start the drawing classes and if possible the music classes. These kinds of subjects I have in mind that I must do something to take new staff in these subjects, I mean specialists. Commerce is also an important subject of the day. I am also thinking about starting the commerce classes in the school this year. This is what I have in my plans, I hope, God willing, I succeed.

Regarding school development planning, the preparation of the budget is the first stage and it is planned for three years. The process adopted is to first do a needs analysis through the section heads who review and report back on needs such as furniture, library books, tube lights, fans, repairs, white washing, cementing, painting, glass windows etc. The budget is then prepared with an estimate of how much they spent last year and how much they will spend this year.

School development planning became an important feature of the institution last year. They started making plans for the institution with many projects in the budget that should improve the standard of all sections: 'For the juniors we will buy a few things like swings, see-saw and we will change the gates of the college, we have a lot of plans for the senior, for the junior, and for the college section.'

Tradition at Royal School

An important theme that emerged from this research was the importance of tradition at Royal School and the particular attachment to the school of the principal, all head teachers, teachers, students, and parents. The school places high emphasis on students displaying a sense of decorum and responsibility, and observing high norms of ethics. Grooming of the girls, especially in their daily endeavours, including handwriting, still continues as it has been done for a hundred years. It was amazing to see their writing which was neat and legible. The teachers also had good handwriting and have undergone training to improve it. This is a distinguishing characteristic of the school and what needs to be appreciated is that in a class of ninety to ninety-five students, the teachers achieve outstanding results.

One of the traditions very closely followed is the annual crowning of Miss Royal School. The criteria to qualify for Miss RS is that she must secure outstanding results, i.e., secure the first rank throughout from class 1 to class 10 and she must have exceptional qualities of 'head and heart'.

The thread that binds this distinct community of learners together is their love for the institution. The school does face a lot of challenges, such as large classes, but the teachers go out of their way to manage them. Overall, this research has enriched our experience and taught us that tradition and love for the institution can make a successful school.

CASE STUDY 3: CENTRAL SCHOOL

Central School is a private school in the southern part of Karachi, the largest city and commercial capital of Pakistan. Karachi is a cosmopolitan city of about 13 million people whose economic backgrounds range from the affluent to the extremely poor. English is widely spoken by the literate members of the society, though Urdu is most commonly used. The residents of Karachi are engaged in a wide range of industrial businesses and trade.

PECHS, where Central School was located, is a residential suburb mainly occupied by the upper middle class of society. Within a 5 mile radius of the school, there are at least twenty other schools. It is co-educational with kindergarten, junior, and senior sections in different buildings. At the time of the research all three sections were housed in former residential houses, hence their location in three different places. The school was twenty-two years old and was started in 1981 in another residential house on the south side of the city. It moved to its current location in 1986. Plans were underway for 2004 to relocate the school once more to new premises that would see all sections located on the same purpose-built campus.

The school followed the British Curriculum (GCE 'O' Level) and had plans, in collaboration with two other schools, to offer the GCE 'A' levels in fourteen subjects. This new set-up would be housed separately near the new campus facility. Students came from a wide range of suburbs in Karachi (as far as 15 kilometers away) and they got to school either by buses provided by the school or family cars.

The principal and teachers believed that grades and the mere completion of the syllabus was never a true indication of a child's ability. They primarily promoted on-going and formative assessment and felt that teaching for exams only would not help them in adhering to their philosophy.

The school ensured that admission did not disadvantage anyone so it was open to all. The students were mostly from middle and upper-middle class families. A total of seven students (two in junior and five in senior) had special needs and were taught inclusively within the mainstream. There were thirty classrooms and seventy-one teachers. Overall the teacher-student ratio for the school was 1:10.

An interesting point was that almost half (thirty-four out of seventy-one) of the teachers were parents of students attending the school. English was the medium of instruction and all students comfortably spoke English. Importantly, despite English being the instructional language, the principal had established a non-profit organization named 'The Book Group' to publish books in Urdu. According to the principal, the manner in which Urdu language was dealt with in the curriculum prescribed by the government did not allow students to be imaginative, creative or critical of the literature or the language.

Student absenteeism was minimal with only one or two students absent each day. Most students expressed joy at coming to school every day because they 'enjoy' themselves. Besides this, the parent community was well-educated and regarded it important that their children attend school regularly.

All classes were co-educational with girls and boys sitting together (quite unusual in Pakistan). The average class size was twenty-eight students. This could be attributed to either the lack of physical space or the principal's belief in small class sizes.

The school day began at 7.30 a.m. and ended at 1.30 p.m. Teachers' workload varied from section to section; in kindergarten teachers taught all day while in the junior and senior schools they had an average of five periods per day. Additionally, teachers had co-curricular responsibilities such as student clubs and field trips.

The principal has been the proprietor of the school since its inception. They had a 'parents consultative committee (PCC) which met once a month to discuss the school's progress and new initiatives and proposals. There were approximately twenty parents on this committee, mostly women.

What makes this a successful school?

> Our motto is something from Einstein who says 'Imagination is more important than knowledge...' My role is to redefine education and to translate it at organizational levels. (Principal)

The school was proud of being unconventional. Structures were less important and the students' holistic development through a broad curriculum was more important. Education was viewed as a socialization process. The principal stated: 'My priorities are very clear, I want to take education away from being a chore and exam-oriented and make it a pleasure and something which is in internal lives.'

There were numerous features of this school that were not typical of schools in Pakistan or other developing countries. Some of these were:

- Teacher and student autonomy in practice, policy formulation, and decisions.
- Purpose-driven experimentation with new curriculum, projects, and other initiatives.

- An integrated approach to students' and teachers' holistic development.
- A sense of connection with reality outside the school.

At times we were surprised by the nature of the principal's role. We found him to be quite critical and despite a few successful initiatives his view was that they had not done enough. He would not spare himself from criticism nor other schools, both public and private. Above all, he believed in challenging himself and his colleagues, setting very high standards, never giving up, and being bold.

An important point was establishing priorities and expectations in the school. The principal believed that a good teacher would first of all be a person who knew students as human beings. If a teacher had a very nice course plan, research, and exact training or whatever, that was not necessarily a good teacher. He summed up his philosophy in this way: 'If you want to build a ship, don't herd people together to collect wood and don't assign them tasks and work but rather teach them to long for the endless immensity of the sea. That says it all to me, that is a good teacher.' One of the teachers commented that the lesson planning that they do is geared towards getting the best out of each child and aimed to develop their personalities. Similarly, the principal asserted that 'the process of teaching is a matter of being a good person, plus having very specific learning skills, no question about it!'

One of the teachers said that she would categorize this school as very progressive and during her stay here she had witnessed considerable change for the better. She added:

> What I have really liked about the school is that we give individual attention to the children. Each child is important for us and we try to bring out the hidden potential in each child. At the end of each class we want each child to become a well-rounded person where he realizes his potential and we try to bring out that potential.

The school's priorities were clearly articulated and have been made practical through various mechanisms such as teacher workloads that enabled teachers to perform well. Commenting on teacher workload, the principal said:

> Very reasonable, very reasonable. I think in the senior section the workload is greatest. The average contact period, number of periods in which they have contact [with students] is 15 or 16 periods per week, which is very, very good. It could have been 17 or 18 periods but I think beyond that is not possible...not so good schools will have 24-25 periods per week. Here most of our teachers would be teaching no more than 15-16 contact periods of 45 minutes each per week.

On this issue, one of the teachers said:

> I think the workload is something I can handle very easily. We have time to give individual attention to children like sometimes you know we also have the children who have some kind of problems like earlier on I had a child who had the hearing problem, some kind of impairment and so I can give time to those children and also give time to the weaker students, so it gives me time for doing that.

Talking about the weaker students, most of the teachers indicated that the school was very committed to working with each child. It was also evident that the principal had made a commitment to ensure that each and every child would be looked after and the school was structured to focus on child development.

There were some interesting initiatives in managing peda-gogical processes where the centerpiece was the student. For example, the school recently introduced 'Seminars for Intellectual Development', where the idea was to expose students to names like Darwin and Einstein, famous artists, and famous figures of history. One teacher explained that it gave students 'exposure to get them thinking about social issues, political issues around the world and so on and also we didn't want to examine, there is no exam, [and] there is not even a grading'.

Another example was student research work which was strategically built into a student inventory of skills. According to one of the teachers leading this assignment, students in the senior grades were required to learn how to do research. The school had also introduced it at grade 5 and 6. The teacher said:

> We had topics like the Second World War and the Renaissance period, they do research work then there is a panel set up and they talk about it and I think on the Second World War they even had computer clippings...these are 11-year-olds we are talking about... grade 5 and 6...they are learning so much in the process.

Relations with the learners could be characterized as 'friendly and accessible'. One teacher said: 'friendly' has a connotation which might mean you are not taking them very seriously. It's therefore friendly and having an accessibility which means that they can come and talk to you'.

Students had a range of views on the school. One said: 'teachers over here; you can say anything to them about the school, complain and you know they will not hold it against you'. Another student shared: 'you can say anything you want, your choice and I think the teachers over here are very good too'. However, there were students who did not quite agree:

> I won't say that it's an excellent school. I think it's a good school. The first thing is that teachers are good most of the time, [at times] it happens that students know more than the teachers and sometimes the teachers make it out...so I would say that it's a good school, I would not say it's an excellent school but this school is definitely one of the best schools in Karachi.
>
> ...I think it's a friendly environment, it gives us what we want and I think the teachers are good. They treat us the way we respond to them, the way we behave...it's a good school, I want to stay here and I like it.

Since the school was privately owned, the principal had complete autonomy and no external supervision. In its twenty-two years of existence, government officials had visited only once to ascertain that it met the standards set by the government to operate as a private school.

IMPLICATIONS FOR POLICY AND PRACTICE

Whilst each of the schools is clearly different from the others, the findings of the cross-case analysis revealed a number of characteristics of the three successful schools which have implications for policy and practice.

a) Shared responsibility and accountability for the management of the school is evident. In all cases, we found that the principal delegated significant responsibility to others in the school, e.g. head of department, coordinator, etc. and ensured that accountability accompanied the delegation of responsibility. This produced a sense of shared responsibility for the outcomes of the school by empowering others to make decisions and take appropriate actions, though always within a framework or a set of guidelines provided by the principal. The principals did not abdicate their responsibility but they shared it and then ensured that those given delegated responsibility would be accountable for their decisions and actions.

b) Successful schools have a high degree of autonomy. Whilst the degree of autonomy varied across the schools, it was evident that all principals were involved in school-based management and had power devolved to them. Whilst in Case 3 the principal owned the school and therefore had complete autonomy, in Case 2 the school had been granted autonomy by the Government of Punjab and is an 'autonomous government school'. In Case 1, though the school was part of a large school system in the Northen Areas, for all practical matters it was largely in charge of its own affairs. The finding here is that successful schools are part of decentralized systems of education and have a high degree of autonomy which is consistent with world-wide trends towards decentralization, flattening of bureaucratic structures in education systems and increased focus on school-based management.

c) Effective management of physical resources was a high priority. In all cases we found that the management of physical resources was an important role for the principal—it could be said that 'a good school looks good'. Whether it is the proper maintenance of buildings and grounds, adequate classroom space, the provision of libraries and laboratories or simply clean washrooms it seems that successful schools give high priority to these matters. What is important here is that this aspect of a school is highly visible to all concerned, particularly parents who make decisions about which school to send their children to (in Case 2 the imposing architecture is an important part of the tradition of the school which parents find so attractive). Interestingly, any plans or actual improvements in physical resources such as relocating to new premises (Case 3) or building a boundary wall (Case 1) sends a strong, visible message both inside and outside the school that this school is successful.

d) Teacher management and the management of pedagogy was an important focus. There was a clear and sustained focus on teaching and learning in all three cases and the principals were very much involved in it. Whilst the nature of the principals' involvement varied considerably from Case 1, where the principal was very much 'hands-on' in conducting workshops for teachers, to Case 3 where he was more concerned with the philosophy of the school, they all demonstrated a strong interest in what was happening in classrooms on a daily basis with a particular concern for student achievement in external examinations as an important indicator of success. In fact, this focus on teaching and learning goes beyond management into the realm of 'pedagogical leadership' (Memon and Bana, 2005) which is becoming increasingly recognized as a feature of successful schools around the world.

e) The principal was in touch with everything happening through very effective communication. In all cases, the structures of communication were hierarchical but the nature of the communication was decidedly non-hierarchical and personal. The principals did not 'give orders' to be carried out, as is possible in a hierarchy, but they discussed matters with their staff, students, and parents in ways that allowed diverse views to emerge and be taken into account in decision-making. This form of symmetrical communication results in clearer understanding of meaning than does a 'top-down', hierarchical communication which often results in distortion of meaning through the exercise of power (Habermas, 1984).

f) Parents had open access to the principal but they did not exert control over the school. It was evident in all cases that the schools viewed parents as important stakeholders and they were given opportunities for regular meetings with the principal and through the principal they had access to the teachers, but there was no evidence that parents were given significant roles in the management of the schools. There was a range of approaches to parental interaction with the schools from Case 1 where the SMC provided a great deal of cooperative assistance to the school, to Case 2 where parental interaction was carefully controlled and Case 3 where parents were regarded more as 'part of the problem rather than the solution'. In no case, however, did we find that parents were denied access to the school and particularly when it came to student examination results, all schools provided formal mechanisms to enable parents to discuss issues with the teachers.

g) The principals were dynamic and well-educated individuals with a strong commitment to the school and the profession of education. The finding here is that the principal definitely made a difference in the school. In all cases, the principals were found to be outstandingly dedicated people who had gone to great lengths to get a sound education themselves (two had Master's degrees and one a Ph.D.) before becoming a principal. Though their qualifications were not always in teacher education (only Case 1 demonstrated that) it seems that post-graduate programmes might be important for producing the kind of openness, thoughtfulness, and confidence that a person needs to be an effective principal. Clearly, there are issues here about the recruitment and education of principals for successful schools, though further research is necessary to explore the possible connections between a principal's level of education and commitment to their work.

h) The schools had a broader view of the curriculum than textbooks and classroom learning. In all cases, we found that serious efforts were made to relate the in-school learning of students to the reality of their lives outside of school. This was done in various ways such as students being involved in a programme to uplift some schools in poor areas in Case 3, educational trips to visit other schools and communities in Case 1, and extensive involvement in competitions outside the school in Case 2.

i) The schools engaged in some form of school development or improvement planning. In Case 1, it was quite pronounced and called the School Action Plan with a focus on school improvement on an annual basis. In Case 2, planning was mainly to do with budget forecasting to ensure that ample resources continued to be available in the school and in Case 3, the plan was a complete relocation of the school to new purpose-built premises enabling expansion of the school. Successful schools plan for their future; they do it in different ways and with different emphases but it is clear that they are not satisfied with success in the present. They are searching for success in the future as well and they have a vision of what that might look like.

CONCLUSION

This research sought to identify three successful schools and identify why they are successful. We found that the *person* who was the principal and the *processes* used, both played a very important part in understanding school success. Essentially, we went looking for processes and we found that it was the outstanding personal qualities of the people who were the principals that really caught our attention. They were educational leaders, not just managers, who had a vision of a better school, indeed a better world, and they were able to share it and inspire others to join them in pursuing it. Management processes, strategies, and techniques are important though it is also important to have the 'right people' leading schools. Of course, defining and selecting the right people are problematic issues, for qualities such as commitment, caring, openness, tolerance, vision, and a broad education are just some of those required. It has often been said that such matters should not be considered because they are too difficult to deal with and that 'people cannot be trained' in such things. Let us not take that for granted. If this research is telling us anything of value it is that education systems across the region and the world need to pay more attention to the personal qualities of the people who would be principals of the schools.

NOTES

1. I wish to acknowledge the contribution of the following to the research and writing case studies: Jane Rarieya, Qamar Safdar, Shahzad Mithani, Muhammad Babur, and Rosina Sewani.
2. Lahore and Karachi are the provincial capitals of Pakistan's two major provinces i.e., Punjab and Sindh respectively.
3. Ismailis are a religious sect in Islam.
4. ITREB stands for 'Ismaili Tariqa and Religious Education Board'. It is responsible for looking after the religious formation and education of the Shia Imami Ismaili community in Pakistan.
5. The Professional Development Centre, North is a satellite institution of AKU-IED and is located in Gilgit town in the Northern Areas.

10

Impact and Sustainability of the Whole School Improvement Programme
Fauzia Shamim

INTRODUCTION

Change in schools and schooling practices in Pakistan is often initiated through school improvement projects funded by external change agents such as international donor agencies or non-government organizations working for improving the quality of education in Pakistan. One such organization is the Professional Development Centre of the Institute for Educational Development, Aga Khan University (AKU-IED), located in the Northern Areas of Pakistan. The Professional Development Centre, North (PDCN) was established in Gilgit town in district Gilgit in 1999 with a mission to 'develop and adopt activities and strategies that will lead to improvement in the quality of education in the Northern Areas'.

The PDCN initiated a Whole School Improvement Programme (WSIP) in selected schools in the Northern Areas in 2000. The programme was designed with a focus on the school as a unit of change instead of professional development of individual teachers only, as done in earlier school improvement initiatives in the Northern Areas. A central agenda for WSIP was to work with the three education systems, i.e., government; Aga Khan Education Services (AKES), a large non-governmental organization in Pakistan; and the not-for-profit private schools run by communities, trusts, and smaller non-governmental organizations in the Northern Areas. The aim was to bring about sustainable change in project schools as part of a larger strategy of 'moving' the school systems in the Northern Areas and showing them by example a model for improving the quality of education in schools.

The present study was conducted to investigate the impact of WSIP on school improvement and its sustainability in selected project schools in the Northern Areas of Pakistan.

Before we describe the WSIP, it would be useful to look at the educational and socio-cultural context of Northern Areas to locate the programme in context.

NORTHERN AREAS OF PAKISTAN

The Northern Areas of Pakistan, spread over 72,496 sq. km, have a population of one million people, 91 per cent of whom live in small, isolated villages. There are few basic facilities for social welfare, health care, and education. Though the snow-clad mountains with heights varying from 1000 meters to 8000 meters, were a major tourist attraction till a few years ago, the recent world events, particularly after September 11, have adversely affected the tourism industry in this area. Hence, this remains a poor region of the country. Both the geographical terrain and the extreme cold for most part of the year pose a number of challenges for the local population.

The Northern Areas are divided into five administrative districts, i.e., Gilgit, Ganche, Skardu, Diamer and Ghizer. Metalled roads are few, mainly connecting the big towns only. Hence access to remote parts is difficult and sometimes only possible through jeepable tracks. The government is the biggest education provider in the Northern Areas with 1,371 schools out of a total of 1,648 schools. The private sector mainly comprises schools run by the AKES, Pakistan. However, many educational trusts and community-based organizations are now establishing private schools to meet the educational needs of their specific areas. Some examples are schools run by Olding Development

Organization or supported by Hunza Educational Resource Project. Figure 1 (p. 218) gives a break-up of schools in the Northern Areas according to sector and gender.

WHOLE SCHOOL IMPROVEMENT PROGRAMME

The general aim of WSIP was to improve learning conditions in schools and classrooms for enhanced student outcomes. Specific objectives were identified for input and focused work in six focus areas in project schools (figure 1). These served as guiding principles for the project team. The main principle of WSIP was to treat the school as a unit of training rather than the individual, with the long term aim being the development of effective group dynamics and collegiality amongst teachers, students, and communities for the purposes of ongoing educational dialogue and continuous improvement. (Muhammad et al., 2000:4).

As mentioned earlier, WSIP identified the whole school as the context for change. There was a realization at the outset that each school will present a unique context for change resulting in variability in impact in the six areas identified for improvement in project schools belonging to different school systems. Schools in close proximity to one another were organized into clusters mainly for pragmatic reasons. The project design included three stages: pre-intervention, intervention, and post-intervention or follow-up stage. In the pre-intervention stage, a baseline survey was conducted in all the selected schools to get an understanding of the school conditions. This information was used to help the teams strategize their input in different areas for whole school improvement, and to plan the intervention phase in each school in particular. During the intervention stage, intensive school-based support was provided to all project schools. This included co-planning and co-teaching of lessons and organizing regular workshops on selected topics, every alternate Friday, for teachers of all schools in the cluster. This was supplemented by brief centre-based orientation sessions for all teachers and, more importantly, a formal field-based training programme for head teachers of WSIP schools conducted at PDCN. The Professional Development Teachers (PDTs) from PDCN worked two days a week in each project school to provide school-based support to the teachers and head teachers in achieving project objectives. It was envisaged that during the second year of the project, the PDTs would visit the schools on a fortnightly basis and in the third year, these visits would be further reduced. Thus, support from project team members would be reduced significantly in the post-intervention phase. However, while a few follow-up activities were carried out in some project schools, no systematic programme of follow-up support in the post-intervention phase could be established due to various reasons.

Teachers' learning and their participation in the programme was acknowledged through the award of a formal teacher qualification titled 'Visiting Teachers Certificate' by AKU-IED. The award was given to the participating teachers on the basis of evidence of their participation and involvement through the intervention year of the programme and on fulfilling some additional requirements, such as, writing a reflective paper. During the intervention year, WSIP also provided some material inputs to schools. Resources such as library books and teacher resource bags were provided to build a reading culture in the school and to enable the teachers to develop low-cost, no-cost resources for enhancing their teaching and learning. In addition, a mobile library service was established for participating schools (for further details see Shamim, 2005; Kanji and Ali, 2006).

As mentioned earlier, the model of WSIP focused on six areas for whole school improvement for the holistic development of the child. The level of intervention in each area varied in every school largely due to the school contexts and conditions, for example, in one school (Case 2), WSIP intervention focused mainly on staff development and curriculum enrichment at the primary and pre-primary levels only. However, the implementation process was largely similar for all the project schools.

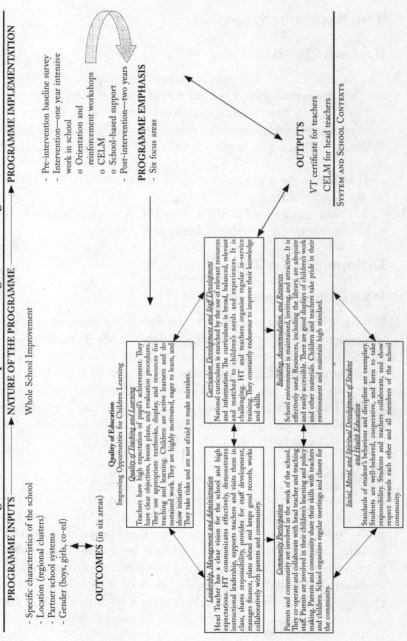

Figure 1: Whole School Improvement Programme—Programme Context

The Research Study

Research Questions

The purpose of the study was to evaluate the impact of WSIP on selected project schools. A second aim of the study was to identify critical factors that facilitate and/or impede sustainability of change efforts in schools in the context of the Northern Areas of Pakistan. Following were the research questions for the study:

1. What is the nature and level of impact of WSIP in varied school contexts?
2. What factors lead to the sustainability of change efforts in schools in the Northern Areas of Pakistan?

Definition of Key Terms

Whole School Improvement

Whole School Improvement is often defined as improvement for 'all learners and all teachers' (e.g. Anderson, 2003). Kanji (2001) identified six dimensions of a school for focused input and improvement for enhancing student outcomes in schools in the Northern Areas (see figure 1). Kanji's framework of Whole School Improvement informed the design and implementation of the WSIP. Hence, it was used in the study for evaluating the impact and sustainability of the programme.

Sustainability

A common experience in developing countries is that most school reform initiatives fade away soon after the exit of the project. While acknowledging the importance of capacity building at the school and systems level for 'continuous improvement' (cf. Fullan, 2005), for the purpose of this research study, sustainability was defined in terms of the continuation of changes initiated by the WSIP, a school reform initiative for improving the quality of student outcomes undertaken in the Northern Areas of Pakistan.

METHODOLOGY

Research Design

Measuring impact and sustainability of change is not easy. Several models and tools have been developed for this purpose, for example, Hall and Hord's 'stages of concern' model (1989), or Earl and Lee's (2000) school improvement index to measure change in a successful school improvement project in Canada. As the focus of WSIP was the school as a unit of change, a case study approach was used (Merriam, 1998) to identify the impact of the programme and its sustainability in selected project schools. Case studies of eight schools from the three educational systems in the Northern Areas, i.e., government, AKES, and private, were undertaken. The sampling criteria included systemic affiliation and the year of WSIP intervention. Gender, regional location, and level of school were used as secondary criteria, wherever possible. The details of sample schools are given in Table 1.

Table 1: Sample Schools for Impact Study of WSIP

System/Year of WSIP Intervention	2000	2001	2002
AKES,P (Private)	CASE 1 Gilgit (Primary, co-ed)	CASE 2 Gilgit (Secondary, girls)	CASE 3 Yasin (Middle, co-ed)
Govt.	CASE 4 Hunza (Primary, co-ed)	CASE 5 Gilgit (Middle, boys)	CASE 6 Skardu (Middle, boys)
NGO (Private)	CASE 7 Gilgit (Primary, co-ed)	No school was available in this category	CASE 8 Skardu (Middle co-ed)

Data Collection: Methods and Tools

Both quantitative and qualitative data were collected for each case study. Quantitative data was collected about the current profile of the school (number of teachers, students, accommodation and resources etc.) using a fact-sheet filled in by the researcher with assistance from other stakeholders, if required. Qualitative data was collected through observation, interviews, and document analysis. Observation was done in the classroom and at other locations in each school such as playground, resource room, laboratory, staffroom, and head's office. Semi-structured interviews were conducted of the head teacher and the four selected WSIP teachers in each sample school. Additionally, focus group interviews were conducted of volunteer teachers and other stakeholders, i.e., community members (VEC, mothers), system representatives, and students.

Efforts were made to triangulate the data by using multiple methods of data collection (observation, interview, document analysis) and varied perspectives (teachers, head teacher, students, system, and community representatives). The participating schools were informed that the findings of the study would not affect the current or future relationship of these schools with PDCN. Moreover, it was emphasized that the purpose of this impact study was not to evaluate the participating schools but PDCN's programme and model of school improvement.

The members of the research team were supported by the project leader mainly through four research seminars held at different stages of the process, i.e., developing research plan or initiation stage, data collection, data analysis, and writing up.

Data Analysis

Standards and Procedure for Impact Assessment

The issue of what counts as impact has been raised by authors of several recent research studies and position papers on impact and/or evaluation of professional development programmes (e.g. Gusky, 2002; Davies and Preston, 2002; Retallick and Mithani,

2003). The problems of evidencing impact have also been identified by various researchers engaged in the study of impact, mainly of programmes of teacher or professional development (Halai, 2002; Flecknoe, 2002; Burchell, Dyson and Rees, 2002). For evaluating the impact of WSIP, we started with the following question:

> What should we expect to 'see' in a school that would convince us that whole school improvement has taken place or in other words, that WSIP has had an impact?

The guiding principles developed to aid project implementation in the six focus areas of WSIP were used as 'standards' for evaluation of impact in each school. In each case study student outcomes were reviewed within the project framework only (see Figure 1). Impact was calculated on the basis of the relative presence or absence of changes (expected outcomes), in relation to the existing situation at the pre-intervention stage, in each area of intervention.

For each case, the impact of WSIP was identified at two stages of the programme, i.e., during intervention and post-intervention or follow-up stage. PDT's progress reports and interviews of various stakeholders were the main data sources for assessment of impact during the intervention stage of the project. Classroom observation, stakeholders' semi-structured interviews, and documents were used to asses the sustainability of WSIP impact during the post-intervention stage. Impact at each stage was judged by comparing the existing situation at the time of data collection (post-intervention stage) to the conditions and practices during WSIP intervention and the situation prevailing at the pre-intervention stage. This comparative analysis was done to assess the impact of WSIP when, a) the project schools were receiving intensive support from the programme, including rewards and incentives such as resource bags for teachers and formal teacher certification for teachers in WSIP schools; and when b) there was limited or no follow-up support from the programme for continuation of changes introduced during the intervention year. It was assumed that the assessment of WSIP impact at the 'post-intervention' stage would help in assessing the extent to which the changes introduced by WSIP continued in project schools or the sustainability of the programme. Case studies of each school were written by the case researchers. In the second stage, a systematic cross-case analysis was undertaken. This chapter presents the findings of the cross-case analysis of the eight cases in the study.

FINDINGS

WSIP Impact during the Intervention Stage

This section reports the impact of WSIP in its six focus areas during intervention.

Quality of Teaching and Learning

It was found that WSIP had an impact in all the schools during the intervention stage, particularly in the quality of teaching and learning in the classroom despite, with varying degrees of success, the differences in school characteristics. Impact was evident in the accounts of teachers' efforts in using child-centred methodology and in engaging the learners actively, thereby enhancing their learning opportunities in the classroom. It seems that the teachers showed more tolerance for learner errors and stopped the use of corporal punishment for learners for not doing their homework or for making mistakes during their learning in the classroom. The students developed confidence in seeking help from the teacher and peers through asking questions and working in small groups. Success in learning was celebrated through display of children's work in the classroom and showing it to visitors to the school. One of the teachers in a public sector school confessed: 'I feel shy when I look and reflect on the situation of the school which was before WSIP and feel the same about other schools when I compare them with my school now.

I used to reprimand students when I entered any class and mostly gave corporal punishment to students, but now it is changed' (Teacher Interview). Other participating teachers also shared, during their interviews, anecdotes of how their classroom practices had changed due to WSIP during the intervention stage.

Leadership, Management, and Administration

During intervention, it seems that the leadership, management, and administration practices also underwent major changes in each school. All the head teachers participated in the Certificate in Education: Leadership and Management (CELM) programme which seemed to have significantly enhanced their knowledge and skills in this area (see also Madhani, 2003). More importantly, there seemed to be a major shift in attitudes with the heads moving from a very authoritarian style of leadership to a willingness to delegate tasks and authority to other teachers in the school. More emphasis was placed by trained head teachers on information sharing and shared decision-making in systematically organized staff meetings held on a regular basis.

Community Participation

The importance of community mobilization and support was also realized and efforts made in this regard with the help of formal structures such as village education or school management committees, and also through regular and more systematic contact with parents in general and mothers in particular. It was reported that the involvement of mothers in their childrens' learning had affected positively the cleanliness and behaviour patterns of the children. Often the community helped in resolving some of the issues in the school, 'Community helped us a lot, for example our blackboards were repaired by the community members' (Teacher Interview, Case 3). In one school, the mothers made small cushions (seats) for their children to keep them warm in the extreme cold weather conditions.

Curriculum and Staff Development

Curriculum and staff development was a regular feature of WSIP, and formal workshops for teachers' ongoing professional development were held in school clusters for this purpose. More importantly, it seems that the school-based support provided by WSIP motivated the teachers to try out innovative ways of teaching and learning and seek additional support from the PDTs through co-planning, co-teaching, and demonstration lessons, wherever required.

Building, Accommodation, and Resources

Improvement of building, accommodation, and resources was another focus of the programme. Resource room and library were established in all the schools by using the available space more effectively. Washrooms were made functional. Physical environment of the schools was improved through maintaining cleanliness in the classrooms and the whole school, displaying children's work, and planting trees and flowers. Wherever possible, the buildings were white-washed and broken furniture removed from the classrooms. Mats were placed in some classrooms to create space for children to move around easily during group work.

Social, Moral, and Spiritual Development of Students and Health Education

WSIP interventions did not focus explicitly on increasing student achievement levels as reflected in exam results. However, one of the areas identified for intervention was children's physical, behavioural, and moral development. This was done mainly through encouraging the students to take responsibility at the class and school level, making presentations in morning assembly, and engaging them in co-curricular activities such as sports and games. The impact of these efforts was evident in all the schools in the study. The children demonstrated confidence in greeting and talking to visitors during our visit to their schools. When the school was over, they were observed to leave their classes (except for a few exceptions) in an orderly manner. The teachers appreciated students' help in maintaining discipline in the assembly and in the class in the absence of teachers, and in taking care of cleanliness in their school. The parents also reported improved behaviour at home, such as completing home work and taking good care of library books.

To summarize, WSIP seems to have had an impact, during the intervention stage of the programme, in all the schools belonging to the three school systems in the Northern Areas, despite differences in their other characteristics. There was evidence of visible improvement in the learning conditions in project schools and classrooms. This, along with WSIP's focus on the holistic development of the child, seemed to have had a positive impact on students' behaviour. Often, the PDTs and the head also succeeded in mobilizing community support, particularly through the involvement of mothers in their child's education. The impact of WSIP during intervention could be ascribed mainly to the programme's focus on the capacity-building of teachers and head teacher in all project schools through formal programmes/workshops for professional development and school-based support. The school systems 'cooperated' with PDCN in programme implementation by allowing access to their schools and a policy of non-interference during the intervention year. At the post-intervention stage, however, the changes introduced during the intervention stage of the programme were found to have been sustained, at variable levels, in a few schools only. At this point, it is important to note that these changes were sustained, to a greater or lesser extent, in schools from all the three participating school systems. This provides evidence of the potential for success of the programme across varied school contexts and conditions in the Northern Areas of Pakistan.

While there was a positive and noticeable impact on the knowledge, skills, and attitudes of all participating teachers during the intervention stage of the programme, many teachers were found to revert back to their earlier 'routines' and practices after the intervention phase and/or the exit of the programme from their school. Hence, it was decided to take a more in-depth look at the sustainability of impact on learning conditions in the school and classrooms and the capacity of the school head to support changes in a sub-sample of four schools belonging to the two major school systems in the Northern Areas, i.e., AKES and government. The aim was to identify and gain further understanding of school and system level factors that facilitate and/or impede sustainability of change in schools in the context of the Northern Areas of Pakistan.

Post-intervention Stage: Sustainability of Impact of WSIP

A sub-sample of four cases, two WSIP schools each from the two major school systems in the Northern Areas, i.e., private (AKES) and government, were selected for further analysis. The aim was to identify factors that may facilitate and/or impede sustainable change in varied school contexts in the Northern Areas. A comparative analysis of the two schools within each school system was done in terms of learning conditions in the school and classroom. The role of the head teacher and his/her leadership and management practices were also analysed for these schools. Our assumption, based on school improvement literature, was that improvement in both the school context and conditions and knowledge, skills and attitudes of the head teacher would lead to improved learning conditions in the classroom (see Retallick in this book).

A comparative analysis of two AKES schools revealed major differences in the area of accommodation and resources. In contrast, the comparison of two schools in the public sector revealed a striking similarity in the school building, accommodation, and resource availability for teaching and learning. More importantly, major differences were found within the AKES and public sector school systems in the head teachers' understanding and commitment to school improvement as well as the head teachers' individual capacity for school improvement in terms of their biography and current practices. At the time of data collection, for example, WSIP teachers were working as head teachers in the absence of the head teachers trained through WSIP in both the public sector schools. However, in one school, it was found that the previous head teacher, after staying in the school for three years, had left recently for her B.Ed studies. She was known for her hard work and enthusiasm for school improvement, and her ability to motivate the teachers and mobilize the community for supporting changes introduced through WSIP (stakeholders' interviews). The head teacher in the other public sector school, though very enthusiastic about the whole school improvement, did not have an opportunity to consolidate the changes introduced through WSIP due to his transfer from the school soon after WSIP intervention year. Both the head teachers, though having the advantage of being WSIP teachers, were facing difficulties in continuing with the changes instituted by their predecessors. This was more marked in the case of the second head teacher. Also, several teachers had been transferred from this school (Case 5) reducing the group of WSIP teachers from nine during intervention to only four in the first post-intervention year.

A comparative analysis of learning conditions in the four selected schools from the private and public sector also revealed significant improvement in learning conditions in two schools (Cases 2 and 4) belonging to the private and public sectors respectively. Some improvement was also evident in the second private-sector school (Case 1). However, the learning conditions in the second public-sector school (Case 5) seemed to be closer to the pre-intervention stage.

The findings of the present study indicate that while school improvement challenges abound for all schools in the Northern Areas of Pakistan, they are different in nature and scope in relation to the specific school contexts and conditions (also see Shafa, 2003). The challenges of head teachers in WSIP schools ranged from providing basic facilities such as making the washrooms functional and providing clean drinking water for the students to low attendance of teachers and students and lack of resources for teaching and learning. The major challenge for all the head teachers, common across the range of school conditions and contexts represented in the sample schools, was to develop a professional culture in the school. Moving from a traditional hierarchical mindset to collaborative and shared decision-making was not easy. However, it was found to be more manageable for those head teachers who believed in the 'extended' view of leadership espoused by CELM and supported by the PDTs during WSIP intervention year. Sustainable school improvement was also facilitated when the head teacher, as in Case 2 in the present study, could analyse the context quickly and devise and or select strategies for school improvement that were responsive to the specific school (and larger) context (West, Ainscow, and Stanford, 2005).

CRITICAL FACTORS IN WSIP IMPACT AND ITS SUSTAINABILITY

As mentioned earlier, WSIP impact was found to be positive and largely present in all sample schools during the intervention phase. However, a lack of sustainability of this impact was found in the majority of project schools.

Factors Facilitating Sustainability of Change

Individual capacity-building of teachers and heads, head teacher's personal and professional characteristics, support from the community and the schools system were found to be the major factors influencing the level of WSIP impact during the intervention stage. More importantly, it was found that changes introduced by WSIP during the intervention year were sustained only in those schools where the head teacher and/or the system provided intended or unintended support for school improvement to the teachers. These factors are described in detail and discussed in the following sections.

Role of the Head Teacher

The central role of the head in school improvement has been identified by a number of studies in school improvement literature (e.g. Harris, 2001; Hadfield, 2003; West et al., 2005). As mentioned earlier, all head teachers of WSIP project schools were enrolled in a one-year field-based CELM programme, aimed to foster an 'extended view of leadership', during the WSIP intervention year (Madhani, 2003:25). The work of the head teachers was supported by PDTs in each school. A comparison of head teachers' background knowledge and skills revealed major differences in their capacity for leading and supporting school improvement. However, congruence was found between head teachers' personal and professional characteristics and the sustainability of change observed in their schools at the post-intervention stage. More specifically, sustainability of changes introduced by WSIP was found in those schools where the head teacher:

- had a vision for school improvement
- had knowledge and understanding of processes and strategies for school improvement and was consequently able to identify the challenges in school improvement and develop strategies to address them
- took initiative and was proactive in enlisting support of all stakeholders for his/her actions including the community and the wider school system
- had high expectations of students and teachers and worked to raise their confidence and morale
- used existing resources creatively and worked continuously with the system and community to raise additional resources
- could harness support from multiple innovations while ensuring 'programme coherence'.

Thus, it can be concluded that head teachers' personal and professional characteristics were the key factors in the process of school improvement in varied school contexts and conditions in the Northern Areas of Pakistan.

Support from the School System

School is the location where changes are enacted by changed individuals. However, recently, there is also growing evidence of the importance of a systemic orientation to change and the need for 'system thinkers' for sustainability and continuous improvement (Fullan, 2005). In WSIP, the intervention was focused on individual capacity-building of teachers and head teachers within a school which was essentially considered as the unit of change. The head teacher's capacity for supporting change on an ongoing basis was found to be a major determinant for the 'institutionalization' of changes introduced by WSIP (Cases 2 and 4). At the same time, it seemed that the stakeholders found changes that were congruent with the system's view of school improvement (for example, lesson planning and innovative classroom practices) easier to sustain than those that appeared to be in conflict with the goals of the school system.

While attempts were made to negotiate goals for improvement with the school systems at the outset of the project, and later through several formal and informal meetings with system representatives (Kanji, personal communication), very often, a lack of congruence was evident in the aims of the WSIP and policy and procedures at the systems' level (stakeholders' interviews). For example, the WSIP goal was holistic development of the child. In contrast, the participating school systems were more interested in improving exam results.

In schools where the teachers and head teachers were highly enthused, the changes could be sustained even after the exit of the programme. However, in schools with high teacher turnover or head teacher's mobility due to various reasons such as transfer to other schools, only those changes could be sustained that were 'sanctioned' and/or actively encouraged by the school system. For example, one school system insisted that teachers develop lesson plans and meet with parents of weak children to discuss their learning difficulties. Compliance to this policy was reviewed at the time of teachers' annual appraisal. Hence teachers were seen writing lesson plans and meeting with parents in project schools in this system. In contrast, display of student's work, not a system level requirement, was found to continue only in one school where the head teacher actively encouraged the teachers to do so and presented students' work proudly to parents and visitors to the school. In this school, students' work was displayed in the head's office as well as on the school notice boards outside. This indicates that school reform initiatives that fell within the purview of system level thinking about school improvement were supported at systems level and, therefore, continued even after the exit of WSIP from the school.

To summarize, the strong role of the head teacher (past and present) and the (unintended) role of the school system on the nature and level of changes both during intervention and post-intervention stages of the programme were found to be important facilitating factors in the project schools. These were particularly evident at the post-intervention stage when project support was found to be either limited or totally absent in these schools.

Factors Impeding Sustainability of Change

Lack of a Critical Mass

Lack of sustainability of WSIP impact was found particularly in one of the four schools from the public sector (Case 5). It was found that the school did not have a critical mass of WSIP teachers and head teacher to consolidate changes introduced during WSIP intervention in this school (also see, West, Ainscow, and Stanford, 2005). In contrast, such a critical mass was present in the other three schools (Cases 1, 2, and 4).

In schools where the head teacher stayed in the school for one to two years post-intervention, changes in school culture were more visible than in schools where the head teacher had to leave the school soon after the WSIP intervention year. If many WSIP teachers were also transferred from the school along with the head, the teachers left in the school were more likely to revert to 'old ways' due to lack of shared goals for school improvement and limited or no collegial support from their non-WSIP head and colleagues.

Lack of Follow-up Support

Lack of systematic and sustained follow-up support from WSIP team during the post-intervention phase was found to be another important factor affecting the sustainability of WSIP impact. No systematic programme of support for the follow-up phase could be established due to various reasons. Hence, while in some cases the PDTs continued to visit the schools, as scheduled, during the first year of the post-intervention phase, they were unable to use strategically planned procedures for problem identification and develop appropriate response mechanisms to sustain the changes introduced by the programme. In the absence of any agreed guidelines for providing follow-up support, the PDTs mainly engaged in doing 'more of the same' as in the intensive intervention year. In one school, however, attention was paid to the induction of a new head teacher and new teachers in the school into the philosophy of WSIP and its related strategies for whole school improvement mainly at the behest of the PDTs responsible for providing follow-up support in that school.

Absence of a Clear and Shared Vision for School Improvement

'Absence of a clear vision has been shown to lead to confusion, demoralization and failure within much School Improvement work' (Harris, 2000: p. 6). This could be true both at the level of the school and/or the school system. In WSIP, it seems that there was no shared purpose amongst various stakeholders for school improvement. For various reasons, the external change agents, in this case PDCN and PDTs, could not negotiate this successfully with the systems, prior to the WSIP intervention. Consequently, there was conflict between the goals of WSIP and those of the participating systems for school improvement. This was mainly evident in WSIP's focus on holistic development of the child in contrast with the system's exclusive focus on improving school results. This often led to confusion and sometimes even frustration amongst WSIP teachers and head teachers. However, some 'strong' head teachers were able to bring about both visible and sustainable changes in the school environment and in the quality of teaching and learning in the classroom through their high level of commitment and enthusiasm for school improvement, hard work, and through developing a shared vision for school improvement with all the stakeholders. For example in Case 2, the focus on improved school results created shared goals with the system, community, and students and led to synergy in their efforts for school improvement; the system provided new furniture while the community supported the head teacher's efforts for bringing about visible changes in the physical conditions of the school by providing skilled labour for building a boundary wall and through active community participation for planting trees etc. during summer vacations. This and other initiatives within the focus areas of WSIP led to high student morale and a significant increase in student result moving from 27 per cent and 60 per cent result in class nine for Science and Arts sections respectively to 90 per cent and 100 per cent in the next school year (Jamaluddin, 2003:6).

To summarize, important determinants of the sustainability of WSIP impact during the post-intervention phase of the programme were: support from the head and/or the school system, the presence of a critical mass of teachers and/or head, developed through WSIP, and follow-up support from WSIP. Though systematic follow-up support was not provided to the majority of schools for various reasons, wherever available, it facilitated the consolidation of changes introduced during the intervention phase. Many of these factors have also been identified in earlier school improvement literature (e.g. Earl and Lee, 2000; Harris, 2000; Fullan, 2005). At the same time, lack of a critical mass, absence of follow-up support and a shared vision for school improvement were identified as major challenges for sustaining the benefits gained during the intervention stage of the project. However, the present study highlights the need for a two-pronged approach to capacity-building in school improvement projects. There seems to be a need for building capacity of individual teaches and head teachers as well as that of the school system as a whole. Consequently, the aim of improving schools in the

Northern Areas of Pakistan, and in similar contexts elsewhere, will remain elusive till individual capacity-building of teachers and school heads is complemented with a systematic effort to build capacity at the systemic level. Additionally, efforts should be made for bringing together various elements in the school and the school system in ways that are synergistic (cf. Hadfield, 2003).

LESSONS LEARNT AND RECOMMENDATIONS

The following lessons were learnt about school improvement in varied school contexts in the Northern Areas of Pakistan. Many of these lessons are applicable to other schools in Pakistan and elsewhere in other developing countries.

1. Individual capacity-building is necessary for bringing about change at the school/systems' level. However, this needs to be complemented with capacity-building of the school system for sustainability of change efforts introduced during focused intervention from projects such as WSIP.

2. A knowledgeable, strong, and committed head teacher can lead change efforts in the face of odds at different levels including getting the necessary support from the school system. Training programmes for head teachers should, therefore, focus on developing head teachers' knowledge, skills, and attitudes for initiating, supporting, and sustaining school improvement projects such as WSIP.

3. A critical mass is required for innovative practices to take root and influence school culture. In addition, the support of a project is needed beyond the intervention stage for sustainability. It may not be possible to 'control' teacher mobility due to transfers in the government sector and better job opportunities for trained teachers in the private sector. Provision of systematic follow-up support in the post-intervention phase should, therefore, be part of school improvement project design, particularly in contexts similar to the Northern Areas of Pakistan.

4. Innovative practices that are in conflict with the goals and objectives of the community and/or school system are difficult to sustain. In contrast, support and pressure from the community and the system can lead to sustainability of changes introduced by school improvement projects. WSIP was initiated in all the schools, except one, by external change agents from PDCN. WSIP was not successful, despite various efforts in this regard, in engaging the school systems in the processes of whole school improvement on an ongoing basis. Findings indicate that changes that were 'sanctioned' and, consequently, supported by the school system were more sustainable than those which conflicted with the systems' goals and procedures for school improvement. Hence, for purposes of sustainability, negotiation and agreement on shared goals for school improvement is vital before initiating any school improvement project.

5. Monitoring and follow-up of change efforts is necessary for addressing teething problems in implementing innovative practices and preventing 'backsliding' to earlier routines and practices. Schools and school systems need to be facilitated in undertaking monitoring and evaluation activities for the success of school improvement projects.

6. School reform efforts need to focus on 'maintenance' strategies along with 'development' strategies for the success of school improvement initiatives.

CONCLUSION

No school is an island unto itself in the Northern Areas of Pakistan, as in many developing country contexts around the world. Schools are located within school systems and are consequently governed by the policies and decisions made at the systems' level. Thus, it seems that while no school reform effort can be initiated without individual capacity-building of the teachers and head teachers, capacity-building at the systemic level is equally important for school systems to have a stronger role in the school improvement process—from planning and implementation of the intervention to ongoing monitoring and follow-up support for sustainability of change effort and continuous improvement.

The findings of the present study indicate that a bottom-up approach to whole school improvement with support from the 'central office' can lead to more sustainable change than an approach where only the school is considered as the unit of change. It must be remembered that the system emphasis is not aimed at achieving control (which is impossible), but on harnessing the interactive capability of systemic forces. A more integral role of the system is recommended in all school improvement projects, from developing shared purposes and strategies for school improvement to strategic planning for support in the post-intervention phase of these projects.

ACKNOWLEDGEMENTS

I wish to acknowledge the contribution of the research team members in compiling this study. Each team member contributed to the study not only as a case researcher but also through mutual sharing of ideas and discussion of themes for analysis through various stages of the project.

The team included eight team members, four professional development teachers and two research associates from PDCN, one professional development teacher from the government sector in the Northern Areas, and one faculty member from AKU-IED. These are: Abdul Hameed Lone, Abdul Jahan, Bahadur Ali, Mehrunnisa Baig, Muhammad Shakoor, Roshni Kumari, Shamshad Sajid, and Shams-ur-Rehman.

NOTE

1. Adapted form Kanji (2001).

11

Lessons Learnt

Rashida Qureshi and Fauzia Shamim

Schools and schooling practices reflect the lives and realities of the contexts and people in the larger society. People in Pakistan have throughout its short history of sixty years been struggling to improve the life chances of their children through improving the quality of education. However, regrettably there are more stories of failure than success (see Jumani and Iqbal, 2006; Hoodbhoy, 1998; Warwick and Reimers, 1995; and Hayes, 1987 for different reform initiatives and their history). Although the present situation of schools in Pakistan still leaves much to be desired, the research studies presented in the preceding chapters give out a message of 'hope'. This is in sharp contrast to the feelings of 'despair' about the future of education in Pakistan alluded to by Warwick and Reimers (1995) after their extensive research in Pakistani educational institutions more than a decade ago. Hence, this book is a moment for us to rejoice. At the same time it raises the issue of finding ways to upscale these 'success' stories to benefit more children across schools in Pakistan. What can practitioners and policy makers learn from the research studies reported in this book? How can these 'success stories' help improve the life chances of Pakistani children? In this concluding chapter, we will look briefly at the major lessons learnt from research on improving schools and schooling practices in Pakistan and similar contexts elsewhere.

First, it is heartening to note that all the studies reported in the book indicate that individual teachers, despite their weak content knowledge and other resource constraints, are willing to learn and enthusiastic about implementing innovative ideas to improve learning conditions in schools and classrooms for enhanced student outcomes (also see Rizvi and Elliot, 2005). It may be argued that the findings of the small-scale research studies described and discussed in the book are context specific; however, several important lessons for practitioners and policy-makers can be extracted from these research studies. Especially important is the critical look with which the authors, both teachers and teacher educators, have examined some of the strategies for teaching and teacher-education and practices for leadership and school improvement. The issues highlighted need to be considered particularly in upscaling these 'experiments' as well as in introducing other reform efforts in schools and schooling practices in Pakistan and similar contexts elsewhere. The first to consider is the key role of teachers' agency in any innovation or reform effort; but teachers need to be enabled to play this role through opportunities for school-based professional learning with and from their colleagues on an ongoing basis. How can schools and school systems provide support for teachers' ongoing professional development? This question brings us to the equally central role of organizational context and conditions in school improvement: a) teachers and teacher leaders need to be facilitated in their work through creating facilitative instead of bureaucratic structures, and; b) teachers need to be 'nurtured' and supported in their innovative practices at the classroom and school level. Secondly, many reform efforts do not require a huge amount of additional resources. What they do need to be successful is a shared understanding of the nature and purpose of these reforms and the necessary infra-structure required to support their successful implementation at the classroom level. Thirdly, all the evidence in the empirical studies described in the preceding chapters indicates that school improvement strategies and reform efforts need to be adapted for and during practice in different contexts. This requires both strategic planning and a flexible approach whereby local contextual factors are taken into account at the outset instead of being treated as constraints at a later stage; at the same time there should be enough flexibility in the system to respond to and fine-tune or change strategies during the process of implementation. The studies highlight the important role of systematic inquiry on practice and ongoing evaluation and monitoring of reform efforts at all stages, for example, by engaging teachers in action research studies.

Once we recognize that schools and schooling practices should be the hub of reform efforts, the implementation of innovations at classroom and school level takes the centre stage with all efforts and resources, one hopes, zooming in on the teachers and school leaders. According to Sarita and Tomar (2004), 'the process of teaching is at the heart of education and the expertise, pedagogical know-how and organizational and technical competence of teachers are widely considered to be central to educational improvement' (280-281). A recurrent theme throughout the book, especially in Part 1, is the issue of teacher quality in terms of both, content knowledge and pedagogical knowledge and skills. This raises the issue of the role of teacher education in terms of pre-service and in-service training for improving schooling, particularly in a country like Pakistan where the majority of teachers are either untrained or poorly trained (Kirk, 2007; Warwick and Reimers, 1995). Thus a pivotal question that needs to be addressed for school improvement initiatives to succeed is, 'How to prepare teachers for effective teaching and learning in varied contexts?' For a very long time 'Teacher education has suffered from a widespread perception that no special knowledge base is required for teaching; that anyone can teach as long as they understand the mechanics of chalkboard use' (Sarita and Tomar, 2004:4). However, a recent proposal for establishing a four-year Bachelors' degree in Education in Pakistan seems to acknowledge this pressing need for teachers to acquire both a good knowledge base in their own subject area as well as skills for engaging learners in inquiry-based and collaborative learning, in order to develop useful citizens for the twenty-first century. It is widely recognized that novice teachers, once in school, need constant support and facilitation through their induction phase. Similarly, as emphasized by the research studies in all the chapters of this book, more experienced teachers also need continuous support to translate their 'new' learning into improved classroom teaching and learning practices. Also, it seems that teacher leaders such as subject coordinators can play a key role in the continuous professional development of their colleagues.

Head teachers are also amongst the key players in changing schools and schooling practices. As the chapters in Part II point out, leadership is contextual; therefore, the preparation of school leaders has to be based on the needs and requirements of the local context and not on contents dictated by global notions of leadership and management only. A major lesson learnt is that for Pakistani school leaders, the educational management and leadership training programmes need to be cognizant of the skills and resources required for functioning effectively in the 'local' context. Such an endeavour necessitates taking stock of local practices and strategies, a research area where a small database is emerging (Khaki, 2005; Shafa, 2003).

Any discussion of schools and schooling practices would be incomplete without students, because the whole purpose of improving schools and subsequently raising the standards of education is to benefit the end-users, i.e., the students. Unfortunately, virtually no studies are available that give 'voice' to the students' feelings and concerns with regard to schools and schooling practices in Pakistan and other developing countries and, therefore, a gap in this regard is very noticeable. A discerning reader would also have noticed the same gap in this book. How students can be made more visible and more active participants in school-based reform should, thus, be given priority as future research agenda by organizations committed to school improvement such as the Aga Khan University, Institute for Educational Development.

Research-based evidence collected in this book indicates success in small-scale studies conducted at school level. To upscale these efforts, schools and school systems need to think about ways of helping one another through building alliances for promoting professional development of their teachers, teacher educators and school leaders (see Farah and Jaworski, 2006; Farah and Rettalick, 2000 for examples). Some of the possible mechanisms include the formation of professional associations, school networks and other forms of partnerships (cf. Babar, Sarwar, and Safdar, 2005). Similarly, the recently completed professional development component of the Education Sector Reform Assistance project in Pakistan provides a good example of improving schools and schooling practices through partnership with NGOs for training of in-service teachers and head teachers in Sindh and Balochistan (ESRA, 2005).

A to Z References
(All Chapters)

A

Abdulalshoev, K. (2000). A study of head teacher's role in managing financial resources. Unpublished Master's thesis submitted to the Aga Khan University-Institute for Educational Development, Karachi, Pakistan.

Adams, R.S., and Biddle, B.J., (1970). *Realities of Teaching*. New York: Holt Rinehart, Winston.

Ali, M.A. (2000). *Enabling a Mathematics Teacher to Teach for Conceptual Understanding*. Unpublished Master's thesis submitted to the Aga Khan University-Institute for Educational Development, Karachi, Pakistan.

Apple, M.W. and Beane, J.A. (1995). *Democratic School*. Alexandria, Virginia: Association for Supervision and Curriculum Development.

Ashcroft, K. (1992). Working Together: Developing Reflective Student Teachers. In C. Biott and J. Nias (Eds.), *Working and Learning Together for Change* (pp. 33-45). Buckingham: Open University Press.

Avalos, B., and Aylwin, P. (2007), How Young Teachers Experience their Professional Work in Chile, *Teaching and Teacher Education*, 23 (4):515-28.

B

Babar, S.A., Sarwar, Z. and Safdar, Q. (2005). Networks of Learning: Professional Associations and the Continuing Education of Teachers, in J. Retallick, and I. Farah, (Eds.)(2005). *Transforming Schools in Pakistan: Towards the Learning Communities*. Oxford University Press, Pakistan: 215-45.

Ballard, T. I. (2001). Coaching in the Classroom. *Teaching and Change*, 8 (2), 160-75.

Ball, D.L. (2000). Bridging Practices: Intertwining Content and Pedagogy in Teaching and Learning to Teach. *Journal of Teacher Education*, 51 (3), 241-7.

Ball, D.L. (1988). *Research on Teaching Mathematics: Making Subject Matter Knowledge Part of the Equation*. NCRTL (special report). Michigan State University. [Online] Available: http://ncrtl.msu.edu/full.htm.

Ball, S.J. (1987). *The Micro-politics of the School: Towards a Theory of School Organization*. London: Methuen.

Barber, B.R. (1984). *Strong Democracy*. Berkeley, Los Angeles: University of California Press.

Barrow, R. (1989). Curriculum Theory and Values. In N. Entwistle (Ed.), *Handbook of Educational Ideas and Oractices*. (pp. 110-17). London: Routledge.

Bartlett, S. (1998). Teacher Perception of the Purpose of Staff Appraisal: A Response to Kyriacou. *Teacher Development*, 2, 3, 479-90.

Bauersfeld, H. (1992). Classroom Cultures from a Social Constructivist's Perspective. *Educational Studies in Mathematics, 23*, 467-81.

Beattie, M. (2002). Educational Leadership: Modelling, Mentoring, Making and Remaking a Learning Community. *European Journal of Teacher Education, 25*, 199-221.

Begum, A. (2004). A Study of a Head Teacher's Perceived and Performed Roles in a Community School in Karachi, Unpublished Master's thesis submitted to the Aga Khan University-Institute for Educational Development, Karachi, Pakistan.

Bennet, B., Rolheiser-Bennet, C. and Stevahn, L. (1991). *Cooperative Learning, where Hearts meet Minds.* Toronto: Educational Connections.

Bergman, J. and Mohammad, M. (1998). Primary and Secondary Education-structural Issues, in Hoodbhoy, P (ed), *Education and the State: Fifty Years of Pakistan*, 68-101, Karachi: Oxford University Press.

Biddulph, F., Symington, D., and Osborne, R., (1986). The Place of Children's Questions in Primary Science Education. *Journal of Research in Science and Technological Education, 4.* (1), 77-87.

Borko, H. and Putnam, R.T. (1995). Expanding a Teacher's Knowledge Base: A Cognitive Psychological Perspective on Professional Development. In T.R. Guskey and M. Huberman (Eds.), *Professional Development in Education: New Paradigms and Practices.* New York: Teachers College Press.

Brooks, J.S., Scribner, J.P., and Eferakorho, J. (2004). Teacher Leadership in the Context of Whole School Reform, *Journal of School Leadership*, 14, 242-65.

Brown, G.A and Edmondson, R. (1996) Asking Questions. In E.C. Wragg. (Ed.). *Classroom Teaching Skills.* London: Routledge.

Brown, G., and Wragg, E.C., (1993) *Questioning.* London: Routledge.

Burchell, H. and Dyson, J. and Rees, M. (2002) Making a Difference: A Study of the Impact of Continuing Professional Development on Professional Practice. *Journal of In-service Education, 28*, (2), 2002.

Burgess, R. (1988). *A Head Teacher at Work during the Teachers' Dispute.* Paper presented at the Histories and Ethnographies of Teachers' Conference, Oxford.

Burn, K., Hagger, H., Mutton, T., and Everton, T. (2000). Beyond Concerns with Self: The Sophisticated Thinking of Beginning Student Teachers. *Journal of Education for Teaching*, 26(3), 259-78.

C

Carr, W. (1995). *For Education: Towards Critical Education Inquiry*. Buckingham: Open University Press.

Carr, W. and Kemmis, S. (1986) *Becoming Critical: Education, Knowledge and Action Research*. London: Falmer Press.

Carson, T., and Sumara, D. (1997). *Action Research as a Living Practice*. New York: Peter Lang.

Carter, M., and Francis, R. (2001). Mentoring and Beginning Teachers' Workplace Learning. *Asia-Pacific Journal of Teacher Education*, 29(3), 249-62. Chancellors Commission Report (1994). The future of the Aga Khan.

University Evolution of a Vision. Karachi: The Aga Khan University. Chembere, A. (1995). Classroom Action Research and Teacher Development. Unpublished Master's thesis submitted to the Aga Khan University-Institute for Educational Development, Karachi, Pakistan.

Cobb, P. (1986) *Context, Goals, Beliefs and Learning Mathematics* For the Learning of Mathematics, 6(2), 2-9.

Cochran-Smith, M. and Lytle, S. L. (1993). Communities for Teacher Research: Fringe or Forefront? In M. Cochran-Smith and S. L. Lytle (Eds.), *Inside Outside: Teacher Research and Knowledge*. New York: Teachers College Press.

Cohen, L., Manion, L., and Morrison, K., (2000). *Research Methods in Education* (5th ed). London: Falmer Press.

Cohen, L., and Manion, L., (1989). *A Guide to Teaching Practice* (3rd Ed). London: Routledge.

Cole, A.L. (1997). Impediments to Reflective Practice: Toward a New Agenda for Research on Teaching. *Teachers and Teaching: Theory and Practice*, 3(1), 7-27.

Collier, S.T. (1999). Characteristics of Reflective Thought during the Student Teaching Experience. *Journal of Teacher Education*, 50(3), 173-81.

Connelly, F.M. and Clandinin, D.J. (1988). *Teachers as Curriculum Planners: Narratives of Experience*. Ontario: Ontario Institute for Studies in Education.

Cooper, B., and Dunne, M. (2000). *Assessing Children's Mathematical Knowledge, Social Class, Sex and Problem Solving*. Buckingham: Open University Press.

Cotton, K. (1999). *School Improvement Research Series (SIRS)*, http://www.nwrel.org/scpd/sirs/3/cu5.html.

Crowther, F., Ferguson M., Kaagan, S.S. and Hann, L. (2002). *Developing Teacher Leaders: How Teacher Leadership Enhances School Success*, North America: Crown Press.

Cuban, L. (1996). Curriculum Stability and Change. In P. W. Jackson (Ed.), *Handbook of Research on Curriculum* (pp. 216-47). New York: Simon & Schuster Macmillan.

Cubin, P., Featherstone, D., and Russell, T. (1997). Voice of Critical Friends Reflecting on Teaching and Learning Experiences. In D. Featherstone, H. Munby and T. Russell (Eds.), *Finding a Voice While Learning to Teach.* (pp. 137-57). London: The Falmer Press.

Cullingford, C., (2006). Mentoring as Myth and Reality: Evidence and Ambiguity. In C. Cullingford (Ed.), *Mentoring in Education: An International Perspective.* Ashgate: England.

D

Davies, R. and Preston, M. (2002) An Evaluation of the Impact of Continuing Professional Development on Personal and Professional Lives. *Journal of In-service Education*, 28 (2), pp. 231-54.

Day, C. (1999). *Developing Teachers: The Challenges of Lifelong Learning.* Norwich: The Falmer Press.

Day, C.W. (1993). Reflection: A Necessary but not Sufficient Condition for Professional Development. *British Educational Research Journal*, 19(1), 83-93.

Dean, B., Joldoshalieva, R. and Kizilbash, M. (2005). Researching Practice, Practicing Research: Impact on Teaching and Learning. *Journal of Educational Research*, 8(1):30-9.

Dean, J. (1991). *Professional Development in School.* Philadelphia: Open University Press.

Denvir, H., Askew, M., Brown, M. and Rhodes, V. (2001). Pupil Participation in Interactive Whole Class Teaching. In M. H. Panhuizen (Ed.) *Proceedings of the 25th Conference of the International Group for the Psychology of Mathematics Education.* Vol. 2, 337-44. Utrecht: The Freudenthal Institute.

Dillon, J.T. (1988). *Questioning and Teaching: A Manual of Practice,* London: Croom Helm.

Dobbins, R. (1996). The Challenge of Developing a 'Reflective Practicum', *Asia-Pacific Journal of Teacher Education*, 24, 269-80.

E

Earl, L. and Lee, L. (2000). Learning, for a Change: School Improvement as Capacity building. *Improving Schools*, 3(1), 30-8.

Early, P. (2003). Leaders or Followers? Governing Bodies and their Role in School Leadership, *Educational Management and Administration*, 31(4), 353-67.

Edwards, C., and Mercer, N. (1987). *Common Knowledge: The Development of Understanding in the Classroom.* London: Routledge.

Elliot, J. (1991). *Action Research for Educational Change.* London: Open University Press.

Elliott, J. (1981). Developing Hypotheses about Classrooms from Teachers' Practical Constructs: An Account of the Work of the Ford Teaching Project. *Interchange*, 7, (2), Ontario Institute for Studies in Education.

Elliot, J. (1978). What is Action Research in Schools? *Journal of Curriculum Studies*, 10, 355-7.

Eraut, M. (1994). *Developing Professional Knowledge and Competence*. London: The Falmer Press.

Ernest, P. (1994). Social Constructivism and the Psychology of Mathematics Education. In P. Ernest (Ed.) *Constructing Mathematical Knowledge: Epistemology and Mathematics Education (pp. 62-72)*. London: Falmer Press.

ESRA-Pakistan. (2005). Technical Report on Teacher Behaviour, Student Achievement and Head Teachers' Performance. Evaluation Unit, Islamabad.

Eyre, D. and Marjoram, T. (1990). *Enriching and Extending the National Curriculum*. London: Kogan Page.

F

Farah, I. and Jaworski, B. (Eds.) (2006). *Partnerships in Educational Development*. Oxford: Symposium Books.

Feiman-Nemser, S., and Parker, M. B. (1990). Making Subject Matter Part of the Conversations in Learning to Teach. *Journal of Teacher Education*, 41, 32-43.

Feldman, A. and Atkin, M. (1995) Embedding Action Research in Professional Practice. In S. Noffke and R. Stevenson (Eds.) *Educational Action Research: Becoming Practically Critical*. New York: Teachers College Press.

Fendler, L. (2003). Teacher Reflection in a Hall of Mirrors: Historical Influences and Political Reverberations. *Educational Researcher*, 32 (3), 16-25.

Fidler, B. (1997). School Leadership: Some Key Ideas. *School Leadership* and *Management*, 17, 23-37.

Flecknoe, M. (2002) Measuring the Impact of Teacher Professional Development: Can it be Done?, *European Journal of Teacher Education*, 25, 2&3, pp. 119-34.

Fraidonov, F. (2004). Understanding a Principal's Role in Managing Financial Resources in a Private School in the Context of Pakistan. Unpublished Master's thesis submitted to the Aga Khan University-Institute for Educational Development, Karachi, Pakistan.

Freire, P. (1970). *Pedagogy of the Oppressed*. New York: The Seabury Press.

Fullan, M. (2005). *Leadership and Sustainability: System Thinkers in Action* Thousand Oaks, California: Corwin Press and Ontario Principals' Council.

Fullan, M. (2002). The Change Leader. *Educational Leadership*, 59(8), 16-20.

Fullan, M. (1991). *The New Meaning of Educational Change*. Toronto, ON: OISE Press.

G

Galton, M.J., Simon, B., and Croll, P., (1980). *Inside the Primary Classroom.* London: Rutledge.

Geraldine, H. (1997). The Industrial Relations of Appraisal: The Case of Teachers, *European Journal of Analysis, Policy and Practice,* 28 (3), 206-20.

Glover, D., Gleeson, D., Gough, G., and Johnson, M. (1998). The Meaning of Management: The Development Needs of Middle Managers in Secondary Schools. *Educational Management and Administration,* 26, 276-92.

Gorodetsky, M., Keiny, S. and Hoz, R. (1997) Conceptions, Practice and Change. *Educational Action Research,* 5 (3).

Goodwin, S.S., Sharp G.W., Cloutier, E. F., and Diamond, N. A. (1999). Effective Classroom Questioning. USA, University of Illinois: Urbana-Champaign.

Government of Pakistan, Ministry of Education (2001). Education Sector Reforms. Islamabad.

Graue, M.E. and Walsh, D.J. (1998). *Studying Children in the Context.* London: Sage.

Gray, J. (2002). Training for Reflective Practice: Getting the Most out of Pre-service Courses. *The Teacher Trainer,* 14 (1), 14-18.

Gray, W.A., and Gray, M.M. (1985) Synthesis of Research on Mentoring Beginning Teachers. *Educational Leadership,* 43 (3), 37-43.

Greaney, V. and Hasan, P. (1998). Public Examinations in Pakistan: A System in Need of Reform. In Hoodbhoy (Ed.), 136-76.

Gregory, M. (1996). Developing Effective College Leadership for the Management of Educational Change, *Leadership and Organization Development Journal,* 17(1), 46-51.

Groundwater-Smith, S. and Dadds, M. (2004). Critical Practitioner Enquiry: Towards Responsible Professional Communities of Practice (pp. 238-63). In C. Day and J. Sachs (Eds.), *International Handbook on the Continuing Professional Development of Teachers.* Maidenhead, England: Open University Press.

Gunter, H.M. (2002). Teacher Appraisal 1988-1998: A Case Study. *School Leadership* and *Management,* 22, 61-72.

Gusky, T.R. (2002). Does it Make a Difference? Evaluating Professional Development. *Educational Leadership,* March 2002, pp. 45-51.

H

Habermas, J. (1984). *The Theory of Communicative Action,* Vol. 1. Boston: Beacon Press.

Hadfield, M. (2003). Capacity Building, School Improvement and School Leaders, in D. Hopkins, M. Hadfield, A. Hargreaves and C. Chapman (Eds.), *Effective Leadership for School Improvement.* London and New York: Routledge Flamer Press.

Hagger, H., Burn, K., and McIntyre, D. (1993). *The School Mentor Handbook: Essential Skills and Strategies for Working with Student Teachers.* Oxford: Kogan Page Ltd.

Halai, A. (2006). Mentoring In-service Teachers: Issues of Role Diversity. *Teaching and Teacher Education,* 22(6), 700-10.

Halai, A. and Anderson, S. (2005). Case Studies of School Improvement in Pakistan. Unpublished research report. Karachi: Aga Khan University-Institute for Educational Development.

Halai, A. (2002). Impact of Teacher Education Inputs: A Systematic Review. Paper presented at the School Improvement Conference, Kampala, Uganda, November 2002.

Halai, A. (2001). Role of Social Interactions in Students' Learning of Mathematics in Classrooms in Pakistan. Doctoral dissertation submitted to the Oxford University, Department of Educational Studies, UK.

Halai, A. (1999). Mathematics Education Project: Teaching Teacher Development through Action Research. In O. Zaslavsky (Ed.), *Proceedings the 23rd Conference of the International Group for the Psychology of Mathematics Education.* (pp. 65-72). Israel: Israel Institute of Technology.

Halai, A. (1998). Mentor, Mentee, and Mathematics: A Story of Professional Development. *Journal of Mathematics Teacher Education,* 1(3), 295-315.

Halai, A., Ali, A.M., Kirmani, N. and Mohammad, F.R. (2003). *On-going Impact of the 'Advanced Diploma in Education: Mathematics'.* Paper presented at the Impact: Making a Difference Conference, Karachi.

Hall, G.E. and Hord, S.M. (2001). *Implementing Change: Patterns, Principles and Potholes.* Boston, Allyn and Bacon.

Haque, K. (2002). A Study of the Possibilities and Challenges of Mentoring. Unpublished Master's thesis submitted to the Aga Khan University-Institute for Educational Development, Karachi, Pakistan.

Harlech-Jones, B., Baig, M., Sajid, S. and ur-Rahman, S. (2005). Private Schooling in the Northern Areas of Pakistan: A Decade of Rapid Expansion. *International Journal of Educational Development* 25, 557-68.

Harlen, W. and Holroyd, C., (1997). Primary Teachers Understanding of Concepts of Science: Impact on Confidence and Teaching. *International Journal of Science Education* 19(1) 93-105.

Harris, A. (2002). *School Improvement: What is in it for Schools?* UK: Routledge.

Harris, A. (2001). Building the Capacity for School Improvement. *School Leadership and Management,* 21(3), 261-70.

Harris, A. (2000). What Works in School Improvement? Lessons from the Field and Future Direction. *Educational Research,* 42(1), 1-11.

Hayes, L.D. (1987). *The Crisis of Education in Pakistan.* Pakistan: Vanguard.

Helsby, G. (1999). *Changing Teachers' Work.* Bristol, PA: Open University Press.

Holly, M.L. (1994). *Keeping a Personal-Professional Journal.* Victoria: Deakin University Press.

Hoodbhoy, P. (1998). Out of Pakistan's Educational Morass: Possible? How? In P. Hoodbhoy (Ed.), *Education and the State: Fifty Years of Pakistan* (pp. 1-22). Karachi: Oxford University Press.

Hoodbhoy, P. (1998). *Education and the State: Fifty Years of Pakistan.* Karachi: Oxford University Press.

Hopkins, D. (2002). *Improving the Quality of Education for All.* Second edition. London: David Foulton Publishers.

Hopkins, D., Ainscow, M., and West, M. (1994). *School Improvement in Era of Change.* London: Cassell.

I

Ishmatov, A. (2000). A study of a school professional development activities with particular reference to the role of the principal in ensuring effective professional development. Unpublished Master's thesis submitted to the Aga Khan University-Institute for Educational Development, Karachi, Pakistan.

J

Jackson, D.S. (2000). The School Improvement Journey: Perspectives on Leadership, *School Leadership and Management*, 20(1), 61-78.

Jackson, W. (1995). *Methods: Doing Social Research.* Ontario: Prentice-Hall.

Jamaluddin (2003) The Positive Changes at the Aga Khan D.J. Girls High School, Danyore, Gilgit. Paper presented at the School Improvement Conference, Uganda.

Jaworski, B. (1996). The Implications of Theory for a New Master's Programme for Teacher Educators in Pakistan. In C. Brock (Ed.), *Global Perspectives on Teacher Education* (pp. 65-76). Oxford: Triangle Books.

Johnson, D.W., Johnson, R.T., and Houlbec, E.J. (1993). *Circles of Learning Cooperation in the Classroom* (4th Ed.), Edina, Mn: Interaction.

Joyce, B., Calhoun, E., and Hopkins, D. (1999). *The New Structure of School Improvement: Inquiring Schools and Achieving Students.* Buckingham: Open University Press.

Joyce, B., Calhoun, E. and Hopkins, D. (1998). *Models of Teaching: Tools for Learning.* Buckingham: Open University Press.

Jumani, N.B. and Iqbal, P. (2006). Teacher Education in Pakistan: An Overview, *Pakistan Review of Education*, 23(1), 105-117.

K

Kabylov, T.B. (2003). Exploring the Contribution of Mentoring in Improving Teaching and Learning. Unpublished Master's thesis submitted to the Aga Khan University-Institute for Educational Development, Karachi, Pakistan.

Kanji, G. (2001) The Whole School Improvement Programme: A Case Study. Gilgit: Professional Development Centre, North. Unpublished report.

Kanji, G. and Ali. T. (2006). School Improvement: A Case from the Northern Areas in Pakistan (pp. 193-206). In I. Farah and B. Jowarski (Eds.).

Kanu, Y. (1996). Educating Teachers for the Improvement of Quality of Basic Education in Developing Countries. *International Journal of Educational Development*, 16(2), 73-184.

Kemmis, S. and McTaggart, R. (1988). *The Action Research Planner*. Geelong: Deakin University Press.

Kemmis, S., McTaggart, R. and Retallick, J. (2004). *The Action Research Planner*. Karachi: Aga Khan University-Institute for Educational Development.

Kemmis, S. and Wilkinson, M. (1998). Participatory Action Research and the Study of Practice. In B. Atweh, S. Kemmis and P. Weeks (Eds.), *Action Research in Practice*. London and New York: Routledge.

Kelly, A.V. (1999). *The Curriculum: Theory and Practice*. London: Paul Chapman Publishing Ltd.

Kekale, J., (1998). Academic Leaders and the Field of Possibilities. *International Journal of Leadership in Education*, 1, 237-55.

Kerry, T. (1982). *Effective Questioning: a Teaching Skills Workbook*. Basingstoke: Macmillan Education.

Khaki, J.A. (2005). Exploring the Beliefs and Behaviours of Effective Head Teachers in Government and Non-governement Schools in Pakistan. Unpublished doctoral dissertation, Department of Curriculum, Teaching and Learning, Institute for Studies in Education, University of Toronto: Canada.

Khamis, A. (2000). The Various Impacts of the Institute for Educational Development in its Cooperating Schools in Pakistan. Unpublished doctoral dissertation, University of London, London.

Khan, B. (2005). The Principal's Role in Creating Conditions for Teachers to Undertake Leadership Roles. Unpublished Master's thesis submitted to the Aga Khan University-Institute for Educational Development, Karachi, Pakistan.

Khan, G. (2005). Exploring Principal-Student Relationships in a Private Secondary School in Pakistan. Unpublished Master's thesis submitted to the Aga Khan University-Institute for Educational Development, Karachi, Pakistan.

Khan, H.K. (2002). Exploring the Contribution of Mentoring in Improving Teaching and Learning. Unpublished Master's thesis submitted to the Aga Khan University-Institute for Educational Development, Karachi, Pakistan.

Khan, M.A. (2005). The Influences of Performance Appraisal on Teachers' Professional Development: A Case Study of a Private School in Karachi, Pakistan. Unpublished Masters' thesis, Karachi: The Aga Khan University-Institute for Educational Development.

Khan, S. (2003). A Study of Principal's Role as an Effective Educational Leader. Unpublished Master's thesis submitted to the Aga Khan University-Institute for Educational Development, Karachi, Pakistan.

Khan, S.R. (2005*). Basic Education in Rural Pakistan: A Comparative Institutional Analysis of Government, Private and NGO Schools*. Karachi: Oxford University Press.

Khan, S.T. (2005). Exploring the Co-relation of a Head Teacher's Decision-making and her Prior Professional Experiences in Dealing with Challenges in the Initial Years of Headship. Unpublished Master's thesis submitted to the Aga Khan University-Institute for Educational Development, Karachi, Pakistan.

Kizilbash, H.H. (1998). Teaching Teachers to Teach. In P. Hoodbhoy (ed.) *Education and the State: Fifty Years of Pakistan* (pp. 102-135). Karachi: Oxford University Press.

L

Lakatos, I. (1976). *Proofs and Refutations*. Cambridge: Cambridge University Press.

Lalwani, F.A. (1999). A Study of the Impact of the Mentoring Process on Primary Teachers' Professional Development in District Lasbella, Balochistan. Unpublished Master's thesis submitted to the Aga Khan University-Institute for Educational Development, Karachi, Pakistan.

Leask, M., and Terrell, I. (1997). *Development Planning and School Improvement for Middle Managers*. London: Kogan Page.

Little, J.W. (1990). The Persistence of Privacy, Autonomy and Initiative in Teachers' Professional Relations. *Teachers Professional Relations*, 91(4), 509-36.

Loughran, J. and Russell, T. (2002) *Improving Teacher Education Practices Through Self-study*. London: Routledge, Falmer.

M

Madhani, N. (2003). Impact on Head Teachers' Role Perceptions and Professional Practice of the Certificate in Education Management, Northern Areas of Pakistan. Unpublished dissertation for MBA in Education, Leicester University, UK.

Maksutova, K. (1999). Study of Head Teachers Management Practices: A Comparative Perspective. Unpublished Master's thesis submitted to the Aga Khan University-Institute for Educational Development, Karachi, Pakistan.

Mangin, M.M. (2005). *Designing Instructional Teacher Leadership Positions: Lessons Learned from Five School Districts*. Paper presented at the annual meeting of the American Educational Research Association, Montreal, Canada.

Mawdsley, J. (1992). Learning to Help Others. In C. Biott, and J. Nias (Eds.), *Working and Learning Together for Change* (pp. 86-90). Buckingham: Open University Press.

McGarvey, B., Marriot, S., Morgan, V., and Abbot, L. (1997). The Role of Core Subject Coordinator in Supporting Differentiation in Northern Ireland Primary Schools. *School Leadership and Management*, 17, 375-386.

McNiff, J. (1988). *Action Research Principles and Practice*. New York: Routledge.

McNiff, J., Lomax P. and Whitehead, J. (1996). *You and Your Action Research Project*. London: Routledge.

Mehta, Y. (1995), The Impact of Mentoring on Teachers' Understanding of Learning and Teaching Mathematics. Unpublished Master's thesis submitted to the Aga Khan University-Institute for Educational Development, Karachi, Pakistan.

Memon, M. and Bana, Z. (2005). Pedagogical Leadership in Pakistan: Two Head Teachers from Northern Areas. In J. Retallick and I. Farah (Eds.). *Transforming Schools in Pakistan: Towards the Learning Community*. Karachi: Oxford University Press.

Mercer, D. and Ri. L. (2006). Closing the Gap: The Role of Head of Departments in Chinese Secondary Schools, *Educational Management, Administration and Leadership*, 34(1), 105-20.

Merriam, S.B. (1998). *Qualitative Research and Case Study Applications in Education*. San Francisco, CA: Jossey-Bass Publishers.

Miles, M.B. and Huberman, M.A. (1994). *Qualitative Data Analysis*. Sage.

Mohammad, R.F. (2006). Problems of Teachers' Re-entry in Schools after In-service Education. In I. Farah and B. Jaworski (Eds.), *Partnerships in Educational Development*. Karachi: Oxford University Press.

Mohammad, R.F. (2004). Practical Constraints upon Teacher Development in Pakistani Schools. *Journal of In-service Education*, 30(1), 101-114.

Mohammad, R.F. (2002). From Theory to Practice: An Understanding of the Implementation of In-service Mathematics Teachers' Learning from University into the Classroom in Pakistan. Unpublished D.Phil thesis, University of Oxford, Oxford.

Moller, G. (2006). Teacher Leadership Emerges within Professional Learning Communities. *Journal of School Leadership*, 16, 520-33.

Morrison, M. (1996). An Examination of the Development of Teachers' Reflective Practice. *Education Today*, 46(2), 43-47.

Muhammad, S. Kiani; A. Ali; T. Ashraf; D. Ayoub; S. Hammed; A. Ali; B. Jahan. (2000) Professional Development Centre, Northern Areas: Overview. Unpublished paper presented at the Educational Forum held at the Professional Development Centre, North, in Gilgit in March 2000.

N

Nias, J. and Groundwater-Smith, S. (1988). *The Enquiring Teacher: Supporting and Sustaining Teacher Research*. London: The Falmer Press.

Nickson, M. (1994). The Culture of Mathematics Education. In Lerman, S.(Ed.), *Cultural Perspectives on the Mathematics Classrooms* (pp. 7-35). The Netherlands: Kluwer.

Nicol, C., Moore, J., Zappa, S., Yusyp, M. and Sasges, M. (2004). Living Action Research: Authoring Identities through Yaya Projects. *Educational Action Research*, 12(3), 311-327.

O

Oluga, M.A. (2004). The Role of the Principal in Enhancing Efficient School Improvement through Collaboration: A Critical Perspective. Unpublished Master's thesis submitted to the Aga Khan University-Institute for Educational Development, Karachi, Pakistan.

P

Pardhan, S. and Theissen, D. (2006). The Establishment of the Aga Khan University-Institue for Educational Development. In Farah and Jaworski (Eds.) *Partnerships in Educational Development*. Karachi: Oxford University Press: (11-28).

Park, S., Oliver, S., Johnson, T.S., Graham, P., Oppong, N.K., (2007). Colleagues' Roles in the Professional Development of Teachers: Results from a Research Study of National Board Certification, *Teaching and Teacher Education*, 23 (4):368-3.

Piggot-Irvine, E. (2003). Key Features of Appraisal Effectiveness. *International Journal of Educational Management*, 17(4), 170-78.

Ponte, P., Ax, J., Beijaard, D. and Wubbels, T. (2004). Teachers' Development of Professional Knowledge through Action Research and the Facilitation of this by Teacher Educators. *Teaching and Teacher Education*, 20(6), 571-88.

Price, A. (2000). Communication, Construction and Community: Learning Addition in Primary Classrooms. Unpublished doctoral thesis, University of Oxford, UK.

Pugach, M.C. and Johnson, L.J. (1990). Developing Reflective Practice through Structured Dialogue. In R.T. Clift, R.W. Houston and M.C. Pugach (Eds.), *Encouraging Reflective Practice in Education: An Analysis of Issues and Programmes* (pp. 186-205). New York: Teachers College Press.

R

Rahman, T. (2004). *Denizens of Alien Worlds: A Study of Education, Inequality and Polarization in Pakistan*, Karachi: Oxford University Press.

Randall, M., and Thornton, B. (2001). *Advising and Supporting Teachers*. Cambridge: Cambridge University Press.

Rarieya, J.F.A. (2005). Reflective Dialogue: What's in it for Teachers? A Pakistan Case, *Journal of In-service Education*, 31(2).

Rarieya, J.F.A. (2005b). Promoting and Investigating Students' Uptake of Reflective Practice: A Pakistan Case, *Reflective Practice*, 6(2), 285-94.

Reed, Y., Davis, H., and Nyabanyaba, T. (2002). Investigating Teachers' 'Take-up' of Reflective Practice from an In-service Professional Development Teacher Education Programme in South Africa. *Educational Action Research*, 10(2), 253-74.

Reinhold, P. (1999). Case Studies of Teachers' Reflective Practice within the Developmental Research Project PING. *Curriculum Studies*, 31(5), 545-70.

Renzulli, J.S. (1977). *The Enrichment Triad Model: A Guide for Developing Defensible Programmes for the Gifted and Talented*. Mansfield Center, CT: Creative Learning Press.

Renzulli, J.S., and Reis, S.M. (1997). The Schoolwide Enrichment Model: New Directions for Developing High-end Learning. In N. Colangenlo, and G. A. Davis (Eds.) *Handbook of Gifted Education* (2nd ed.) (pp. 136-54). Boston: Allyn and Bacon.

Retallick, J. and Farah, I. (Eds.) (2005). *Transforming Schools in Pakistan: Towards the learning Community*. Karachi: Oxford University Press.

Retallick, J., Rarieya, J., Safdar, Q., Mithani, S., Babur, M. and Sewani, R. (2004). *Successful School Management: Pakistan Study*. Report of the ANTRIEP Research Project, Karachi: AKU-IED.

Retallick, J. and Mithani, S. (2003). The Impact of a Professional Development Programme. *Journal of In-service Education*, 29(3), 405-22.

Risko, V., Vukelich, C. and Roskos, K. (2002). Preparing Teachers for Reflective Practice: Intentions, Contradictions and Possibilities. *Language Arts*, 80(2), 134-44.

Rowe, M.B, (1974). Reflections on Wait-time: Some Methodological Questions. *Journal of Research in Science Teaching*, 11(3), 263-79.

Rowe, M.B. (1969). Science, Silence and Sanction, *Science and Children*, 6(6), 11-13.

Russell, T. (1993). Critical Attributes of a Reflective Teacher: Is Agreement Possible? In J. Calderhead and P. Gates (Eds.), *Conceptualising Reflection in Teacher Development* (pp. 144-53). London: Falmer Press.

S

Sarita and Tomar, M. (Eds.) (2004). *Teacher Education–Making Education Effective*. Isha Books: India.

Saeed, M. and Mahmood, K. (2002). Assessing Competencies of Pakistani Primary School Teachers in Mathematics, Science and Pedagogy. *International Journal of Educational Management*, 16(4), 190-95.

Schon, D.A. (1983). *The Reflective Practitioner: How Professionals Think in Action*. London: Mourice Temple Smith Ltd.

Serafini, F. (2002). Reflective Practice and Learning. *Primary Voices K-6*, 10 (4), 2-7.

Shaaban, M.J. (2005). The Influence of the Process of Teachers' Involvement on School Development Planning on their Practices. Unpublished Masters' thesis, Karachi: The Aga Khan University-Institute for Educational Development.

Shah, L.A. (2005). A Principal's Impact on Teachers' Classroom Pedagogical Practices. Unpublished Master's thesis submitted to the Aga Khan University-Institute for Educational Development, Karachi, Pakistan.

Shah, T. (2003). A Study of the Role of Principal in Promoting Team Learning in School Development. Unpublished Master's thesis submitted to the Aga Khan University-Institute for Educational Development, Karachi, Pakistan.

Shafa, M. (2003). Understanding how a Government Secondary School Head Teacher Addresses School Improvement Challenges in the Northern Areas of Pakistan. Unpublished doctoral thesis, Ontario Institute for Studies in Education, University of Toronto, Canada.

Shamim, F. (1996). Towards an Understanding of Learner Resistance to Innovation in Classroom Methodology: A Case Study. In H. Coleman (Ed.), *Society and the Classroom: Social Explanations for Behaviour in the Language Class*. Cambridge University Press.

Shamim, F. (2005) Impact and Sustainability of Whole School Improvement Programme, PDCN. Karachi: Aga Khan University-Institute for Educational Development.

Sheikh, A.Q. (1977). The Problems of Implementation of Elementary Science Curriculum. Karachi: Government of Sindh.

Shulman, L.S. (1986). Those who Understand: Knowledge Growth in Teaching. *Educational Researcher*, 15, 4-14.

Shulman, L.S. (1987). Knowledge and Teaching: Foundations of the New Reform. *Harvard Educational Review*, 57, 1-22.

Silverman, D. (1993). Interpreting Qualitative Data. Thousand Oaks: Sage Publications.

Simkins, T., Sisum, C., and Memon, M. (2003). School Leadership in Pakistan: Exploring the Head Teacher's Role. *School Effectiveness and School Improvement*, 14, 275-91.

Smylie, M.A. (1992). Teachers Report of their Interactions with Teacher Leaders Concerning Classroom Interaction. *Elementary School Journal*, 93, 85-98.

Snowden, P.E., and Gorton, R.A. (1998). *School Leadership* and *Administration: Important Concepts, Case Studies & Simulations* (5th ed.). United States: Jane Vaicunas.

Sosik, J.J. (2006). *Leading with Character: Stories of Valor and Virtue and the Principles they Teach*. Greenwich: Information Age Publishing.

Sotto, E. (1994). *When Teaching Becomes Learning. A Theory and Practice of Teaching*. London: Cassell.

Stephens, D. and Reimer, K.M. (1993). Explorations in Reflective Practice. In L. Patterson, C.M. Santa, K.G. Short and K. Smith (Eds.), *Teachers are*

Researchers: Reflections and Action (pp. 156-80). Newark, DE: International Reading Association.

Strauss. A. and Corbin, J. (1998). *Basics of Qualitative Research: Techniques and Procedures for Developing Grounded Theory.* 2nd Edition. London: Sage.

Swai, N. (2002). The Role of School Head Teacher in Empowering Teachers: A Case Study. Unpublished Master's thesis submitted to the Aga Khan University-Institute for Educational Development, Karachi, Pakistan.

T

Thomas, J.A. and Montemery, P. (1997). On Becoming a Good Teacher: Reflective Practice with Regard to Children's Voices, *Journal of Teacher Education*, 49 (5), 372-80.

Tobin, K., Tippins, J.D., and Gallard, A.J., (1994). Research on Instructional Strategies for Teaching Science. In Gabel, D. (Ed.). *A Handbook of Research on Science Teaching and Learning* (pp. 45-94). New York: Publishing Company.

Tobin, K. (1983). The Influence of Wait Time on Classroom Learning, *European Journal of Science Education*, 5(1), 35-48.

U

UNESCO Principal Regional Office for Asia and the Pacific (UNESCO PROAP) (2000). *Increasing the Number of Women Teachers in Rural Schools.* Bangkok.

V

Venezky, R. (1996). Textbooks in School and Society. In P. W. Jackson (Ed.), *Handbook of Research on Curriculum: A Project of the American Educational Research Association.* (pp. 436-61). New York: Macmillan Library Reference.

W

Wanzare, Z., and Ward, K.L. (2000). Rethinking Staff Development in Kenya: Agenda for the Twenty-first Century. *The International Journal of Educational Management*, 14(6), 265-75.

Warwick, D.P. and Reimers, F. (1995). *Hope or Despair? Learning in Pakistan's Primary Shools.* Westport CT: Praeger.

Wells, G. (1989). Educational Change and School Improvement. *Let's Talk, Newsletter 2,* 3-6.

Wesley, D. (1998). Eleven Ways to be a Great Teacher. *Educational Leadership*, 55(5), 80-1.

West, M., Ainscow, M., and Stanford, J. (2005). Sustaining Improvement in Schools in Challenging Circumstances: A Study of Successful Practice. *School Leadership and Management*, 25(1), p. 77.

Wildman, T. M., Magliaro, S.G., Niles, R.A., and Niles, J.A. (1992). Teacher Mentoring: An Analysis of Roles, Activities, and Conditions. *Journal of Teacher Education*, 43(30), 205-13.

Wildman, T.M. and Niles, J.A. (1987). Reflective Teachers: Tensions between Abstractions and Realities. *Journal of Teacher Education*, 3(1), 25-31.

Williams, J. (2002). *Professional Leadership in Schools: Effective Middle Management* and *Subject Leadership*. London: Kogan Page.

Wise, C. (2001). The Monitoring Role of the Academic Middle Manager in Secondary Schools. *Educational Management and Administration*, 29, 333-41.

Wood, T. (1999). Creating a Context for Arguments in Mathematics Class. *Journal for Research in Mathematics Education*, 30(2), 171-91.

Wood, T. (1995). An Emerging Practice of Teaching. In P. Cobb., and H. Bauersfeld (Eds.), *The Emergence of Mathematical Meaning, Interaction in Classroom Cultures* (pp. 203-228). New Jersey: Lawrence Erlbaum.

Wragg, E.C. (1993) *Primary Teaching Skills*. London: Routledge.

Y

Yackel, E. (2001). Explanation, Justification and Argumentation in Mathematics Classrooms. In M.H. Panhuizen (Ed.), *Proceedings of the 25th Conference of the International Group for the Psychology of Mathematics Education*, 1, 9-24. Utrecht: The Freudenthal Institute.

Yackel, E., and Cobb, P. (1996). Socio-mathematical Norms, Argumentation, and Autonomy in Mathematics. *Journal for Research in Mathematics Education*, 27(4), 458-77.

York-Barr, J. and Duke, K. (2004). What Do We Know about Teacher Leadership? Findings from Two decades of Scholarship, *Review of Educational Research*. 74(3), 255-316.

Yousafi, S. (1998). Head Teachers Beginning to Make a Difference. Unpublished Master's thesis submitted to the Aga Khan University-Institute for Educational Development, Karachi, Pakistan.

Contributors' Profile

Anjum Halai is associate professor and head, Research and Policy Studies, AKU-IED, Karachi. She has a rich experience of teaching and teacher education at graduate and post-graduate levels. Her special areas of research interest include school improvement, teacher development, and students' learning in mathematics. As head of Research and Policy Studies, she facilitates and encourages the execution and publication of high-quality research programmes and projects at AKU-IED. She was the founding chairperson of the Mathematics Association in Pakistan and has been instrumental in launching the Pakistan Association of Research in Education. She has published widely in national and international scholarly journals.

Bernadette L. Dean is associate professor and head, Academic and Student Affairs, AKU-IED, Karachi. Her teaching and research interests are in social studies education, citizenship and human rights education, and teaching and learning in developing countries. She has presented her research in national and international conferences and has published her work in journals and as book chapters. In addition, she has written social studies textbooks and a teaching learning resource to educate for citizenship, human rights, and conflict resolution.

Fauzia Shamim is professor of Applied Linguistics at the Department of English, University of Karachi. Earlier, she was engaged in teacher education and research at the Institute for Educational Development of the Aga Khan University. She is a founding member of the Society of Pakistan English Language Teachers and the Pakistan Association of Research in Education. She has received several awards including the award for scholarship of teaching from the Aga Khan University in 2004. Her research interests include school improvement, developing contextually appropriate methodology for teaching of English, and teacher development strategies.

Haji Karim Khan is a doctoral student at the Aga Khan University-Institute for Educational Development (AKU-IED), Karachi. He has been working as a teacher, teacher educator, and educational researcher for more than a decade. His areas of interest include teacher education, school improvement, and educational action research.

Jane Frances Akinyi Rarieya, an assistant professor at the Aga Khan University-Institute for Educational Development Eastern Africa has a doctorate in Gender and Educational Management from the University of Keele, UK. Her research activities and publications have been in the areas of reflective practice, gender and educational leadership and management.

John Retallick has been an associate professor, at AKU-IED since 2002. Prior to that he was at Charles Sturt University in Australia for twenty-five years. He has teaching and research interests in teacher learning, educational leadership, and schools as learning communities. He has published four books and a number of articles in international journals.

Mehrun-Nisa started her career as a secondary school teacher in Gilgit, Northern Areas (NAs). After the M.Ed (in 2000) programme at AKU-IED, she worked as Manager Academic Cell, Government Education Department, Northern Areas. In 2004, she received the Prestigious British Chevening scholarship and studied at Cardiff University, UK, where she obtained an M.Sc in Education with distinction. Currently, she is a doctoral student at AKU-IED. Her areas of interest include planning, implementation, and, particularly, sustainability of education programmes and projects.

Rahat Joldoshalieva teaches a Social Studies Education course in the Master's programme at the Aga Khan University-Institute for Educational Development (AKU-IED). She has conducted action research with teachers in Kyrgyzstan in improving their practices by using discussion, cooperative learning, and inquiry in language classrooms which was part of an international study, *Researching Practice, Practicing Research* coordinated by Dr Bernadette Dean. Ms Joldoshalieva has also worked at Osh State University-Faculty of World Languages, Kyrgyzstan.

Rashida Qureshi is assistant professor at the Aga Khan University-Institute for Educational Development, Karachi. She is an experienced community development practitioner and has worked extensively with rural women in remote regions of the North West Frontier Province. She has written several research reports, edited *Gender and Education in Pakistan* and published articles in international journals. She is a member of the Aga Khan University's Ethics Review Committee and the chair of the AKU-IED's Ethics Review Committee.

Razia Fakir Mohammad is assistant professor at the Aga Khan University–Institute for Educational Development. Her academic and professional interests are in the area of teacher education in general, and Mathematics teaching and teacher education, in particular. Her work has been published in national and international journals and books.

Roshni Kumari is senior instructor at the Aga Khan University–Institute for Educational Development. Her academic background is in Linguistics and Educational Management. Her current teaching and research interests involve school effectiveness and improvement, teacher education, educational policy analysis, and overall educational management and development.

Mohammed Juma Abdalla is a Tanzanian national who has done his Master of Education (M.Ed.) in Teacher Education from

Aga Khan University's Institute for Educational Development (AKU-IED) in Karachi, Pakistan in 2004. He has also done his Bachelor of Arts in Education with honours in 1993 from Dar-es-Salaam University in Tanzania. He is currently working at Aga Khan University's Institute for Educational Development (AKU-IED), Eastern Africa as a Professional Development Tutor.